TABLE OF CONTENTS

SECTION

UNIT ONE   Personal Money Records

UNIT TWO   Buying Problems

UNIT THREE   Special Buying Problems

UNIT FOUR   Wages

UNIT FIVE   Commissions

UNIT SIX   Borrowing Money

UNIT SEVEN   Saving and Investing

UNIT EIGHT   Home Expenses

UNIT ONE Personal Money Records

SECTION 1. Personal Cash Records

Many persons and families keep a record of their cash receipts and cash payments. Some use a single-column cash receipts record like the one shown below in Problem 1, and a single-column cash payments record like the one shown in Problem 4 on page 2. Others use a cash payments record with special columns for classifying the payments, like the one shown in Problem 5 on page 2.

EXERCISE. (Practical problems)

1. Shown at the right is the cash receipts record of David Morris for the week of February 1. David is a sales-clerk in the automotive department of a large department store. He also has a part-time job on weekends driving a cab.

You are to add the amounts in the Amount column and write the total on the line labeled "Total."

CASH RECEIPTS RECORD			
DATE	EXPLANATION	AMOUNT	
Feb. 1	Take home pay, week of January 25	83	42
3	Sale of old guitar	30	00
3	Refund on returned record	5	25
4	Savings bond cashed at maturity	25	00
4	Birthday gift	10	00
5	Commission for driving cab	35	00
5	Tips received	8	00
6	Commission for driving cab	22	55
6	Tips received	4	25
	Total		

2. Jim Dickins is employed in a gas station. Jim also works part-time as a night watchman at a paper mill. Jim has a savings account at a local bank. Interest is added to the account every three months, on January 2, April 1, July 1, and October 1. Jim often withdraws the interest a few days later and uses it along with his other cash receipts.

For the first week of April, his cash receipts were as follows: take-home pay from gas station, $94.72; take-home pay as night watchman, $45.63; interest from savings account, $15.16; dividend on stock, $12.50; sale of old hi-fi set, $25; door prize at local benefit dance, $10. The total cash receipts for the week were $_____.

3. The cash receipts of Sally Johnson for last week were: take-home pay, $154.72; take-home pay from part-time work, $42.88; interest from savings account, $15.46; birthday gift, $25; life insurance dividend, $29.60; repayment of a loan to a friend, $12; savings bond cashed at maturity, $50. The total cash receipts for the week were $_____.

4. Shown at the right is the cash payments record of David Morris for the week of February 1.

Add the amounts in the amount column and write the total on the line labeled "Total."

CASH PAYMENTS RECORD			
DATE	EXPLANATION	AMOUNT	
Feb. 1	Automobile insurance premium	64	78
3	Gasoline and oil	8	70
4	Life insurance premium	36	25
4	Clothing purchases	27	50
5	Deposit to savings account	20	00
5	Telephone bill for January	10	67
5	Entertainment	15	45
6	Food purchases	14	72
6	Miscellaneous expenses	7	34
	Total		

5. Janet Oliver uses a cash payments record which has special columns for classifying the payments. Shown below is the cash payments record for April.

The payments were recorded on one line at the end of each full or partial week within the month. On each line, the amounts were entered first in the Classification of Payments columns. They were then added horizontally (across) and the sum entered in the Total Payments column.

		CLASSIFICATION OF PAYMENTS					
WEEK	TOTAL PAYMENTS	RENT	FOOD	CLOTHING	TRANS-PORTATION	SAVINGS	
1–7	164 07	110 00	12 42	14 22	12 43	15 00	
8–14	21 51		11 63		9 88		
15–21	35 13		8 90		11 23	15 00	
22–28	56 74		19 67	22 50	14 57		
29–30	11 46		5 84		5 62		

You are to do the following:

a Add each of the six columns and write the total on the blank line at the bottom of the payments record.

b Check your work by adding horizontally the totals of the five Classification of Payments columns. The sum should equal the total of the Total Payments column.

6. The cash payments of Nina Gonzales for the month of March were as follows:

Food. . . . . $87.67   Transportation. $65.30
Clothing. . . . . 36.48   Medical. 13.45
Housing. . . . . 85.00   Savings. 36.84

The total cash payments for the month were $_____.

Section 1.

DRILL 1. (Number sentences)

The marks we make in a cash receipts or payments record to represent numbers are called *numerals* and may be thought of as names for the numbers they represent. Thus, 8, 69, and 263 are numerals or names for certain particular numbers.

Any number may be represented by many different names or numerals. The number eight, for instance, may be represented by the numerals 8, 5 + 3, 10 − 2, 4 × 2, 24 ÷ 3, and $\frac{32}{4}$ to list just a few. To show that two numerals name the same number, we write an equal sign between them. Thus, we may write 5 + 3 = 8. This statement about 5 + 3 and 8 is called a *number sentence*. It states that 5 + 3 and 8 name the same number.

A sentence like $N + 3 = 8$ or $? + 3 = 8$, in which a numeral is missing, is incomplete and is called an *open sentence*. We complete the sentence by replacing "N" or "$?$" with a numeral that makes the sentence true. Since 8 is 3 more than the missing number, the missing number must be 3 less than 8, or 5. Substituting 5 for "N" or "$?$" gives 5 + 3 = 8, which is a true sentence.

In $N − 9 = 4$, 4 is 9 less than the missing number. Hence, the missing number must be 9 more than 4, or 13. In $6 × N = 54$, the 54 results from multiplying the missing number by 6. Hence, the missing number must be 54 divided by 6, or 9. In $N ÷ 4 = 8$, the 8 results from dividing the missing number by 4. Hence, the missing number must be 4 times 8, or 32.

In the blank space at the right of each of the following number sentences, you are to write the numeral that should be substituted for the letter or question mark to make the sentence true.

1. $N + 3 = 10$ _____	5. $4 × N = 80$ _____	9. $N − 11 = 21$ _____
2. $N − 5 = 15$ _____	6. $? + 12 = 30$ _____	10. $10 + ? = 26$ _____
3. $3 × N = 12$ _____	7. $? ÷ 4 = 10$ _____	11. $N × 9 = 54$ _____
4. $N ÷ 6 = 12$ _____	8. $8 × N = 72$ _____	12. $36 ÷ ? = 4$ _____

DRILL 2. (Using combinations in addition)

You cannot add as rapidly as you should unless you are able to combine two or more figures and add them to others as one amount. Two or three figures amounting to ten are especially easy to recognize. Observe how easy the addition of the problem at the right becomes when combinations equaling ten are recognized. You should practice until you can recognize such combinations at a glance.

$$10\begin{cases}65\\45\end{cases}10$$
$$10\begin{cases}82\\26\end{cases}8$$
$$10\begin{cases}17\\31\\42\end{cases}10$$
$$\overline{308}$$

Add the columns below. Combine two or more figures wherever possible.

1.	2.	3.	4.	5.	6.	7.	8.
16	96	17	34	56	51	36	79
94	14	21	25	24	37	74	24
71	53	72	51	75	42	69	15
39	57	45	18	35	23	41	95
65	12	21	61	72	14	28	77
15	68	24	11	38	33	16	39

DRILL 3. (Using combinations in addition)

In adding the following problems, combine three figures wherever possible.

1.	2.	3.	4.	5.	6.	7.	8.
35	12	33	83	17	25	76	45
12	65	12	27	83	13	34	65
63	33	65	12	10	72	12	26
18	14	67	65	62	81	98	84
31	83	43	33	17	18	41	12
61	15	19	67	31	11	71	64
45	82	91	43	81	72	15	34
12	67	23	15	29	25	84	83
23	14	67	85	15	13	14	27

DRILL 4. (Checking by reverse addition)

Reverse addition is used to check a column total. It consists of adding in the opposite direction from which you first added. Add the following problems and check by reverse addition. Place a check mark (√) at the left of the answer after you have checked it in this manner.

1.	2.	3.	4.	5.	6.	7.	8.
$18.09	$10.10	$ 1.75	$17.26	$12.37	$ 1.27	$32.46	$ 6.05
.78	1.21	16.29	9.04	1.56	10.48	.74	13.12
4.46	15.57	1.25	40.76	42.83	15.09	1.26	1.98
12.26	7.75	75.03	.39	9.03	3.23	16.27	.19
.93	.09	8.42	.68	.72	.35	3.45	.46
.07	30.01	.94	1.39	8.12	9.26	11.92	.84
17.99	9.96	16.05	11.18	28.11	1.84	4.12	15.13
1.24	18.72	.59	18.11	5.39	7.78	.93	17.49
8.92	12.48	8.27	2.79	.07	19.72	3.17	8.27
15.55	8.93	13.03	10.06	13.60	12.29	19.18	18.03

DRILL 5. (Checking horizontal and vertical addition)

When lines and columns of figures are added horizontally and vertically, as in Problem 5 on page 2, the work can be checked by adding the column totals horizontally. In the example at the left, for instance, the first three totals (21, 24, 18) in the column at the right are the result of horizontal addition from left to right. The totals at the bottom (20, 22, 21) are the result of vertical addition of the four columns. The work is checked by adding the first three totals at the bottom horizontally. The sum should be the same as the total of the last column, which is 63.

$$9 + 5 + 7 = 21$$
$$5 + 10 + 9 = 24$$
$$6 + 7 + 5 = 18$$
$$20 + 22 + 21 = 63$$

Complete the following problems, using horizontal and vertical addition as shown in the illustration above.

1.
$$10 + 2 + 4 + 6 + 9 + 8 = \rule{1cm}{0.4pt}$$
$$6 + 9 + 6 + 4 + 1 + 3 = \rule{1cm}{0.4pt}$$
$$9 + 3 + 8 + 7 + 4 + 9 = \rule{1cm}{0.4pt}$$
$$7 + 9 + 5 + 10 + 5 + 5 = \rule{1cm}{0.4pt}$$
$$10 + 4 + 8 + 7 + 6 + 9 = \rule{1cm}{0.4pt}$$

$$\_ + \_ + \_ + \_ + \_ + \_ = \rule{1cm}{0.4pt}$$

2.
$$3 + 7 + 6 + 5 + 2 + 6 = \rule{1cm}{0.4pt}$$
$$2 + 10 + 9 + 4 + 8 + 9 = \rule{1cm}{0.4pt}$$
$$7 + 8 + 5 + 6 + 5 + 3 = \rule{1cm}{0.4pt}$$
$$12 + 4 + 9 + 8 + 10 + 8 = \rule{1cm}{0.4pt}$$
$$9 + 8 + 7 + 3 + 3 + 2 = \rule{1cm}{0.4pt}$$

$$\_ + \_ + \_ + \_ + \_ + \_ = \rule{1cm}{0.4pt}$$

SECTION 2. Personal Checkbook Records

EXERCISE. (Practical problems)

1. When you make a deposit in a checking account, the bank expects you to record it on a deposit slip. As shown by the deposit slip below, the total of the bills and coin is listed after "Currency." Each check is listed separately and is identified by its American Bankers Association number which is printed on the check.

Find the total of this deposit and enter it on the last line of the slip.

FOR DEPOSIT TO THE ACCOUNT OF		DOLLARS	CENTS
Harold J. Jackson	CURRENCY	23	63
	CHECKS 18-3	112	42
*November 22*_____19_ _	46-12	15	75
EDGEVILLE NATIONAL BANK	23-18	8	62
EDGEVILLE, IOWA	82-9	35	96
	TOTAL		

⑈0739⑈1429⑈   302⑈69042⑈

2. As treasurer of the Bern High School D.E. Club, Elsa Meade deposits the following items on September 21 of the current year: cash consisting of $12.00 in bills and $18.30 in coin, and checks bearing numbers of 7-35, $8.50; 7-69, $11.35; 65-119, $8.85; 15-51, $6.55.

Prepare the deposit slip, using the blank form provided at the right. The total of the bills and coin is to be listed after "Cash" on the deposit slip.

RECEIVED FOR DEPOSIT FOR THE CHECKING ACCOUNT OF		DOLLARS	CENTS
	CASH		
BERN HIGH SCHOOL D.E. CLUB	C H E C K S		
_____19___			
STATE STREET TRUST CO.			
612 State Street			
	TOTAL		

⑈0520⑈0033⑈   218⑈23518⑈

3. Dan Taylor, treasurer of the Mt. Carmel High School Junior Theater, has the following items to deposit for the group on March 11 of the current year: cash, $15.75, and checks bearing bank numbers of 27-3, $9.75; 32-10, $8.49; 86-12, $17.22; 14-2, $9.58.

Prepare the deposit slip, using the blank form at the right.

CHECKING ACCOUNT DEPOSIT TICKET		DOLLARS	CENTS
MT. CARMEL HIGH SCHOOL	CASH		
JUNIOR THEATER	CHECKS		
_____19___			
Madison State Bank			
12 North Main Street			
	TOTAL		

⑈1131⑈0121⑈   92⑈32348

4. A bank provides each depositor with blank checks to use in withdrawing money that has been deposited in a checking account. The blank checks have stubs so that the depositor may keep a record of deposits and withdrawals in order to know how much money is in the bank at any given time.

Shown below are three checks, with accompanying stubs taken from the checkbook of Carol P. Martin. The first check has been completed as a model. With the information provided on check stub No. 973, you are to complete the second check.

5. On May 18, Carol P. Martin wants to use the third check to make a payment of $77.40 to the Golden Insurance Co. for a life insurance premium. Earlier the same day she deposited $114.30. Use this information to complete stub No. 974 and check No. 974.

NO. *972*

May 14 19 --

TO *Eileen's Dress Shop*

FOR *dress*

	DOLLARS	CENTS
BALANCE BRO'T FOR'D	522	45
AMOUNT DEPOSITED	115	25
TOTAL	637	70
AMOUNT THIS CHECK	49	95
BALANCE CAR'D FOR'D	587	75

NO. *972* **Cascade National Bank** 24-39 / 1232

PORTLAND, OREGON _____ *May 14* ____ 19 --

PAY TO THE ORDER OF *Eileen's Dress Shop* ____ $ *49.95*

Forty-nine 95/100 _____ DOLLARS

Carol P. Martin

CAROL P. MARTIN

⑈1232⑈0039⑈ 238⑈41067⑈

NO. *973*

May 16 19 --

TO *Connie's Beauty Shoppe*

Cosmetics

	DOLLARS	CENTS
BALANCE BRO'T FOR'D	587	75
AMOUNT DEPOSITED		
TOTAL		
AMOUNT THIS CHECK	22	50
BALANCE CAR'D FOR'D	565	25

NO. ____ **Cascade National Bank** 24-39 / 1232

PORTLAND, OREGON _____ 19 ____

PAY TO THE ORDER OF _____ $ _____

_____ DOLLARS

CAROL P. MARTIN

⑈1232⑈0039⑈ 238⑈41067⑈

NO. ____

_____ 19 ____

TO _____

FOR _____

	DOLLARS	CENTS
BALANCE BRO'T FOR'D		
AMOUNT DEPOSITED		
TOTAL		
AMOUNT THIS CHECK		
BALANCE CAR'D FOR'D		

NO. ____ **Cascade National Bank** 24-39 / 1232

PORTLAND, OREGON _____ 19 ____

PAY TO THE ORDER OF _____ $ _____

_____ DOLLARS

CAROL P. MARTIN

⑈1232⑈0039⑈ 238⑈41067⑈

Section 2

EXERCISE.   (Practical problems) — concluded

6. During the month of October, John Oaks, treasurer of the school Boosters' Club, made a deposit and issued the checks as shown on the check stubs below. The deposit and the checks issued are receipts and expenses from the annual school game day.

Complete the stub records so that John's correct balance at the end of the month will be shown at the bottom of the last stub.

No. 64	No. 65	No. 66	No. 67
October 6 19--	*October 7* 19--	*October 9* 19--	*October 10* 19--
To *Opal Athletic Co.*	To *School Rentals Co.*	To *Joe Garcia*	To *Uptown Printers*
For *Equipment*	For *Uniform rental*	For *Referee's fee*	For *tickets*
BALANCE FOR'D...$ *64.27*	BALANCE FOR'D...$ ____	BALANCE FOR'D...$ ____	BALANCE FOR'D...$ ____
DEPOSITED.......$ *384.75*	DEPOSITED.......$ ____	DEPOSITED.......$ ____	DEPOSITED.......$ ____
TOTAL..........$ ____	TOTAL..........$ ____	TOTAL..........$ ____	TOTAL..........$ ____
THIS CHECK......$ *143.65*	THIS CHECK......$ *48.00*	THIS CHECK......$ *25.00*	THIS CHECK......$ *26.50*
BALANCE.........$ ____	BALANCE.........$ ____	BALANCE.........$ ____	BALANCE.........$ ____

7. Betty Ashley began the month of May with a bank balance of $627.45. The following is a summary of the deposits made and the checks written during the month.

May 4. Wrote check No. 169 for Cash*, $55.
    7. Deposited $75.
  12. Wrote check No. 170 to Ajax Appliances for air conditioner, $259.70.

May 19. Wrote check No. 171 to Bob's Hardware for paint and brushes, $21.23.
  31. Deposited $65.
  31. Wrote check No. 17 to Bond Clothing Store for sweater, $15.90.

Using the information given above, fill out the check stubs shown below. The entry for the deposit of May 7 should be made on the second check stub, and the entry for the deposit of May 31 should be made on the fourth stub. The amount of a deposit should always be recorded on the stub following the one on which the last previously written check was recorded. The entry for the next check is then recorded on the same stub.

No.____	No.____	No.____	No.____
_____ 19__	_____ 19__	_____ 19__	_____ 19__
To_____	To_____	To_____	To_____
For_____	For_____	For_____	For_____
BALANCE FOR'D...$____	BALANCE FOR'D...$____	BALANCE FOR'D...$____	BALANCE FOR'D...$____
DEPOSITED.......$____	DEPOSITED.......$____	DEPOSITED.......$____	DEPOSITED.......$____
TOTAL..........$____	TOTAL..........$____	TOTAL..........$____	TOTAL..........$____
THIS CHECK.....$____	THIS CHECK.....$____	THIS CHECK.....$____	THIS CHECK.....$____
BALANCE.........$____	BALANCE.........$____	BALANCE.........$____	BALANCE.........$____

*When a person writes a check for "Cash," "Cash" is written on the check and check stub in the space where the name of the person to whom the check is payable is usually written. Such a check is payable to any person who presents the check to the bank for payment. A depositor may write a check payable to "Cash" so that the depositor can cash the check.

DRILL 6. (Inverse operations)

If we start with 7 and add 3, we get 10. If we then subtract 3 from 10, we get 7, the number we started with. Subtracting 3 from 10 "undoes" what was done by adding 3 to 7. Hence, if $N + 3 = 10$, we can "undo" the addition by subtracting 3 from 10 and find that N is equal to 7. Substituting 7 for N gives $7 + 3 = 10$, a true sentence.

Similarly, if $N - 4 = 8$, we can "undo" the subtraction by adding 4 to 8 and find that N is equal to 12. Substituting 12 for N gives $12 - 4 = 8$, a true sentence.

Because they "undo" each other, addition and subtraction are called *inverse operations*, subtraction being the inverse of addition and addition the inverse of subtraction.

In the blank space at the right of each of the following number sentences, you are to write the numeral that should be substituted for the letter or question mark to make the sentence true. Use the principle of inverse operations wherever it can be applied.

1. $N + 5 = 14$ _____	7. $N - 10 = 13$ _____	13. $? + 0 = 17$ _____
2. $? + 8 = 15$ _____	8. $? - 8 = 20$ _____	14. $N - 13 = 24$ _____
3. $N - 6 = 7$ _____	9. $N + 6 = 18$ _____	15. $? + 32 = 56$ _____
4. $? - 9 = 16$ _____	10. $N = 7 + 0$ _____	16. $N + 27 = 64$ _____
5. $9 + 8 = N$ _____	11. $9 - 0 = N$ _____	17. $? - 18 = 47$ _____
6. $N + 10 = 25$ _____	12. $N - 0 = 14$ _____	18. $N - 47 = 34$ _____

DRILL 7. (Checking subtraction)

Make the following subtractions, then prove by adding the difference to the subtrahend.** The sum should equal the minuend* if your first calculations are correct. Place a check mark at the left of each problem to indicate that you have proved it and that the answer is correct.

	a	b	c	d	e
1.	7,259 367	19,864 5,976	$18,965.25 9,876.37	$47,863.12 7,974.15	$76,219.49 9,146.98
2.	9,627 519	24,719 6,348	$26,214.97 7,839.58	$16,399.28 5,489.49	$87,945.37 7,814.95
3.	8,572 398	41,587 6,453	$57,362.84 4,857.68	$38,473.32 9,485.86	$39,283.45 3,847.38

*A *minuend* is an amount from which another amount is to be subtracted.

263

**A *subtrahend* is an amount that is to be subtracted from a given number.

−191

[8]

SECTION 3. Proving the Checkbook Balance

EXERCISE. (Practical problems)

In Problem 7 on page 7, Betty Ashley kept a record on her check stubs of the balance of her bank account. The bank also keeps a record and sends the depositor a monthly statement of her account as it appears on that record.

1. Shown at the right is a statement Betty Ashley received from her bank during the month of June. The statement is complete except for the daily balance, which you are to enter. For example, by deducting the $55 check written on May 4, you find that $572.45 should be written in the balance column as the balance for that day. By adding the deposit of $75, you find the balance for May 7. In the same way, find the balance for each of the remaining dates on the statement.

	STATEMENT OF YOUR ACCOUNT			BETTY ASHLEY 42 MAPLE LANE ATLANTA, GA 30305

FIRST NATIONAL BANK
Atlanta, Georgia

ACCOUNT NO. 291-85603

CHECKS	DEPOSITS	DATE	BALANCE
	BALANCE FORWARD	May 1	627.45
55.00		May 4	572.45
	75.00	May 7	647.45
259.70		May 14	
21.23		May 21	
	65.00	May 31	

CC—CERTIFIED CHECK	EC—ERROR CORRECTED	OD—OVERDRAWN
CM—CREDIT MEMO	LS—LIST OF CHECKS	RT—RETURNED ITEM
DM—DEBIT MEMO	NC—CHECK NOT COUNTED	SC—SERVICE CHARGE

2. Betty Ashley's check-stub record at the end of May shows a balance of $415.62. Her bank statement, however, shows a balance of $431.52. On comparing the check stubs with the checks listed in the bank statement, she finds that a $15.90 check written on May 31 is not listed on the statement. It had not been presented to the bank for payment before the end of the month. She therefore reconciles the balance shown on her bank statement with the balance shown on her stubs in the manner shown below. You are to enter the correct figures in the blank spaces.

Bank statement balance May 31 $_____

Less May 31 check, #172, outstanding $_____

Available bank funds (checkbook balance) $_____

3. Upon comparing the record on your check stubs with the items on your October bank statement, you find that the October 31 bank balance, as shown by the bank statement, is $562.39, and that four checks written on October 29 and 30 have not yet been presented at the bank for payment. These checks are listed at the right. You are to show at the right (a) the total unpaid checks, and (b) the available bank balance, after deducting the checks.

Balance, Oct. 31, on bank statement.......$562.39

Outstanding checks:

    #231......................$31.53
    #232......................13.87
    #233......................18.30
    #234......................8.65

Total unpaid checks......................_____

Available bank balance, Oct. 31..........$_____

4. Shown below is a summary of Martin Turner's banking transactions for the month of August.

August 1. Balance $578.45
Deposited $137.15

     5. Check No. 106 to Pete's Diner for lunch, $8.45

     8. Check No. 107 to Hauf's for lamp, $36.80

   12. Check No. 108 to John's Hardware for monthly statement, $14.76

   16. Deposited $116.25

   21. Check No. 109 to Cooper Plumbing Co. for new water heater, $161.25.

   27. Deposited $98.70

   29. Check No. 110 to Home Garden Center for shrubbery, $26.80

   30. Check No. 111 to Cash, $65

On September 1 Martin Turner receives a statement from the bank showing that his balance is $644.29 and that the check issued on August 29 is still outstanding. You are to show his check-stub calculations on the check stubs below. Reconcile the bank-statement balance with the check-stub balance, making the necessary calculations in the space at the right of the check stubs.

No._____	No._____	No._____
_____ 19__	_____ 19__	_____ 19__
To _____	To _____	To _____
For _____	For _____	For _____
BALANCE FOR'D...$_____	BALANCE FOR'D...$_____	BALANCE FOR'D...$_____
DEPOSITED.......$_____	DEPOSITED.......$_____	DEPOSITED.......$_____
TOTAL..........$_____	TOTAL..........$_____	TOTAL..........$_____
THIS CHECK.....$_____	THIS CHECK....$_____	THIS CHECK.....$_____
BALANCE........$_____	BALANCE........$_____	BALANCE........$_____
No._____	No._____	No._____
_____ 19__	_____ 19__	_____ 19__
To _____	To _____	To _____
For _____	For _____	For _____
BALANCE FOR'D...$_____	BALANCE FOR'D...$_____	BALANCE FOR'D...$_____
DEPOSITED.......$_____	DEPOSITED.......$_____	DEPOSITED.......$_____
TOTAL..........$_____	TOTAL..........$_____	TOTAL..........$_____
THIS CHECK.....$_____	THIS CHECK.....$_____	THIS CHECK.....$_____
BALANCE........$_____	BALANCE........$_____	BALANCE........$_____

Name _____

Section 3

EXERCISE. (Practical problems) — concluded

5. The Senior Class Committee of the Ridgeway High School began their spring drive with a balance of $68.44 in the bank. The following checks were written and deposits were made for a dance party they held:

March 16. Deposited $181.75 from advance ticket sales for the party

18. Check No. 76 to Bluenote Music Store for rental of extra speakers, $10

21. Check No. 77 to Carleton Press for printing tickets, $19.08

22. Check No. 78 to Ridgeway Daily News for advertisement, $25

25. Check No. 79 to A-1 Department Store for decorations, $35

26. Deposited $291.85 receipts for dance party

28. Check No. 80 to Carter Catering for refreshments, $50

30. Check No. 81 to The Magicians for music $75

On May 1 they received a statement from the bank showing that their bank balance was $452.11. A service charge of $.85 was deducted on the bank statement, and checks No. 80 and No. 81 were outstanding. Show the check-stub calculations on the check stubs below, and reconcile the check-stub and bank-statement balances, making the necessary calculations at the right of the check stubs.

No._____	No._____	No._____
_____ 19__	_____ 19__	_____ 19__
To _____	To _____	To _____
For _____	For _____	For _____
Balance For'd...$_____	Balance For'd...$_____	Balance For'd...$_____
Deposited........$_____	Deposited........$_____	Deposited........$_____
Total..........$_____	Total..........$_____	Total..........$_____
This Check.....$_____	This Check.....$_____	This Check.....$_____
Balance........$_____	Balance........$_____	Balance........$_____
No._____	No._____	No._____
_____ 19__	_____ 19__	_____ 19__
To _____	To _____	To _____
For _____	For _____	For _____
Balance For'd...$_____	Balance For'd...$_____	Balance For'd...$_____
Deposited........$_____	Deposited........$_____	Deposited........$_____
Total..........$_____	Total..........$_____	Total..........$_____
This Check.....$_____	This Check.....$_____	This Check.....$_____
Balance........$_____	Balance........$_____	Balance........$_____

[11]

DRILL 8. (Checking addition)

It is essential that all addition be checked. One way to make checking easy is to write the sum of each column and then add the sums as shown in the example at the right. Then reverse addition may be used to check accuracy.

In the problems below, show (a) the sum of each column, (b) the total of these sums, and (c) check marks at the left to indicate that you have proved each amount by reverse addition.

```
$6 4.3 8
  4 3.7 2
  9 1.4 8
  1 3.1 2
       √2 0
      √1 5
     √1 1
    √2 0
$ 2 1 2.7 0
```

1.	2.	3.	4.
$ 7 2.4 6	$ 1 2 3.4 6	$ 1 4 3.8 0	$ 5 6.8 3
4 5.1 9	9 1.3 2	1 0 1.1 2	1 4 9.0 7
9 3.2 8	5 4.9 1	9 7.8 3	8 3.9 1
4 7.1 8	1 0 3.3 8	1 7 6.3 4	1 3 2.4 6
8 2.5 6	6 4.5 5	7 6.4 1	6 4.4 5
2 3.4 7	8 7.4 9	2 3 0.7 5	2 8 1.9 0

5.	6.	7.	8.
$ 2 6 3.7 1	$ 7 1 2.3 5	$ 2 4.9 8	$ 3 7 8.1 6
2 4.4 0	2.8 6	7 8 5.6 1	4.0 2
1 7 2.9 3	4 3.0 0	9 3.4 4	7 1.3 9
7 2.1 8	2 7.1 3	5.6 8	8.6 7
2 1 7.9 5	9 1.8 5	1 8 2.9 1	7 8 1.3 9
8 4.1 6	4 7 6.1 7	2 2.5 2	5 4.6 8

DRILL 9. (Checking subtraction)

The problems below provide practice in subtraction. (a) Perform the indicated subtractions. (b) Check each difference by adding it to the subtrahend or amount subtracted. The result should agree with the minuend. Place a check mark at the left of the difference to indicate that you have proved it.

1.	2.	3.	4.
$ 1 3 6.4 8	$ 3 7 9.2 1	$ 2 4 3.1 7	$ 6 4 9.2 6
2 3.3 7	8 6.4 7	1 3 0.2 5	3 7 2.7 8

5.	6.	7.	8.
$ 3 4 8.0 9	$ 5 6 0.2 3	$ 1 2 6.7 0	$ 8 1 9.7 6
2 3 1.6 8	3 1 4.9 1	4 2.5 1	4 7 3.8 8

UNIT TWO   Buying Problems

SECTION 4.   Sales Slips

In making purchases at various stores, you will see different kinds of sales slips prepared by clerks. All of the slips serve the same general purpose. These may be slips from a cash register or forms prepared by the clerk. You should study these forms and make use of them in checking purchases and in keeping your own records. Examples of sales slips are given in the problems in the following exercise.

EXERCISE.   (Practical problems)

1.

WESTBROOK AUTO SUPPLIES
East Side Square -- Bloomington, Indiana
phone 542-5627

DATE *June 3* 19 --

NAME *Mr. Richard Allison*

ADDRESS *113 Norton St., Westville*

CLERK	CASH	CHARGE	TAKE		SEND	

QTY.	DESCRIPTION	PRICE	AMOUNT	
8	Sparkplugs	.65		
2	Condensers	1.70		
5	Cans, oil	.65		
3	Cans, auto paint	1.15		
15	ft., hose	.12		

2.

Village Butcher Shop
410 Beech Street, Columbus

DATE *Nov. 2* 19 --

NAME *Mrs. William Bern*

ADDRESS *12 Hadden Ave., Morris*

CLERK	CASH	CHARGE	TAKE		SEND	

QTY.	DESCRIPTION	PRICE	AMOUNT	
2	lb. bologna	1.07		
3	lb. sausage	1.29		
1	chicken legs	.33		
3	lb. sliced beef	1.65		
2	5 lb. canned hams	6.05		

1. You are to complete sales slip No. 1 above. Make the extensions by multiplying each quantity by the price and find the total sale.

2. Complete sales slip No. 2 above as you did No. 1.

3. You are to complete the sales slip at the right from the following data: Sold on account to Mr. Harvey Wilson, 32 Northern Blvd., City.

   6 lb. potato salad @ 59¢

   3 lb. coleslaw   @ 55¢

   4 lb. fish sticks   @ 89¢

   8 lb. rice pudding @ 63¢

Use the current date.

Glenmont Grocery

DATE_____19____

NAME_____

ADDRESS_____

CLERK	CASH	CHARGE	TAKE	SEND

QTY.	DESCRIPTION	PRICE	AMOUNT

4. Complete the sales slip below from the following data: Sold to Aborn School Cafeteria, Draper St., City: 15 lb. sugar @ 22¢; 8 lb. frankfurters @ $1.29; 9 cans cherries @ 53¢; 6 pkg. fig bars @ 53¢. Use the current date.

5. Complete the sales slip below from the following data: Sold on account to P. R. Price, 88 Lyons Road, City: 3 shirts @ $6.45; 3 pair socks @ $1.39; 6 handkerchiefs @ 85¢; 2 ties @ $2.95. Use the current date.

HARRISON SUPERMARKET

DATE_____ 19_____

SOLD TO_____

ADDRESS_____

CLERK	CASH	CHARGE	TAKE	SEND	UNIT PRICE	AMOUNT	
QTY.		DESCRIPTION					

Waldorf Men's Wear

DATE_____ 19_____

SOLD TO_____

ADDRESS_____

CLERK	CASH	CHARGE	TAKE	SEND	UNIT PRICE	AMOUNT	
QTY.		DESCRIPTION					

6. Change is usually given in the fewest pieces possible. If you give a $5 bill in payment of a purchase amounting to $2.32, the clerk will give you 3 pennies, 1 nickel, 1 dime, 1 half dollar, and 2 $1 bills. As he hands you the change he says: "Two thirty-two, thirty-five, forty, fifty, three, and two are five."

Complete the form given below by showing for each item the number of pieces of each denomination given to the customer. Proceed in the manner described below for the sample item.

Think: $2.32 and 3¢ are $2.35 (write 3 in the 1¢ column);
and 5¢ are $2.40 (write 1 in the 5¢ column);
and 10¢ are $2.50 (write 1 in the 10¢ column);
and 50¢ are $3.00 (write 1 in the 50¢ column);
and $2 are $5.00 (write 2 in the $1 column).

ITEM	AMOUNT OF SALE	AMOUNT RECEIVED	DENOMINATIONS OF CHANGE							
			1¢	5¢	10¢	25¢	50¢	$1	$5	$10
Sample	$ 2.32	*$5 bill*	3	1	1		1	2		
a	3.85	$5 bill								
b	6.58	$10 bill								
c	13.15	$25 check								
d	23.56	Two $20 bills								
e	46.29	Two $20 bills One $10 bill								
f	.35	$10 bill								
g	2.53	$20 bill								
h	12.77	$30 check								

Section 4

DRILL 10. (Checking multiplication)

As in addition and subtraction, it is always wise to check multiplication. The product may be checked by reversing the factors and multiplying again, as shown in the example at the right.

Multiply the two numbers in each of the problems below. The answers to each pair of problems (1 and 2, 3 and 4, 5 and 6) should be equal, proving that the multiplications are correct.

Example:

```
    3 7          4 3
    4 3          3 7
   -----        -----
   1 1 1        3 0 1
   1 4 8        1 2 9
   -----        -----
   1,5 9 1      1,5 9 1
```

1.	2.	3.	4.	5.	6.
9 5	6 5	2 7 5	1 2 5	3 4 5	1 3 5
6 5	9 5	1 2 5	2 7 5	1 3 5	3 4 5

DRILL 11. (Placing the decimal point in the product)

Frequently, in multiplication problems, there may be one or more decimal places in the multiplicand, the multiplier, or both. In such cases, the decimal point is placed in the product by pointing off from the right as many decimal places as there are in both the multiplicand and multiplier. After pointing off, any end zeros may be dropped.

Solve the following problems, using the space at the right for your calculations. Put your answers on the blank lines provided.

Example:

```
   3.0 5
     1.8
  -------
  2 4 4 0
  3 0 5
  -------
  5.4 9 0 = 5.49
```

Check each product by redoing the work or by reversing the factors and multiplying again.

1. 2.63×403 = _____

2. 12.7×3.22 = _____

3. 24.6×40.8 = _____

4. 70.4×1.65 = _____

5. 79.8×69.25 = _____

6. $3.6 \times \$4.35$ = _____

7. $6.5 \times \$33.22$ = _____

8. $2.4 \times \$86.55$ = _____

DRILL 12. (Rounding numbers)

Often, the cost of a purchase contains a fraction of a cent. For example, if two cans of fish cost $2.05, one can costs $1.025. Such an amount is generally rounded to the nearest cent. The fraction is dropped if it is less than five-tenths. The cents digit is raised by one if the fraction is five-tenths or more. $1.025 would be rounded to $1.03; $9.884 would be rounded to $9.88.

Other numbers are often rounded, also. If 45,675 people were at a football game, a sports reporter might write that 46,000 people saw the game. The number has been rounded to the nearest thousand to make it easier to read. To round a number to a given place, look at the digit to the right of that place. If it is 5 or more, add one to the digit to be rounded. If it is less than five, do not change the digit. All digits to the right are replaced with zeros. For example, 2,556 rounded to the nearest hundred is 2,600; 3,442 rounded to the nearest hundred is 3,400.

You are to round each of the following as indicated and write the answer on the blank line at the right.

1. To the nearest cent:

a $8.349 _____

b $7.564 _____

c $9.748 _____

d $3.542 _____

2. To the nearest cent:

a $13.097 _____

b $20.996 _____

c $39.997 _____

d $ 5.595 _____

3. To the nearest dollar:

a $354.85 _____

b $219.43 _____

c $29.87 _____

d $499.50 _____

4. To the nearest 10:

a 178 _____

b 254 _____

c 65 _____

d 92 _____

5. To the nearest 100:

a 1,329 _____

b 2,568 _____

c 971 _____

d 348· _____

6. To the nearest 1,000:

a 13,940 _____

b 5,495 _____

c 6,700 _____

d 19,420 _____

DRILL 13. (Estimating the product)

A large error in multiplication or an error in placing the decimal point can often be caught by estimating the answer. Round the multiplicand and the multiplier to simpler numbers that can be multiplied mentally. Then write the product of the rounded numbers. For example, the product of 1,922.4 and 64.85 can be estimated as $2,000 \times 60 = 120,000$.

In Problems 1 to 7, show the rounded factors and the estimated product. In Problems 8 to 14, give (a) the estimated product and (b) the exact product. Make the necessary calculations on a separate piece of paper.

	Rounded Factors	Estimated Product		Estimated Product	Exact Product
1. 48×87	_____ × _____	= _____	8. 28.7×7.15 =	_____	_____
2. 585×34	_____ × _____	= _____	9. $28 \times \$91$ =	_____	_____
3. 129×18	_____ × _____	= _____	10. $43 \times \$575.25$ =	_____	_____
4. 70.4×62	_____ × _____	= _____	11. $49 \times \$6.12$ =	_____	_____
5. 16.1×35.6	_____ × _____	= _____	12. $215 \times \$20.35$ =	_____	_____
6. $27 \times \$9.15$	_____ × _____	= _____	13. $68 \times \$9.40$ =	_____	_____
7. $.35 \times 4.75$	_____ × _____	= _____	14. $36 \times \$32.50$ =	_____	_____

SECTION 5. Sales Taxes

Many states and some cities and counties have a retail sales tax. The rate varies from 3% to 7% of the amount of the sale. The retailer collects the taxes from the buyer and sends them to the proper tax agencies.

EXERCISE.   (Practical problems)

1. You are to complete the sales slip given below. Figure the tax to the nearest cent.

2. Using the current date, complete the sales slip given below from the following data: Sold to Ray Hartley, 56 Brookview Rd.:

> 1 stamp album, $15.95
>
> 1 packet stamps, $11.75

Include a 4% sales tax on the total sale.

Wellington Hi-Fi Center

Radios • TV's • Tapes • Recorders

1324 Hollywood Avenue

DATE _Nov. 18_ 19_--_

SOLD TO _Marie Solan_

ADDRESS _342 Sylvan Terrace._

QTY.	DESCRIPTION	AMOUNT	
1	cassette recorder	49	75
3	cassettes @ $4.95	14	85
	Sales tax 6%		

Wallingford's Stamp Shop

Postage Stamps for Collectors

68 Union Street

DATE _____ 19___

SOLD TO _____

ADDRESS_____

QTY.	DESCRIPTION	AMOUNT	

3. Find the total of each of the following purchases:

a			
2 dresses	@ $16.50	=	_____
1 pant set	@ $22.49	=	_____
2 skirts	@ $12.98	=	_____
3 blouses	@ $ 5.69	=	_____
			_____
Sales tax (5%)			_____
Total cost			_____

b			
3 shirts	@ $5.95	=	_____
2 ties	@ $2.75	=	_____
3 pr. socks	@ $1.19	=	_____
1 belt	@ $4.50	=	_____
			_____
Sales tax (3%)			_____
Total cost			_____

DRILL 14. (Multiplication by 10, 100, and 1,000)

Multiplying by 10 or a multiple of 10, such as 100 or 1,000, can be done easily. Move the decimal point in the multiplicand to the right as many places as there are zeros in the multiplier. If necessary, attach zeros to the product. Omit the decimal point if the product is a whole number.

Examples: $2.35 × 10 = $23.50

.065 × 100 = 6.5

3.6 ×1,000 = 3,600

Write the products of the following multiplications.

1. 327 × 10   = _____
2. $6.45 × 100   = _____
3. .0742 × 1,000 = _____
4. 39¢ × 10   = _____
5. 62.1 × $100   = _____
6. $.07 × 1,000 = _____

7. 17¢ × 10   = _____
8. $8.15 × 10   = _____
9. $100 × 5.9   = _____
10. 16.3 × $1,000 = _____
11. .051 × 10   = _____
12. 100 × $4.30   = _____

DRILL 15. (Multiplication by a multiple of 10, 100, or 1,000)

To multiply by a number such as 40, 400, or 4,000, first multiply by 4. Then, multiply that product by 10, 100, or 1,000, as the case may be.

Example: .32 × 40 = ?

.32 × 4 = 1.28

1.28 × 10 = 12.8

Write the product for each of the following.

1. .28 × 20 = _____
2. .52 × 40 = _____
3. 6.3 × 30 = _____
4. 4.1 × 80 = _____
5. 5.2 × 70 = _____
6. 5.5 × 60 = _____

7. 4.3 × 300   = _____
8. 6.4 × 200   = _____
9. 8.2 × 500   = _____
10. 8.5 × 2,000 = _____
11. 30 × .72   = _____
12. 40 × .53   = _____

13. 80 @ $.45   = _____
14. 90 @ $.35   = _____
15. 300 @ $.53 = _____
16. 400 @ $1.22 = _____
17. 12 @ $70   = _____
18. 84 @ $200   = _____

DRILL 16. (Multiplication of numbers containing end zeros)

If either or both factors of a product are whole numbers with end zeros on the right, multiply only the numbers at the left of the zeros. Attach to the product as many zeros as there are end zeros in the factors. If one of the factors is a decimal, attach the zeros before pointing off in the product.

Solve the following problems, using the space at the right for your calculations. Enter your answers on the blank lines provided.

Examples:

```
  2 3 0 0        $ 2.3 1
    3 4 0            2 4 0
  ───────        ─────────
    9 2              9 2 4
  6 9              4 6 2
  ───────        ─────────
7 8 2,0 0 0      $ 5 5 4.4 0
```

1. 2,600 × 120 = _____
2. 130 × 240   = _____
3. 314 × 230   = _____
4. 340 × $2.31 = _____
5. 260 × $3.12 = _____
6. 180 × $4.36 = _____

[18]

Section 5

DRILL 17. (Multiplication of numbers containing end zeros)

If either or both factors of a product are decimals containing end zeros, ignore those zeros in multiplying. End zeros at the right of a decimal point have no effect upon the value of the number.

Solve the following problems, using the space at the right for your calculations. Enter your answers on the blank lines provided.

Example: $640 \times \$3.20 = ?$

$$
\begin{array}{r}
\$\ 3.2 \\
6\ 4\ 0 \\
\hline
1\ 2\ 8 \\
1\ 9\ 2 \\
\hline
\$\ 2{,}0\ 4\ 8.0 \text{ or } \$2{,}048
\end{array}
$$

1. $260 \times \$3.10 =$ _____
2. $3{,}500 \times \$1.70 =$ _____
3. $1{,}800 \times \$22.10 =$ _____
4. $6.50 \times 2{,}300 =$ _____
5. $320 \times 1.22 =$ _____
6. $155 \times \$1.60 =$ _____

DRILL 18. (Multiplication by 1¢ and 10¢)

To multiply by 1¢, move the decimal point in the multiplicand two places to the left. To multiply by 10¢, move the decimal point in the multiplicand one place to the left.

Examples: 215 pounds @ 1¢ = $2.15

43.5 yards @ 10¢ = $4.35

The following problems provide practice in finding the cost of an article when the price is 1¢ or 10¢. Perform the multiplication mentally and write the answers on the blank spaces provided.

1. 345 lb. @ 1¢ = _____
2. 233 yd. @ 10¢ = _____
3. 65 ft. @ 10¢ = _____
4. 108 lb. @ 1¢ = _____
5. 95 gal. @ 10¢ = _____

6. 43 ft. @ 1¢ = _____
7. 342 lb. @ 1¢ = _____
8. 4.5 yd. @ 10¢ = _____
8. 625 ft. @ 1¢ = _____
10. 43.5 lb. @ 10¢ = _____

11. 110.5 yd. @ 10¢ = _____
12. 1,850 lb. @ $.01 = _____
13. 2,340 bu. @ $.10 = _____
14. 870 gal. @ $.01 = _____
15. 16.5 ft. @ $.10 = _____

DRILL 19. (Multiplication by a multiple of 1¢ and 10¢)

To multiply by a unit price such as $.04 or $.40, multiply by 4 or 40, as the case may be, and write the product. Then point off two places in the product and prefix a dollar sign.

Perform the multiplication mentally in each of the following, and write the answers on the blank spaces provided.

Example 1.

37 ft. @ $.04 = ?

$37 \times 4 = 148$

Ans. $1.48

Example 2.

26 yd. @ $.40 = ?

$26 \times 40 = 1{,}040$

Ans. $10.40

1. 55 lb. @ $.03 = _____
2. 52 yd. @ $.06 = _____
3. 85 ft. @ $.04 = _____
4. 112 yd. @ $.05 = _____
5. 35 lb. @ $.08 = _____

6. 60 bu. @ $.40 = _____
7. 43 qt. @ $.30 = _____
8. 13 gal. @ $.60 = _____
9. 25 bu. @ $.70 = _____
10. 83 yd. @ $.20 = _____

11. 80 lb. @ 6¢ = _____
12. 75 yd. @ 5¢ = _____
13. 28 qt. @ 40¢ = _____
14. 110 gal. @ 70¢ = _____
15. 134 ft. @ 2¢ = _____

DRILL 20. (Review of number sentences)

In the blank space at the right of each of the following number sentences, write the numeral that should be substituted for the letter or question mark to make the sentence true.

1. $N + 8 = 19$ _____	7. $N \div 5 = 10$ _____	13. $5 \times ? = 40$ _____
2. $N + 6 = 34$ _____	8. $N \div 3 = 12$ _____	14. $N + 12 = 22$ _____
3. $N - 8 = 20$ _____	9. $? + 9 = 24$ _____	15. $4 \times N = 36$ _____
4. $N - 4 = 19$ _____	10. $7 \times N = 35$ _____	16. $N - 10 = 24$ _____
5. $6 \times N = 30$ _____	11. $N \div 6 = 9$ _____	17. $N \div 8 = 8$ _____
6. $9 \times N = 72$ _____	12. $? - 9 = 15$ _____	18. $8 \times ? = 48$ _____

DRILL 21. (Review of estimating the product)

In each of the following, show the rounded factors and the estimated product.

	Rounded Factors	Estimated Product		Rounded Factors	Estimated Product
1. 34×258	_____ × _____	= _____	7. 7.05×4.31	_____ × _____	= _____
2. 22×307	_____ × _____	= _____	8. $81 \times .47$	_____ × _____	= _____
3. 208×431	_____ × _____	= _____	9. $72 \times .83$	_____ × _____	= _____
4. 72×63.1	_____ × _____	= _____	10. $.415 \times 54$	_____ × _____	= _____
5. 5.43×44	_____ × _____	= _____	11. $.723 \times .62$	_____ × _____	= _____
6. 76×6.09	_____ × _____	= _____	12. $.684 \times 1.01$	_____ × _____	= _____

DRILL 22. (Review of multiplication)

The drill below provides review practice in deciding whether a product is reasonable by comparing it with the estimated product.

In each of the following, show the rounded factors, the estimated product, and the exact product. Make the necessary calculations in the space provided at the right.

	Rounded Factors	Estimated Product	Exact Product
1. 604×12.02	_____ × _____	= _____	_____
2. 710×520	_____ × _____	= _____	_____
3. $1,650 \times 3.4$	_____ × _____	= _____	_____
4. $45 \times \$2.35$	_____ × _____	= _____	_____
5. $86 \times \$9.40$	_____ × _____	= _____	_____
6. $54 \times \$32$	_____ × _____	= _____	_____
7. $96 \times \$2.98$	_____ × _____	= _____	_____
8. $1,015 \times \$.96$	_____ × _____	= _____	_____
9. $120 \times \$18.85$	_____ × _____	= _____	_____
10. $1,800 \times \$3.40$	_____ × _____	= _____	_____

SECTION 6. Aliquot Parts

In figuring the amount of a sale, it is often helpful to be familiar with the aliquot parts of $1. When one number is contained in another without a remainder, the first is known as an aliquot part of the second. For example, $12\frac{1}{2}$¢ is contained exactly eight times in $1. It is therefore $\frac{1}{8}$ of $1, and is said to be an aliquot part of $1.

The term aliquot part is also used to describe a number that is a convenient multiple of an aliquot part. For example, $37\frac{1}{2}$¢ is three times $12\frac{1}{2}$¢. It is therefore $\frac{3}{8}$ of $1, and may be referred to as an aliquot part of $1.

The more commonly used aliquot parts of $1 are the following:

50¢ = $\frac{1}{2}$	20¢ = $\frac{1}{5}$	$12\frac{1}{2}$¢ = $\frac{1}{8}$	$33\frac{1}{3}$¢ = $\frac{1}{3}$
25¢ = $\frac{1}{4}$	40¢ = $\frac{2}{5}$	$37\frac{1}{2}$¢ = $\frac{3}{8}$	$66\frac{2}{3}$¢ = $\frac{2}{3}$
75¢ = $\frac{3}{4}$	60¢ = $\frac{3}{5}$	$62\frac{1}{2}$¢ = $\frac{5}{8}$	$16\frac{2}{3}$¢ = $\frac{1}{6}$
	80¢ = $\frac{4}{5}$	$87\frac{1}{2}$¢ = $\frac{7}{8}$	$83\frac{1}{3}$¢ = $\frac{5}{6}$

When the unit price is an aliquot part, such as $37\frac{1}{2}$¢, the work of multiplying to find the total cost can be simplified by multiplying by the fraction instead of by the unit price.

Example: A salesclerk sold 16 yards of ribbon at $37\frac{1}{2}$¢ a yard. Since $37\frac{1}{2}$¢ is $\frac{3}{8}$ of $1, the amount of the sale may be figured in the manner shown at the right.

$37\frac{1}{2}$¢ $= \frac{3}{8}$ of $1
16 yd. @ $1 = $16
16 yd. @ $37\frac{1}{2}$¢ $= \frac{3}{8} \times $16 = $6

By using $37\frac{1}{2}$¢ as an aliquot part of $1, you can perform the multiplication mentally instead of using the much longer process of multiplying 16 by $37\frac{1}{2}$¢.

EXERCISE. (Practical problems)

1. Complete the sales slip given below. Make the extensions mentally, using aliquot parts of $1, and find the total sale.

2. Complete the sales slip given below. Make the extensions mentally, using aliquot parts of $1, and find the total sale.

WESTEND FOOD SUPPLY

DATE Dec. 11 19 --
SOLD TO Brooks Fast Foods
ADDRESS 1212 Central Blvd., City

CLERK QTY.	CASH	CHARGE	TAKE	SEND	UNIT PRICE	AMOUNT
24	cans tomato juice				.37½	
16	lb. franks				.87½	
16	doz. muffins				.62½	
24	boxes tea				.87½	
18	pt. tomatoes				.50	

ALFRED'S FABRICS

DATE Sept. 12 19 --
SOLD TO Mrs. Richard Clark
ADDRESS 13 Yellowstone Ave., City

CLERK QTY.	CASH	CHARGE	TAKE	SEND	UNIT PRICE	AMOUNT
16	yd. seam binding				.12½	
8	pkg. pins				.25	
8	spools thread				.37½	
8	zippers				.15	
16	yd. muslin				.87½	
	Sales tax 4%					

DRILL 23. (Aliquot parts)

The following problems provide practice in using unit prices that are aliquot parts of $1.

1. 184 ft. @ $12\frac{1}{2}$¢ = ___ × $184 = $_____

2. 64 bu. @ $37\frac{1}{2}$¢ = ___ × $64 = $_____

3. 48 yd. @ 75¢ = ___ × $48 = $_____

4. 72 lb. @ $87\frac{1}{2}$¢ = ___ × $72 = $_____

5. 38 lb. @ 25¢ = ___ × $38 = $_____

6. 84 gal. @ $12\frac{1}{2}$¢ = ___ × $84 = $_____

7. 155 ft. @ 50¢ = ___ × $155 = $_____

8. 40 yd. @ $37\frac{1}{2}$¢ = ___ × $40 = $_____

9. 220 lb. @ 75¢ = ___ × $220 = $_____

10. 128 doz. @ $62\frac{1}{2}$¢ = ___ × $128 = $_____

DRILL 24. (Aliquot parts)

The following provide practice in using unit prices that are aliquot parts of $1.

1. 24 bu. @ $66\frac{2}{3}$¢ = _____ × $ 24 = $_____

2. 42 lb. @ $16\frac{2}{3}$¢ = _____ × $ 42 = $_____

3. 360 yd. @ $33\frac{1}{3}$¢ = _____ × $360 = $_____

4. 60 yd. @ $83\frac{1}{3}$¢ = _____ × $ 60 = $_____

5. 84 ft. @ $16\frac{2}{3}$¢ = _____ × $ 84 = $_____

6. 132 lb. @ $33\frac{1}{3}$¢ = _____ × $132 = $_____

7. 45 bu. @ $66\frac{2}{3}$¢ = _____ × $ 45 = $_____

8. 60 ft. @ 20¢ = _____ × $ 60 = $_____

9. 200 lb. @ 40¢ = _____ × $200 = $_____

10. 300 lb. @ 80¢ = _____ × $300 = $_____

DRILL 25. (Aliquot parts)

The following provide additional practice in using unit prices that are aliquot parts of $1.

1. 17 doz. @ 25¢ = ____ × $____ = $_____

2. 52 cans @ $12\frac{1}{2}$¢ = ____ × $____ = $_____

3. 45 gal. @ $16\frac{2}{3}$¢ = ____ × $____ = $_____

4. 25 yd. @ $33\frac{1}{3}$¢ = ____ × $____ = $_____

5. 35 cans @ $12\frac{1}{2}$¢ = ____ × $____ = $_____

6. 47 doz. @ 25¢ = ____ × $____ = $_____

7. 50 lb. @ $33\frac{1}{3}$¢ = ____ × $____ = $_____

8. 82 ft. @ $16\frac{2}{3}$¢ = ____ × $____ = $_____

9.* 45 bu. @ $37\frac{1}{2}$¢ = ____ × $____ = $_____

10. 35 doz. @ 75¢ = ____ × $____ = $_____

11. 65 yd. @ $66\frac{2}{3}$¢ = ____ × $____ = $_____

12. 18 ft. @ $62\frac{1}{2}$¢ = ____ × $____ = $_____

13. 29 gal. @ 75¢ = ____ × $____ = $_____

14. 175 yd. @ $66\frac{2}{3}$¢ = ____ × $____ = $_____

15. 92 lb. @ $37\frac{1}{2}$¢ = ____ × $____ = $_____

16. 55 bu. @ $87\frac{1}{2}$¢ = ____ × $____ = $_____

---

*$\frac{3}{8}$ × $45 = $$\frac{135}{8}$ = $16.875 = $16.88. If the denominator of the fraction in the multiplier is not contained in the multiplicand, as 8 into $45, then first multiply by the numerator (3 × $45) and then divide (by 8 evenly).

SECTION 7. Unit Prices

Prices are often given in terms of several units of an article. It is important that you be able to find the price in terms of a single unit. You will want to know this price when making price comparisons.

EXERCISE. (Practical problems)

1. In looking over the advertisement of a special sale given by a nearby store, you notice the following price quotations for the quantities indicated. Find the cost of each item in terms of one unit. In this and the following problems, you may make calculations in the space at the side of or below each form.

	QUANTITY	PRICE	PRICE OF ONE UNIT
a	3 shirts	$19.50	
b	6 pr. socks	7.20	
c	5 handkerchiefs	3.75	
d	3 neckties	8.40	
e	2 sport shirts	7.50	
f	2 belts	6.80	
g	3 pr. shoe laces	.93	
h	2 pr. cufflinks	5.96	

2. Find the price of one unit for each item below. The prices quoted are for the quantities indicated.

	ITEM	QUANTITY (No. of Units)	PRICE	PRICE OF ONE UNIT
a	Carrots	3 bunches	63¢	
b	Potatoes	15 lb.	$2.25	
c	Tomatoes	4 cans	$1.36	
d	Apples	3 lb.	75¢	
e	Peas	5 cans	$1.30	
f	Beans	3 cans	84¢	

3. The following price quotations appear in the special-sale advertisement of the Elmwood Pharmacy. Find the saving per unit at the special sale.

	ITEM	REGULAR PRICE	SPECIAL SALE PRICE	SAVING PER UNIT AT SPECIAL SALE
a	Tooth paste	59¢ a tube	3 for $1.59	
b	Hair spray	$1.49 a bottle	2 for $2.78	
c	Hand cream	65¢ a jar	2 for $1.18	
d	Aspirin	49¢ a bottle	3 for $1.35	
e	Memo pads	15¢ each	3 for 39¢	
f	Notebooks	37¢ each	4 for $1.32	

DRILL **26.** (Inverse operations)

If we start with 6 and multiply it by 4, we get 24. If we now divide 24 by 4, we get 6, the number we started with. Dividing 24 by 4 "undoes" what was done by multiplying 6 by 4. Hence, if $4 \times N = 24$, we can "undo" the multiplication by dividing 24 by 4, and thereby find that N is equal to 6. Substituting 6 for N gives $4 \times 6 = 24$, a true sentence.

Similarly, if $N \div 6 = 8$, we can "undo" the division by multiplying 8 by 6. We find that N is equal to 48. Substituting 48 for N gives $48 \div 6 = 8$, a true sentence.

As you saw in Section 2, operations that "undo" each other are called *inverse operations*. Division, then, is the inverse of multiplication and multiplication is the inverse of division.

On the blank line at the right of each of the following number sentences, write the numeral that should be substituted for the letter or question mark to make the sentence true. Apply the principle of inverse operations to obtain your answer. Keep in mind that addition and subtraction, as well as multiplication and division, are the inverse of each other.

1. $8 \times N = 72$ _____   6. $7 \times N = 56$ _____   11. $N + 9 = 25$ _____

2. $6 \times N = 90$ _____   7. $N \div 4 = 20$ _____   12. $5 \times N = 60$ _____

3. $N \div 6 = 12$ _____   8. $N - 8 = 24$ _____   13. $N - 10 = 25$ _____

4. $N \div 5 = 25$ _____   9. $N \div 7 = 14$ _____   14. $N \div 8 = 24$ _____

5. $N + 6 = 19$ _____   10. $9 \times N = 108$ _____   15. $8 \times N = 120$ _____

DRILL **27.** (Identifying factors and products)

When you multiply two factors, such as 4 and 6, you are finding their product, which is 24. Thus, $4 \times 6 = 24$; or *Factor $\times$ Factor = Product*.

When you divide the product, 24, by one of the factors, say 4, you are finding the other factor, which is 6. Thus, $24 \div 4 = 6$ or *Product $\div$ Factor = Factor*. Division, then, is the process of finding the other factor when the product and one factor are known.

In the number sentence, $24 \div 4 = 6$, 24 is the *dividend*, 4 is the *divisor*, and 6 is the *quotient*. The product of 4 and 6 is 24. The dividend in any division problem represents a product. The divisor and quotient are the factors of that product.

Above each numeral and letter in the following number sentences, you are to print "F" or "P" to show whether it represents a factor or a product. Keep in mind that the dividend in a division expression represents a product. Observe the following examples.

Examples:
$$\overset{F}{4} \times \overset{F}{6} = \overset{P}{24} \qquad \overset{F}{4} \times \overset{F}{N} = \overset{P}{24} \qquad \overset{F}{N} \times \overset{F}{4} = \overset{P}{24} \qquad \overset{P}{24} \div \overset{F}{4} = \overset{F}{6} \qquad \overset{P}{N} \div \overset{F}{4} = \overset{F}{6} \qquad \overset{P}{24} \div \overset{F}{N} = \overset{F}{6}$$

1. $8 \times 9 = 72$ 5. $N \times 5 = 65$ 9. $7 \times 6 = 42$ 13. $N \div 9 = 7$

2. $6 \times N = 48$ 6. $48 \div 6 = 8$ 10. $N \div 6 = 12$ 14. $9 \times N = 45$

3. $18 \div 6 = 3$ 7. $84 \div N = 12$ 11. $N \times 8 = 120$ 15. $60 \div N = 20$

4. $N \div 8 = 15$ 8. $12 \times N = 98$ 12. $56 \div N = 4$ 16. $N \times 7 = 91$

Section 7

DRILL 28. (Finding missing products and factors)

In the number sentence, $4 \times 6 = N$, the product is missing. Since *Factor × Factor = Product*, we find the missing product by multiplying the factors, 4 and 6. Thus, $N = 4 \times 6 = 24$, the missing product.

In the number sentence, $N \div 4 = 6$, the dividend is missing. Since the dividend represents a product, 4 and 6 are the factors of that product. We therefore find the missing dividend by multiplying the factors, 4 and 6. Thus, $N = 4 \times 6 = 24$, the missing dividend.

In the number sentence, $4 \times N = 24$, one factor is missing. Since *Product ÷ Factor = Factor*, we find the missing factor by dividing 24 by 4. Thus, $N = 24 \div 4 = 6$, the missing factor. When the product and one factor are known, we divide the product by the known factor to find the missing, or unknown, factor.

Above each numeral and letter in each of the following number sentences, you are to print "F" or "P" to show whether it represents a factor or a product.   Then on the blank line at the right, write the numeral that represents the missing number. Apply the principles indicated above. A missing product is found by multiplying the factors. A missing factor is found by dividing the product by the known factor.

1. $18 \times 6 = N$ _____   5. $4 \times N = 52$ _____   9. $15 \times N = 120$ _____

2. $N \div 12 = 6$ _____   6. $16 \times 4 = N$ _____   10. $N \div 6 = 30$ _____

3. $8 \times N = 104$ _____   7. $N \div 8 = 16$ _____   11. $5 \times N = 80$ _____

4. $24 \times 3 = N$ _____   8. $7 \times N = 140$ _____   12. $12 \times N = 60$ _____

DRILL 29. (Division)

When prices are quoted in terms of several units, it is necessary to divide to find the price of one unit. The division is shown in the example at the right. It shows the division of 865 by 35. The divisor is written at the left of the dividend. The quotient is written on a line above the dividend. The undivided remainder, if there is one, may be expressed in the quotient as a fractional part of the divisor. The fraction should always be expressed in simplest form; that is, in lowest terms.

Divide in the problems given below. Express the remainder, if any, as a fractional part of the divisor.

$$\begin{array}{r} 24\frac{5}{7} \\ 35\overline{)865} \\ 70 \\ \hline 165 \\ 140 \\ \hline 25 \quad \frac{25}{35}=\frac{5}{7} \end{array}$$

1. $32\overline{)1344}$ 2. $24\overline{)1014}$ 3. $45\overline{)972}$ 4. $39\overline{)4732}$

5. $48\overline{)1524}$ 6. $21\overline{)4277}$ 7. $32\overline{)1932}$ 8. $56\overline{)6755}$

DRILL **30.** (Checking division)

Division may be checked by multiplying the whole number in the quotient by the divisor and then adding the remainder to that product. The result should equal the dividend.

In the following problems, divide and then check the division. Express the remainder, if any, as a fractional part of the divisor.

1.
$$203 \overline{)21518}$$

2.
$$96 \overline{)2988}$$

3.
$$65 \overline{)2235}$$

4.
$$108 \overline{)11352}$$

Check: Check: Check: Check:

DRILL **31.** (Locating the decimal point in the quotient)

When the dividend contains a decimal and the divisor is a whole number, the decimal point in the quotient is placed directly over the decimal point in the dividend. This is shown in the example at the left.

$$\begin{array}{r} 3.45 \\ 5 \overline{)17.25} \end{array}$$

When the divisor contains a decimal, move the decimal point to the right in both the dividend and divisor as many places as are required to make the divisor a whole number. Then divide in the usual way. Place the decimal point in the quotient directly over the new position of the decimal point in the dividend. The example at the right shows this procedure.

$$\begin{array}{r} 121.5 \\ .04 \overline{)4.86.0} \end{array}$$

Check:
$$\begin{array}{r} 121.5 \\ \underline{.04} \\ 4.860 = 4.86 \end{array}$$

In the following problems, divide and then prove the division.

1.
$$125 \overline{)18.75}$$

2.
$$3.5 \overline{)8.75}$$

3.
$$27 \overline{).2835}$$

4.
$$2.33 \overline{)54.755}$$

Check: Check: Check: Check:

Name _____

SECTION 8. Large-Unit Prices

Many kinds of articles are priced by the hundred (C), the hundredweight or hundred pounds (cwt.), the thousand (M), and the ton (T). To find the cost of a purchase when the price is per 100 or 1,000 units, divide the number of units purchased by 100 or 1,000, as the case may be. Then multiply the result by the quoted price. For example, the cost of 240 bolts at $3 per 100 would be (240 ÷ 100) × $3 = 2.40 × $3 = $7.20.

If the price is per ton and the quantity purchased is expressed in pounds, divide the quantity by 2,000 and then multiply by the price per ton. For example, the cost of 5,600 lb. of bulk cement at $25 per ton is (5,600 ÷ 2,000) × $25 = 2.8 × $25 = $70. When the price is an even number, it may be easier to divide the quantity in pounds by 1,000 and then multiply by half the price per ton. Calculated in this manner, the cost of 2,425 lb. of cement at $24 per ton is (2,425 ÷ 1,000) × $12 = 2.425 × $12 = $29.10.

EXERCISE.   (Practical problems)

Space for making the necessary calculations is provided after each of the following problems.

1. Frank Harris, owner of an office supplies store, purchases from the Capital Paper Products Co. 3,500 filing folders at $2.45 per C and 6,500 Manila envelopes at $16.40 per M. Mr. Harris pays (a) $_____ for the folders and (b) $_____ for the envelopes.

2. Grace Thomas built a new fireplace for her home. She bought 1,120 bricks from the Build-Rite Construction Supply Store at the rate of $135 per C. How much did she pay for the bricks? $_____.

3. On July 15, John Irwin, a farmer, delivers to the General Commodities Company three truck loads of hay weighing 2,140 lb., 2,210 lb., and 2,070 lb., respectively, and receives payment at the rate of $24.85 per ton. The total weight of the hay is (a) _____ lb., for which he receives (b) $_____.

4. At $13.50 per ton, the cost of 12,250 lb. of top-soil will be $_____.

DRILL 32. (Division by 10, 100, and 1,000)

In dividing a number by 10, 100, 1,000, etc., the quotient is found by moving the decimal point to the left in the dividend as many places as there are zeros in the divisor, attaching zeros if necessary.

Examples: $543.7 \div 10 = 54.37$

$3.8 \div 100 = .038$

$2,410 \div 1,000 = 2.41$

Write rapidly the correct answers to the following problems.

1. $573 \div 10$ = _____
2. $1,425 \div 1,000$ = _____
3. $608 \div 100$ = _____
4. $2,740 \div 1,000$ = _____

5. $23.4 \div 10$ = _____
6. $4.2 \div 1,000$ = _____
7. $2.35 \div 100$ = _____
8. $30 \div 1,000$ = _____

9. $7.5 \div 1,000$ = _____
10. $80 \div 100$ = _____
11. $6.2 \div 10$ = _____
12. $1.3 \div 1,000$ = _____

DRILL 33. (Articles priced by the C, Cwt., M, and T)

The following problems provide additional practice in finding the cost of an article when the price is per hundred, hundredweight, thousand, or ton. Write the answers in the spaces provided. Make any necessary calculations in the space at the right.

1. 860 concrete blocks @ $27.50 per C = $_____
2. 1,450 lb. nails @ $17.75 per cwt. = $_____
3. 11,300 bricks @ $63.50 per M = $_____
4. 9,500 lb. coal @ $26.75 per T = $_____
5. 3,550 lb. hay @ $38.00 per T = $_____
6. 850 sheets paper @ $4.05 per C = $_____
7. 4,350 envelopes @ $7.25 per M = $_____
8. 31,420 lb. top-soil @ $28.85 per T = $_____
9. 980 lb. grain @ $4.15 per cwt. = $_____
10. 17,595 lb. fertilizer @ $62.00 per T = $_____

DRILL 34. (Review of multiplication and division by 10, 100, and 1,000)

The review drill below is to aid you in developing further skill in multiplying and dividing by 10, 100, and 1,000. Write the answers rapidly in the spaces provided.

1. 3.28×10 = _____
2. $.049 \times 1,000$ = _____
3. $745 \div 10$ = _____
4. $630 \div 1,000$ = _____
5. 5.2×100 = _____
6. $.04 \times 10$ = _____

7. $345 \div 1,000$ = _____
8. $.05 \div 10$ = _____
9. $4.27 \times 1,000$ = _____
10. $6.4 \div 100$ = _____
11. $.75 \div 1,000$ = _____
12. 21.4×100 = _____

13. $37.5 \div 1,000$ = _____
14. $.062 \times 100$ = _____
15. $.125 \times 10$ = _____
16. $.65 \div 100$ = _____
17. $4.35 \div 100$ = _____
18. $.0075 \times 1,000$ = _____

[28]

SECTION 9.   Average Prices

An average is the quotient obtained by adding a series of numbers and dividing the sum by the number of items added. For example, during one week Helen Green purchased three one-quart baskets of strawberries. She paid $.79 for the first, $.77 for the second, and $.72 for the third. The average price she paid per quart was $.76, as shown by the calculations at the left. If more than one unit is purchased at one of the unit prices, the average price is found by dividing the total cost of all the units by the total number of units purchased. Thus, if Helen purchases one quart of strawberries at $.79, one at $.77, and two at $.72, the average price paid per quart is $.75, as shown at the right.

1 qt. @ $.79 = $ .79
1 qt. @ .77 =   .77
1 qt. @ .72 =   .72
3 qt. $2.28

$2.28 ÷ 3 = $ .76, average
                    price per qt.

1 qt. @ $.79 = $ .79
1 qt. @ .77 =   .77
2 qt. @ .72 = 1.44
4 qt. $3.00

$3.00 ÷ 4 = $ .75, average
                    price per qt.

EXERCISE.   (Practical problems)

Space for making the necessary calculations is provided after each of the following problems.

1. During one week, Mrs. Verna Thornton purchased three melons. She paid 89¢ for the first melon, 92¢ for the second, and 83¢ for the third. For the three melons she paid an average price of _____¢ per melon.

2. During one heating season, Earl Ford purchased four tons of coal at $28.50 a ton, three tons at $27.75, and one ton at $26.75. For the season, the average price he paid was $_____ a ton.

3. On an automobile trip, Mary Thompson purchased 20 gallons of gasoline at 52¢ a gallon, 10 gallons at 53.5¢, and 10 gallons at 54.5¢. The average price per gallon of gasoline purchased on the trip was _____¢.

4. Carl Ramsey, a farmer, sold his wheat crop as follows: 600 bushels at $1.55 per bushel; 400 bushels at $1.63 per bushel; and the remainder, 200 bushels, at $1.69 per bushel. For the entire crop he received an average price of $_____ per bushel.

5. A book salesman works five days each week, Monday through Friday. During the first four days of one week he sells 12 dictionaries on Monday, 18 on Tuesday, 25 on Wednesday, and 21 on Thursday. He wishes to sell enough books on Friday so that his average will be 18 a day for the five days. (a) To average 18 a day, he must sell a total of _____ dictionaries during the five days. (b) The total number he has sold during the first four days is _____. (c) The number he must sell on the fifth day, Friday, is _____.

6. For the first five months of the year a saleswoman's monthly sales were $5,900, $6,250, $6,650, $6,900, and $6,850, respectively. Her sales for the sixth month must be $_____ in order that her monthly average for the six months may be $6,500.

DRILL 35. (Estimating the quotient)

A large error in division or an error in placing the decimal point in the quotient can usually be detected readily by estimating the quotient. The quotient is estimated by rounding the dividend and divisor to numbers that can be divided mentally or by short division. Then, the quotient of the rounded numbers is found. For example, the quotient of $6,275 \div 890$ may be estimated at $6,300 \div 900 = 7$.

In each of the following problems give (a) the estimated answer and (b) the exact answer, making the necessary calculations in the space at the right. Check the exact answer by multiplication.

	Estimated Answer	Exact Answer
1. $419.84 \div 32$ =	_____	_____
2. $53.55 \div 1.7$ =	_____	_____
3. $23.925 \div 2.75$ =	_____	_____
4. $5.985 \div .45$ =	_____	_____

DRILL 36. (Division to a stated number of decimal places)

```
          .0 4 7 = .05   Check:  1 5 5
1 5 5 ) 7.3 0 0                   .0 4 7
        6 2 0                     1 0 8 5
        1 1 0 0                     6 2 0
        1 0 8 5                   7 2 8 5
            1 5                         1 5
                                 7.3 0 0
```

If the divisor is not contained evenly in the dividend, the quotient may be carried to a stated number of decimal places. When this is done, the division must be carried one place further. The quotient is then rounded to the stated number of places. The procedure for dividing 7.3 by 155 to 2 decimal places is shown at the left. The quotient is carried to 3 decimal places, giving .047. Rounded to 2 decimal places, the final result is .05. The check by multiplication is shown at the right.

In the following problems give (a) the estimated answer and (b) the exact answer correct to two decimal places. Check the exact answer by multiplication.

	Estimated Answer	Exact Answer
1. $127.9 \div 42$ =	_____	_____
2. $37.8 \div 2.9$ =	_____	_____
3. $3.56 \div 6.7$ =	_____	_____
4. $44 \div 2.7$ =	_____	_____

DRILL 37. (Dropping end zeros in the divisor)

When there are end zeros at the right of the divisor and the divisor is a whole number, the division can be simplified. Take the end zeros off the divisor before dividing. Move the decimal point in the dividend to the left as many places as there were zeros taken off. For example, in dividing 7,504.5 by 1,500, you may take two zeros from the divisor. Make the computation by dividing 75.045 by 15. The quotient is 5.003. An estimated quotient would be $8,000 \div 2,000$, which is 4.

In each of the following problems give (a) the estimated answer and (b) the exact answer, calculated in the manner indicated above, correct to two decimal places. Check the exact answer by multiplication.

	Estimated Answer	Exact Answer
1. $23,000 \div 3,700$ =	_____	_____
2. $5,475 \div 270$ =	_____	_____
3. $56,210 \div 4,300$ =	_____	_____
4. $49,770 \div 1,800$ =	_____	_____

Name _____

UNIT THREE   Special Buying Problems

SECTION 10.   Buying Fractions of a Unit

Frequently you may want to buy a fractional part of something, such as $\frac{1}{2}$ dozen eggs or $\frac{2}{3}$ of a yard of cloth. In order to find the cost in such cases, it is necessary to multiply the price by the fraction. For example, if you buy $\frac{3}{4}$ lb. meat at 84¢, you should multiply

$\frac{3}{4}$ lb. @ 84¢

84¢ ÷ 4 = 21¢ cost of $\frac{1}{4}$ lb.

3 × 21¢ = 63¢ cost of $\frac{3}{4}$ lb.

84¢ by $\frac{3}{4}$. This is done by dividing 84¢ by 4 and multiplying the quotient by 3. The calculation is shown at the left.   If the price is not evenly divisible by the denominator, multiply the price by the numerator of

$\frac{3}{4}$ yd. @ 85¢

3 × 85¢ = $2.55 cost of 3 yd.

$2.55 ÷ 4 = 63$\frac{3}{4}$¢, or 64¢, cost of $\frac{3}{4}$ yd.

the fraction, and then divide that product by the denominator. This procedure is shown at the right, in the calculation of the cost of $\frac{3}{4}$ of a yard of cloth at 85¢ a yard.

EXERCISE.   (Practical problems)

1. Find the cost of the fractional quantities in the following problems. Make your calculations in the spaces provided.

a $\frac{1}{2}$ doz. eggs   @ 98¢ = 98¢ ÷ 2 = _____

b $\frac{1}{4}$ lb. butter   @ 92¢ = 92¢ ÷ 4 = _____

c $\frac{1}{3}$ yd. cotton   @ 81¢ = 81¢ ÷ 3 = _____

d $\frac{5}{6}$ doz. oranges   @ 96¢ = 96¢ ÷ 6 = _____ × 5 = _____

e $\frac{2}{3}$ yd. binding   @ 87¢ = 87¢ ÷ 3 = _____ × 2 = _____

f $\frac{3}{4}$ lb. chicken   @ 97¢ = 97¢ × 3 = _____ ÷ 4 = _____

g $\frac{5}{6}$ yd. gingham @ 77¢ = 77¢ × 5 = _____ ÷ 6 = _____

2. Karen Lawson bought the following items in the yard goods department of the Montrose Department Store. Find the cost of each item and the total cost of the purchase. Write the results in the spaces provided. Make your calculations in the space at the right.

$\frac{1}{2}$ yd. gabardine   @ $3.95 = $_____

$\frac{3}{4}$ yd. corduroy   @ $1.87 = $_____

$\frac{5}{6}$ yd. velvet   @ $5.49 = $_____

$\frac{7}{8}$ yd. polyester   @ $2.49 = $_____

$\frac{5}{8}$ yd. wool tweed @ $5.45 = $_____

   Total $_____

3. Mrs. Sybil Turner purchases the following items at the Cortland Market. Find the cost of each item and the total cost of the purchase, writing the results in the spaces provided. Make your calculations in the space at the right.

$\frac{3}{4}$ lb. butter   @ $ .87 = $_____

$\frac{7}{8}$ lb. steak   @ $1.89 = $_____

$\frac{5}{8}$ lb. chicken   @ $ .89 = $_____

$\frac{3}{4}$ lb. bacon   @ $1.49 = $_____

   Total $_____

[31]

DRILL 38. (Multiplication of a fraction by a fraction)

A numeral in a form such as $\frac{2}{3}$ is a *fraction*. The numeral above the horizontal line is the *numerator*. The numeral below the line is the *denominator*.

You will often find it necessary to multiply a fraction by a fraction. Multiply the numerators to obtain the numerator of the product. Multiply the denominators to obtain the denominator of the product. For example, in $\frac{2}{3} \times \frac{4}{5}$, the product of the numerators is 8; and the product of the denominators is 15. Therefore, the product of $\frac{2}{3} \times \frac{4}{5}$ is $\frac{8}{15}$. In $\frac{2}{3} \times \frac{4}{5} \times \frac{4}{7}$, the product of the numerators is 32; and the product of the denominators is 105. Therefore, the product of $\frac{2}{3} \times \frac{4}{5} \times \frac{4}{7}$ is $\frac{32}{105}$.

Find the product in each of the following.

1. $\frac{3}{4} \times \frac{3}{5} =$ 3. $\frac{5}{6} \times \frac{7}{8} =$ 5. $\frac{7}{8} \times \frac{3}{4} =$ 7. $\frac{1}{3} \times \frac{5}{8} \times \frac{1}{2} =$ 9. $\frac{2}{3} \times \frac{4}{7} \times \frac{2}{5} =$

2. $\frac{2}{3} \times \frac{5}{7} =$ 4. $\frac{4}{7} \times \frac{5}{9} =$ 6. $\frac{2}{9} \times \frac{4}{5} =$ 8. $\frac{1}{2} \times \frac{3}{4} \times \frac{5}{8} =$ 10. $\frac{4}{5} \times \frac{2}{3} \times \frac{4}{9} =$

DRILL 39. (Reducing fractions to lowest terms)

The numerator and the denominator of a fraction are its *terms*. A fraction is in lowest terms when no number except 1 will exactly divide both of its terms.

A fraction not in lowest terms can be reduced to lowest terms by dividing the numerator and denominator by their greatest common factor. The greatest common factor is the largest number that will divide each of them without a remainder. The value of the fraction is unchanged.

$$\frac{18}{24} = \frac{18 \div 6}{24 \div 6} = \frac{3}{4}; \text{ or } \frac{\overset{3}{\cancel{18}}}{\underset{4}{\cancel{24}}} = \frac{3}{4}$$

The problems below provide practice in reducing fractions. Reduce each fraction to lowest terms.

1. $\frac{10}{12} =$ 4. $\frac{21}{30} =$ 7. $\frac{9}{15} =$ 10. $\frac{14}{32} =$

2. $\frac{6}{9} =$ 5. $\frac{15}{35} =$ 8. $\frac{28}{40} =$ 11. $\frac{36}{45} =$

3. $\frac{12}{20} =$ 6. $\frac{24}{36} =$ 9. $\frac{12}{28} =$ 12. $\frac{30}{80} =$

DRILL 40. (Reducing the product of fractions to lowest terms)

Whenever the answer to a problem is a fraction, or contains a fraction, the fraction should be expressed in lowest terms. The product of two or more fractions can be obtained in lowest terms by dividing numerators and denominators by their common factors before multiplying. In the example at the right, 5 is a common factor of the first numerator, 5, and of the second denominator, 15. It divides into 5 once and into 15, 3 times. 2 is a common factor of the first denominator, 6, and of the third numerator, 8. It divides into 6, 3 times and into 8, 4 times. The answer is $\frac{44}{81}$.

$$\frac{5}{6} \times \frac{11}{15} \times \frac{8}{9} = \frac{\overset{1}{\cancel{5}}}{\underset{3}{\cancel{6}}} \times \frac{11}{\underset{3}{\cancel{15}}} \times \frac{\overset{4}{\cancel{8}}}{9} = \frac{44}{81}$$

Find the product in each of the following. Be sure that the product is expressed in lowest terms.

1. $\frac{4}{5} \times \frac{5}{16} =$ 3. $\frac{7}{8} \times \frac{4}{9} \times \frac{3}{4} =$ 5. $\frac{5}{8} \times \frac{7}{15} \times \frac{4}{5} =$ 7. $\frac{4}{5} \times \frac{45}{54} \times \frac{14}{15} =$

2. $\frac{3}{4} \times \frac{8}{9} =$ 4. $\frac{2}{3} \times \frac{3}{4} \times \frac{8}{9} =$ 6. $\frac{5}{6} \times \frac{12}{25} \times \frac{3}{4} =$ 8. $\frac{15}{16} \times \frac{32}{35} \times \frac{45}{48} =$

Section 10

DRILL 41. (Changing an improper fraction to mixed number form)

When the numerator of a fraction is smaller than the denominator, the fraction is a *proper fraction*. When it is equal to or greater than the denominator, the fraction is an *improper fraction*. For example, $\frac{2}{3}$ is a proper fraction. The fractions $\frac{5}{5}$ and $\frac{8}{5}$ are improper fractions.

A number represented by a numeral like $3\frac{4}{5}$, consisting of a whole-number numeral and a fraction, is called a *mixed number*. In some computations you will find it necessary to change an improper fraction to a mixed number. This is done by dividing the numerator by the denominator. The process of changing $\frac{57}{18}$ to a mixed number is shown at the right. The fraction in the answer should be given in lowest terms.

$$\frac{57}{18} = 57 \div 18 = 3\frac{1}{6}$$

$$\begin{array}{r} 3\frac{1}{6} \\ 18)\overline{57} \\ 54 \\ \hline 3 \end{array}$$

$$\frac{3}{18} = \frac{1}{6}$$

Change each improper fraction below to mixed number form.

1. $\frac{210}{17} =$　　　　2. $\frac{267}{12} =$　　　　3. $\frac{525}{21} =$　　　　4. $\frac{507}{36} =$　　　　5. $\frac{840}{39} =$

DRILL 42. (Multiplication of a whole number and a fraction)

The general method for finding the product of a whole number and a fraction is to multiply the numerator by the whole number, and divide by the denominator. This is shown in Example *A*, below. Sometimes this process can be made easier by thinking of the whole number as a fraction. For example, the whole number 16 is equal to the fraction $\frac{16}{1}$. Then you use the rules for reducing the product of fractions to lowest terms. In Example *B* below, the whole number is evenly divisible by the denominator of the fraction. In Example *C*, the whole number and the denominator of the fraction contain a common factor.

(A) $35 \times \frac{5}{6} = \frac{175}{6} = 29\frac{1}{6}$　　　　(B) $\overset{4}{\cancel{16}} \times \frac{3}{\cancel{4}} = 12$　　　　(C) $\overset{5}{\cancel{25}} \times \frac{3}{\underset{2}{\cancel{10}}} = \frac{15}{2} = 7\frac{1}{2}$

Make the following multiplications.

1. $24 \times \frac{1}{3} =$　　　　4. $19 \times \frac{1}{4} =$　　　　7. $28 \times \frac{5}{8} =$

2. $16 \times \frac{3}{4} =$　　　　5. $25 \times \frac{5}{9} =$　　　　8. $32 \times \frac{5}{12} =$

3. $14 \times \frac{3}{7} =$　　　　6. $33 \times \frac{4}{5} =$　　　　9. $3 \times \frac{13}{15} =$

DRILL 43. (Addition and subtraction of like fractions)

Fractions such as $\frac{7}{8}$ and $\frac{5}{8}$, whose denominators are the same, are called *like fractions*. They have a *common denominator*. To add or subtract like fractions, add or subtract the numerators and write the result over the common denominator. For example, $\frac{7}{8} + \frac{5}{8} = \frac{12}{8} = 1\frac{1}{2}$; and $\frac{7}{8} - \frac{5}{8} = \frac{2}{8} = \frac{1}{4}$. An answer with a value less than one should be stated as a proper fraction in lowest terms. An answer with a value more than one should be stated as a mixed number, with the fraction part in lowest terms.

Make the additions and subtractions below.

1. $\frac{2}{7} + \frac{3}{7} =$ 4. $\frac{6}{8} + \frac{9}{8} =$ 7. $\frac{21}{18} - \frac{9}{18} =$ 10. $\frac{4}{20} + \frac{10}{20} + \frac{5}{20} =$

2. $\frac{5}{9} + \frac{2}{9} =$ 5. $\frac{7}{12} + \frac{9}{12} =$ 8. $\frac{11}{12} + \frac{9}{12} =$ 11. $\frac{5}{16} + \frac{12}{16} + \frac{8}{16} =$

3. $\frac{7}{10} - \frac{4}{10} =$ 6. $\frac{7}{12} - \frac{5}{12} =$ 9. $\frac{18}{16} - \frac{12}{16} =$ 12. $\frac{14}{24} + \frac{18}{24} + \frac{20}{24} =$

DRILL 44. (Raising a fraction to higher terms)

If two fractions are equivalent, the one with the larger numbers in the numerator and denominator is said to be in higher terms. A fraction may be raised to higher terms by multiplying both terms by the same number. For example, if it is desired to express $\frac{3}{4}$ in terms of twenty-fourths, multiply the numerator and denominator by 6. This process is shown at the right. The value of the fraction is not changed by raising to higher terms. $\frac{3}{4} = \frac{3\ (\times 6)}{4\ (\times 6)} = \frac{18}{24}$

The following problems provide practice in raising fractions to higher terms.

1. Express each of the following with a denominator of 16:

   a $\frac{1}{2} =$ b $\frac{3}{8} =$ c $\frac{3}{4} =$ d $\frac{5}{8} =$

2. Express each of the following with a denominator of 24:

   a $\frac{3}{8} =$ b $\frac{2}{3} =$ c $\frac{3}{4} =$ d $\frac{5}{6} =$

3. Express each of the following with a denominator of 30:

   a $\frac{1}{5} =$ b $\frac{3}{6} =$ c $\frac{8}{10} =$ d $\frac{2}{3} =$

DRILL 45. (Addition and subtraction of unlike fractions)

Fractions whose denominators are different are called *unlike fractions*. Before unlike fractions can be added or subtracted, they must be expressed as fractions with a common denominator. Raise one or more of the fractions to higher terms. For example, to add $\frac{1}{3}$ and $\frac{4}{5}$, $\frac{1}{3}$ is changed to $\frac{5}{15}$; and $\frac{4}{5}$ is changed to $\frac{12}{15}$. The addition then becomes: $\frac{1}{3} + \frac{4}{5} = \frac{5}{15} + \frac{12}{15} = \frac{17}{15} = 1\frac{2}{15}$. Subtraction of unlike fractions is done in a similar manner. Thus, $\frac{3}{4} - \frac{2}{3} = \frac{9}{12} - \frac{8}{12} = \frac{1}{12}$.

Make the additions and subtractions indicated below.

1. $\frac{1}{2} + \frac{3}{4} =$ 4. $\frac{8}{9} - \frac{2}{3} =$ 7. $\frac{9}{10} - \frac{5}{6} =$ 10. $\frac{1}{4} + \frac{1}{2} + \frac{1}{3} =$

2. $\frac{5}{6} - \frac{1}{12} =$ 5. $\frac{11}{12} - \frac{5}{8} =$ 8. $\frac{1}{2} + \frac{5}{6} + \frac{1}{3} =$ 11. $\frac{3}{4} + \frac{1}{5} + \frac{1}{2} =$

3. $\frac{3}{4} + \frac{5}{8} =$ 6. $\frac{5}{6} + \frac{3}{4} =$ 9. $\frac{1}{5} + \frac{1}{2} + \frac{7}{10} =$ 12. $\frac{1}{4} + \frac{2}{5} + \frac{1}{8} =$

SECTION 11. Purchases Involving Mixed Numbers

Often, the price of an item or the quantity purchased is a mixed number. When the quantity purchased is a mixed number, multiply the price by each part of the mixed number separately and add the results. The computation at the left shows the cost of $2\frac{3}{4}$ yards of cloth at 89¢ a yard.

When the price is a mixed number and is the multiplicand, multiply each part of the mixed number separately by the quantity and add the results. The computation at the right shows the cost of 17 yards of cloth at $39\frac{1}{2}$¢ a yard.

$2\frac{3}{4}$ yd. @ 89¢

$.89$
$2\frac{3}{4}$
4)2 67
$\quad 66\frac{3}{4}$ $\quad(\frac{3}{4}\times 89)$
$\quad 1.78$ $\quad(2\times 89)$
$\$2.44\frac{3}{4}$, or $2.45

17 yd. @ $39\frac{1}{2}$¢

$.39\frac{1}{2}$
$\quad 17$
2)17
$\quad 8\frac{1}{2}$ $\quad(17\times\frac{1}{2})$
$\quad 2\ 73$ $\Big\}$ (17×39)
$\quad 3\ 9$
$\$6.71\frac{1}{2}$, or $6.72

EXERCISE. (Practical problems)

1. Complete the sales slip given at the right making any necessary calculations in the space below.

Martin's Famous Fabrics				
DATE _Oct. 4_ 19 --				
NAME _Mrs. Raymond Benson_				
ADDRESS _22 Southland Ave., City_				
CLERK 29	CASH ✓	CHARGE	TAKE ✓	SEND
QTY.	DESCRIPTION		PRICE	AMOUNT
2 ⅔	yd. polyester		2.97	
4 ¼	yd. corduroy		1.37	
4 ¾	yd. cotton		.79	
8	yd. burlap		.47½	
	Sales tax 4%			

2. Jack Peterson redecorated the living room of his home. At the local building supply store he bought the following materials at the prices listed. Find the cost of each item and total cost of the purchase. Write the results in the spaces provided. Make your calculations in the space below.

$2\frac{1}{2}$ gal. paint @ \$5.50   = \$_____

$15\frac{3}{4}$ sq. yd. carpet @ \$8.80   = _____

12 ft. shelving @ $35\frac{2}{3}$¢   = _____

56 ft. molding @ $12\frac{1}{2}$¢   = _____

      \$_____

Sales tax 5%   _____

Total cost   \$_____

DRILL 46. (Multiplication of a whole number and a mixed number)

47
23$\frac{1}{3}$
15$\frac{2}{3}$ ($\frac{1}{3}$×47)
141
94
1096$\frac{2}{3}$

When multiplying a whole number by a mixed number, multiply first by the fraction and then by the whole number, as shown at the left. When multiplying a mixed number by a whole number, use the process shown at the right. First multiply the fraction by the multiplier. Then multiply the whole numbers in the usual manner.

124$\frac{1}{8}$
35
4$\frac{3}{8}$ (35×$\frac{1}{8}$)
620
372
4344$\frac{3}{8}$

Multiply the following.

1. 36
   15$\frac{1}{3}$

2. 24$\frac{3}{5}$
   25

3. 48
   12$\frac{5}{8}$

4. 13$\frac{3}{8}$
   24

5. 36
   17$\frac{2}{3}$

6. 20
   7$\frac{1}{3}$

7. 15$\frac{1}{8}$
   13

8. 16
   12$\frac{2}{3}$

9. 14$\frac{3}{4}$
   11

10. 15
    13$\frac{5}{8}$

DRILL 47. (Addition of mixed numbers)

	12ths
5$\frac{1}{2}$	6
7$\frac{3}{4}$	9
6$\frac{2}{3}$	8
18 +$\frac{23}{12}$=19$\frac{11}{12}$	

Mixed numbers are added as shown at the left. The least common denominator is 12. Therefore the fractions are changed to 12ths. The numerators of the equivalent fractions are written in a column at the right. The numerators are then added, and the sum, 23, is written as $\frac{23}{12}$. The sum of the whole numbers, 18, is then combined with the sum of the fractions, $\frac{23}{12}$ (or 1$\frac{11}{12}$), giving 19$\frac{11}{12}$.

Add the following mixed numbers.

1.
   8$\frac{5}{6}$
   5$\frac{1}{4}$
   12$\frac{7}{8}$

2.
   8$\frac{3}{4}$
   10$\frac{2}{3}$
   12$\frac{5}{6}$

3.
   9$\frac{5}{6}$
   13$\frac{2}{3}$
   10$\frac{4}{9}$

4.
   12$\frac{7}{8}$
   9$\frac{3}{4}$
   17$\frac{5}{8}$

5.
   14$\frac{1}{4}$
   11$\frac{5}{8}$
   13$\frac{2}{3}$

DRILL 48. (Subtraction of mixed numbers)

	12ths
8	15
9$\frac{1}{4}$	3
2$\frac{5}{6}$	10
6 + $\frac{5}{12}$	

The subtraction of 2$\frac{5}{6}$ from 9$\frac{1}{4}$ is shown at the left. The least common denominator is 12. Therefore the fractions are changed to 12ths. The numerators of the equivalent fractions, $\frac{3}{12}$ and $\frac{10}{12}$, are written in a column at the right. The fraction $\frac{10}{12}$ cannot be subtracted from $\frac{3}{12}$, so one unit, or $\frac{12}{12}$, is borrowed from 9 and added to $\frac{3}{12}$, giving 15 as the new numerator. The numerators, 15 and 10, are then subtracted. The difference, 5, is written as $\frac{5}{12}$. The difference between the whole numbers, 6, is then combined with the difference between the fractions, $\frac{5}{12}$, giving 6$\frac{5}{12}$.

Subtract the following mixed numbers.

1.
   34$\frac{2}{7}$
   27

2.
   43
   27$\frac{5}{8}$

3.
   121
   74$\frac{5}{6}$

4.
   15$\frac{1}{4}$
   6$\frac{9}{16}$

5.
   28$\frac{3}{8}$
   10$\frac{3}{4}$

6.
   41$\frac{1}{6}$
   16$\frac{7}{8}$

Section 11

DRILL 49. (Expressing a mixed number as an improper fraction)

$35\frac{2}{9} = \frac{317}{9}$

$\begin{array}{r} 35\frac{2}{9} \\ 9 \\ \hline 315 \\ 2 \\ \hline 317 \end{array}$

In some cases you will find it necessary or desirable to change a mixed number to an improper fraction. The process of changing the mixed number, $35\frac{2}{9}$, to an improper fraction is shown at the left. To find the numerator of the improper fraction, 35 is multiplied by 9, and 2 is added to the product.

Change each mixed number below to an improper fraction.

1. $42\frac{3}{4} =$ 2. $23\frac{5}{6} =$ 3. $18\frac{7}{8} =$ 4. $32\frac{8}{9} =$ 5. $8\frac{11}{12} =$

DRILL 50. (Multiplication of a mixed number by a mixed number)

$35\frac{1}{4} = \frac{141}{4}$
$9\frac{2}{3} = \frac{29}{3}$

$\frac{141}{4} \times \frac{29}{3} = \frac{1363}{4} = 340\frac{3}{4}$

The multiplication of a mixed number by a mixed number may be done in one of two ways.

One method, shown at the left, is to convert the mixed numbers to improper fractions. Multiply these fractions, and express the answers as a mixed number.

● The other method is called the *four-step method*. Multiply separately the fraction and whole number in the multiplicand by the fraction and whole number in the multiplier, as shown at the right.

$\begin{array}{l} 35\frac{1}{4} \\ 9\frac{2}{3} \\ \hline \frac{2}{12} \;\; (\frac{2}{3} \times \frac{1}{4}) \\ 23\frac{1}{3} \;\; (\frac{2}{3} \times 35) \\ 2\frac{1}{4} \;\; (9 \times \frac{1}{4}) \\ 315 \;\; (9 \times 35) \\ \hline 340\frac{3}{4} \end{array}$

Multiply each of the following by the method of converting the mixed numbers to improper fractions.

1. $7\frac{1}{2} \times 3\frac{2}{3} =$ 2. $5\frac{2}{3} \times 3\frac{1}{4} =$ 3. $2\frac{5}{6} \times 2\frac{1}{2} =$ 4. $1\frac{3}{5} \times 3\frac{1}{8} =$

5. $15\frac{5}{6} \times 7\frac{1}{2} =$ 6. $4\frac{3}{8} \times 16\frac{2}{5} =$ 7. $14\frac{2}{3} \times 7\frac{1}{2} =$ 8. $15\frac{3}{4} \times 20\frac{2}{3} =$

● Multiply each of the following by the four-step method.

9. $24\frac{1}{2}$ 10. $24\frac{1}{3}$ 11. $32\frac{1}{4}$ 12. $36\frac{1}{6}$
   $8\frac{1}{2}$ $15\frac{1}{3}$ $16\frac{1}{4}$ $18\frac{1}{6}$

13. $44\frac{1}{2}$ 14. $39\frac{1}{8}$ 15. $48\frac{3}{4}$ 16. $35\frac{5}{6}$
    $26\frac{3}{4}$ $24\frac{2}{3}$ $32\frac{5}{8}$ $30\frac{2}{5}$

SECTION 12. Figuring Unit Prices

Prices are sometimes given for a fractional quantity or for a quantity shown as a mixed number. To find the unit price, divide the quoted price by the given quantity. For example, if you pay 29¢ for a box containing 7 oz. ($\frac{7}{16}$ lb.) of chocolate cookies, you should divide 29¢ by $\frac{7}{16}$. Invert the divisor, $\frac{7}{16}$, giving $\frac{16}{7}$. Then multiply. This is shown at the left. If the quantity is a mixed number, change it to an improper fraction. Then, invert the fraction and multiply. The example at the right shows the price per pound of a $1\frac{1}{4}$ lb. box of cereal costing 87¢.

$$29¢ \div \tfrac{7}{16} = 29 \times \tfrac{16}{7}$$

$$= \tfrac{464}{7}$$

$$= 66\tfrac{2}{7}, \text{ or } 66¢$$

$$87¢ \div 1\tfrac{1}{4} = 87 \div \tfrac{5}{4}$$

$$= 87 \times \tfrac{4}{5}$$

$$= \tfrac{348}{5}$$

$$= 69\tfrac{3}{5}, \text{ or } 70¢$$

EXERCISE. (Practical problems)

1. At the Plaza Food Store the price of a 12 oz. bag of chocolate chips is 49¢. At that rate, the price of one pound is _____ ¢.

2. The advertised price of a $\frac{3}{16}$ lb. package of cream cheese is 14¢. This is equal to _____ ¢ a pound.

3. A $6\frac{1}{2}$ oz. can of tuna fish is priced at 50¢. The equivalent price per ounce is _____ ¢.

4. The price of a $4\frac{1}{4}$ oz. can of shrimp is 69¢. This is equal to _____ ¢ per ounce.

5. At Mom's Candy Store, the price of a 1 lb. box of assorted chocolates is $1.90. The price of a $2\frac{1}{2}$ lb. box is $4.50. If you purchase a $2\frac{1}{2}$ lb. box, the cost of the chocolates is at the rate of (a) $_____ per pound, which represents a saving of (b) _____ ¢ per pound.

6. At the Pearson Department Store, Flora Wirth pays $2.65 for a $1\frac{7}{8}$ yd. remnant of corduroy regularly priced at $1.77 a yard. By purchasing the remnant she saved _____ ¢ per yard.

Name _____

Section 12

DRILL 51. (Writing reciprocals)

If the product of two numbers is 1, each is called the reciprocal of the other. Since $\frac{2}{3} \times \frac{3}{2} = 1$, $\frac{3}{2}$ is the reciprocal of $\frac{2}{3}$; and $\frac{2}{3}$ is the reciprocal of $\frac{3}{2}$. Also, since $\frac{1}{5} \times 5 = 1$, 5 is the reciprocal of $\frac{1}{5}$, and $\frac{1}{5}$ is the reciprocal of 5.

To find the reciprocal of any number, interchange the numerator and denominator of the fraction representing the number. Thus, the reciprocal of $\frac{3}{4}$ is $\frac{4}{3}$; and the reciprocal of 3 (thought of as $\frac{3}{1}$) is $\frac{1}{3}$. Interchanging the numerator and denominator is often referred to as *inverting the fraction*.

The reciprocal of a mixed number is the reciprocal of the improper fraction that is equal to the mixed number. For example, $3\frac{1}{4}$ equals $\frac{13}{4}$. The reciprocal of $\frac{13}{4}$ is $\frac{4}{13}$, therefore, $\frac{4}{13}$ is the reciprocal of $3\frac{1}{4}$.

In the blank space provided, write the reciprocal of each of the following:

1. $\frac{7}{8}$ ____   3. $\frac{8}{3}$ ____   5. 15 ____   7. $4\frac{1}{2}$ ____   9. $38\frac{5}{7}$ ____

2. $\frac{9}{10}$ ____   4. 7 ____   6. 10 ____   8. $15\frac{2}{3}$ ____   10. $12\frac{13}{16}$ ____

DRILL 52. (Division involving fractions)

Many problems involve division where either the divisor or the dividend is a fraction. In such a case, multiply the dividend by the reciprocal of the divisor. In other words, invert the divisor and multiply.

Example 1. $16 \div \frac{3}{4} = 16 \times \frac{4}{3} = \frac{64}{3} = 21\frac{1}{3}$

Example 3. $\frac{14}{15} \div 8 = \frac{14}{15} \times \frac{1}{8} = \frac{\overset{7}{\cancel{14}}}{15} \times \frac{1}{\underset{4}{\cancel{8}}} = \frac{7}{60}$

Example 2. $\frac{3}{4} \div \frac{2}{9} = \frac{3}{4} \times \frac{9}{2} = \frac{27}{8} = 3\frac{3}{8}$

Example 4. $72 \div 12 = 72 \times \frac{1}{12} = 6$

Complete the following divisions by inverting the divisor and then multiplying.

1. $12 \div \frac{1}{4} =$ 5. $\frac{5}{8} \div \frac{3}{7} =$ 9. $\frac{25}{42} \div \frac{5}{12} =$ 13. $\frac{3}{8} \div 4 =$

2. $22 \div \frac{3}{8} =$ 6. $\frac{4}{9} \div \frac{2}{3} =$ 10. $\frac{8}{9} \div 4 =$ 14. $\frac{4}{5} \div 3 =$

3. $12 \div \frac{9}{16} =$ 7. $\frac{7}{12} \div \frac{5}{8} =$ 11. $\frac{15}{16} \div 5 =$ 15. $\frac{3}{4} \div 6 =$

4. $18 \div \frac{16}{25} =$ 8. $\frac{9}{16} \div \frac{7}{12} =$ 12. $\frac{27}{32} \div 3 =$ 16. $\frac{9}{10} \div 15 =$

[39]

DRILL **53.** (Division of a fraction by a fraction)

When dividing a fraction by a fraction, instead of inverting the divisor you may change the fractions to fractions having the same denominator. Then ignore the denominators and divide the numerator of the dividend by the numerator of the divisor. For example, in $\frac{5}{8} \div \frac{3}{4}$, we can mentally change $\frac{3}{4}$ to $\frac{6}{8}$. The expression then becomes $\frac{5}{8} \div \frac{6}{8}$, and the solution of the division is $\frac{5}{8} \div \frac{6}{8} = 5 \div 6 = \frac{5}{6}$. Just as 5 cents $\div$ 6 cents $= \frac{5}{6}$, so 5 eighths $\div$ 6 eighths $= \frac{5}{6}$. Using this process, complete the following:

1. $\frac{1}{3} \div \frac{1}{3} =$

2. $\frac{2}{5} \div \frac{3}{5} =$

3. $\frac{5}{8} \div \frac{3}{8} =$

4. $\frac{1}{2} \div \frac{1}{4} =$

5. $\frac{3}{4} \div \frac{1}{2} =$

6. $\frac{4}{15} \div \frac{1}{3} =$

7. $\frac{7}{10} \div \frac{2}{5} =$

8. $\frac{3}{4} \div \frac{5}{16} =$

9. $\frac{2}{3} \div \frac{5}{6} =$

10. $\frac{5}{6} \div \frac{7}{12} =$

11. $\frac{6}{15} \div \frac{1}{3} =$

12. $\frac{2}{5} \div \frac{7}{10} =$

13. $\frac{18}{25} \div \frac{2}{5} =$

14. $\frac{13}{39} \div \frac{3}{13} =$

15. $\frac{18}{24} \div \frac{5}{6} =$

DRILL **54.** (Division involving mixed numbers)

When the dividend or divisor, or both, are mixed numbers, change each mixed number to an improper fraction. Then proceed as in division involving fractions. Express the result as a common fraction, a mixed number, or a whole number, as the case may be.

Example 1. $39 \div 4\frac{1}{2} = 39 \div \frac{9}{2} = \overset{13}{\cancel{39}} \times \frac{2}{\underset{3}{\cancel{9}}} = \frac{26}{3} = 8\frac{2}{3}$ **Example 2.** $8\frac{2}{5} \div 24 = \frac{42}{5} \div 24 = \frac{\overset{7}{\cancel{42}}}{5 \times \underset{4}{\cancel{24}}} = \frac{7}{20}$

Example 3. $5\frac{1}{2} \div 1\frac{1}{3} = \frac{11}{2} \div \frac{4}{3} = \frac{11}{2} \times \frac{3}{4} = \frac{33}{8} = 4\frac{1}{8}$

Complete the following divisions.

1. $18 \div 8\frac{1}{3} =$

2. $16\frac{3}{4} \div 5 =$

3. $55\frac{1}{2} \div 15 =$

4. $125 \div 7\frac{1}{2} =$

5. $9\frac{3}{5} \div 64 =$

6. $25 \div 82\frac{1}{2} =$

7. $43\frac{1}{3} \div 12\frac{1}{2} =$

8. $76\frac{2}{3} \div 9\frac{1}{5} =$

9. $28\frac{7}{8} \div 5\frac{1}{2} =$

10. $86\frac{1}{4} \div 1\frac{7}{8} =$

11. $5\frac{3}{5} \div 24\frac{1}{2} =$

12. $8\frac{1}{3} \div 32\frac{1}{7} =$

Section 12

RATIO AND PROPORTION

If a mathematics class consists of 9 girls and 15 boys, we say that the ratio of girls to boys is 9 to 15. We can express this ratio by the fraction, $\frac{9}{15}$, which is read "9 to 15" and which means that the number of girls is $\frac{9}{15}$ of the number of boys. The ratio, $\frac{9}{15}$, can be reduced to lowest terms, $\frac{3}{5}$, by dividing both terms by 3. The ratio, $\frac{3}{5}$, does not indicate the number of students in the class; but it does tell us that there are 3 girls for every 5 boys, and that out of every 8 students, 3 are girls and 5 are boys. The number of girls is $\frac{3}{8}$ and the number of boys is $\frac{5}{8}$ of the total class membership. Hence, if the membership is 24, the number of girls is $\frac{3}{8}$ of 24, or 9; and the number of boys is $\frac{5}{8}$ of 24, or 15.

● Since the ratio $\frac{3}{5}$ is simply the ratio $\frac{9}{15}$ reduced to lowest terms, the two ratios are equal; and we may write $\frac{3}{5} = \frac{9}{15}$. A statement such as $\frac{3}{5} = \frac{9}{15}$, which expresses the equality of two ratios, is called a *proportion*. In any proportion, the product of the numerator of one fraction and the denominator of the other is a cross product; and in every proportion the two cross products are equal. Thus, in $\frac{3}{5} = \frac{9}{15}$,

the cross product, 3×15, equals the cross product, 5×9.

● The principle of equal cross products is useful in finding the missing term in a proportion when three of the terms are known.

● **Example:** If 15 yards of carpet cost $125, what will 21 yards cost?

Solution

Let N represent the missing cost

Then $\dfrac{N}{\$125}$ is the ratio of the missing cost to the known cost

And $\dfrac{21}{15}$ is the ratio of the length for the missing cost to the length for the known cost

Equal ratios $\qquad \dfrac{N}{\$125} = \dfrac{21}{15}$

Cross products $\quad 15 \times N = 21 \times \$125$

$\qquad\qquad\qquad 15 \times N = \$2,625$

Missing factor $\qquad N = \$175$

EXERCISE.   (Practical problems)

1. In a class of 30 students, 13 are girls and 17 are boys.

   a The ratio of girls to boys is _____ .

   b The ratio of boys to girls is _____ .

   c The ratio of girls to the total membership is _____ .

   d The ratio of boys to the total membership is _____ .

2. The ratio of 5 in. to 3 ft. is _____ . (Change the feet to inches.)

3. The ratio of 11 oz. to 4 lb. is _____ .

4. The ratio of 47¢ to $1.50 is _____ .

5. As a fraction in lowest terms, the ratio of

   a 14 to 21 is _____ .

   b 12 in. to 30 in. is _____ .

   c 9 in. to 3 ft. is _____ .

   d 8 yd. to 4 ft. is _____ .

6. A football team won 8 games and lost 5. The ratio of the games won to games played is _____.

7. In a group of 135 students, the ratio of boys to girls is 4 to 5. There are _____ boys in the group.

8. A prize of $12,000 is to be shared by two winners of a contest in the ratio of 5 to 3. The larger share is $_____; the smaller share is $_____.

9. Two business partners, *A* and *B*, divide their profits in the ratio of 8 to 7 in favor of *A*. If a profit of $13,500 is to be divided between them, *A* will receive $_____ and *B* will receive $_____.

● **10.** In 5 hours a motorist drove 225 miles. At the same rate, the driver could drive _____ miles in 7 hours.

● **11.** At the rate of 10 oranges for 75¢, you can buy _____ oranges for $2.25.

● **12.** An office clerk types 6 pages of manuscript in 45 minutes. At the same rate, the clerk could type _____ pages in 3 hours.

● **13.** If you are paid $5.95 for working 3½ hours, you would receive $_____ for working 5 hours at the same rate.

UNIT FOUR   Wages

SECTION 13. Figuring Wage Income

In many industrial plants and other business establishments, employees are paid on an hour-rate basis for the hours they work. Usually, time and a half (one and a half times the regular hourly rate) is paid for overtime, that is, for time worked more than the regular hours per day or per week. When there is overtime, an employee's weekly earnings consist of the regular- or straight-time earnings plus the overtime earnings.

Example: James Orr is paid $2.85 an hour for a 40-hour week. For overtime he is paid time and a half, which is at the rate of $1\frac{1}{2} \times \$2.85$, or $4.27½ an hour. Last week he worked 46 hours. How much did he earn?

40 hr. @ $2.85 = $114.00 regular-time earnings
6 hr. @ $4.27½ =   25.65 overtime earnings
                 $139.65 total earnings

EXERCISE.   (Practical problems)

1. Alice Shaw, an employee of the Raymond Corporation, is paid weekly on the basis of a 40-hour week at the rate of $3.68 an hour with time and a half for overtime. During one week she works 48 hours. Her total earnings for the week amount to $_____.

2. The regular factory hours of Becket & Company are eight hours a day, Monday through Friday, with time and a half for overtime. During the first week of November, Earl Finch, an employee whose regular hourly rate is $3.04, worked as shown at the right. During the week, he worked (a) _____ hours regular time and (b) _____ hours overtime. (c) His total earnings for the week were $_____.

	Mon.	Tues.	Wed.	Thurs.	Fri.
Hours worked	6	8½	9	9	9

3. Shown below is a portion of the payroll record of the Becker Tool Company. Eight hours make up a regular day's work, and time and a half is paid for overtime. You are to enter the following information for each employee: (a) total regular-time hours; (b) total overtime hours; (c) total earnings.

PAYROLL RECORD

For Week Ending   November 21, 19--

NO.	NAME	TIME RECORD					HOUR RATE	TOTAL HOURS		TOTAL EARNINGS
		M	T	W	T	F		REGULAR	OVERTIME	
1	John Evans	8	6	8	7	8	$3.42			
2	Lois Marks	8	9	7	9	10	2.86			
3	Mark Winter	7	6	9	5	9	3.18			
4	Jerry Cole	8	5	9	9½	10	3.28			

DRILL 55. (Finding a fractional part of a number)

Sometimes you need to find what number is a fractional part of another number. Sometimes you need to find the number which is a fractional part greater than (or smaller than) another number. In each case you must multiply the given number by the fraction to find the fractional part. For example:

The number that is $\frac{2}{5}$ of 40 is $\frac{2}{5} \times 40 = 16$

The number that is $\frac{2}{5}$ greater than 40 is $40 + (\frac{2}{5} \times 40) = 40 + 16 = 56$

The number that is $\frac{2}{5}$ smaller than 40 is $40 - (\frac{2}{5} \times 40) = 40 - 16 = 24$

In each of the following, complete the statement.

1. $\frac{2}{3}$ of 21 = _____

2. _____ = $\frac{4}{5}$ of 60

3. $\frac{3}{4}$ of 36 = _____

4. _____ is $\frac{1}{6}$ greater than 96

5. _____ is $\frac{3}{8}$ as great as 72

6. _____ is $\frac{5}{6}$ of 42

7. 60 decreased by $\frac{2}{5}$ of itself = _____

8. $\frac{3}{4}$ of 72 is _____

9. _____ are $\frac{7}{8}$ as many as 40

10. 27 increased by $\frac{2}{3}$ of itself = _____

11. _____ = $\frac{3}{5}$ of 85

12. _____ is $\frac{2}{3}$ of 78

13. $\frac{5}{8}$ of 136 = _____

14. _____ is $\frac{3}{8}$ smaller than 56

15. $\frac{5}{4}$ of 60 = _____

16. $\frac{4}{3}$ of 24 is _____

17. _____ = $\frac{9}{8}$ of 72

18. 90 increased by $\frac{6}{5}$ of itself = _____

DRILL 56. (Finding what part one number is of another number)

To find what part one number is of another, express the relationship of the numbers in the form of a fraction. The numerator is the number representing the part. The denominator is the number representing the whole with which the part is compared. For example, in finding what part 32 is of 36, 32 represents the the part, and 36 represents the whole. The fraction $\frac{32}{36}$, or $\frac{8}{9}$, therefore expresses what part 32 is of 36.

In each of the following, show the fraction that correctly answers the question or correctly completes the statement.

1. 24 is what part of (a) 36?_____ (b) 32?_____ (c) 30?_____ (d) 20?_____ (e) 18?_____

2. What part of 24 is (a) 14?_____ (b) 18?_____ (c) 21?_____ (d) 26?_____ (e) 30?_____

3. 18 is what part of (a) 12?_____ (b) 15?_____ (c) 16?_____ (d) 20?_____ (e) 24?_____

4. 10 is _____ of 15

5. 14 is _____ of 16

6. 45 is _____ × 50

7. 40 is _____ × 64

8. 30 = _____ of 45

9. 20 is _____ × 25

10. 12 is _____ of 14

11. _____ of 9 is 6

12. _____ of 10 = 8

13. _____ × 18 is 16

14. 20 is _____ of 18

15. 12 is _____ of 9

16. 30 = _____ of 25

17. 25 = _____ of 20

18. _____ × 30 is 50

SECTION 14. Deductions from Wages

An employer is required by law to deduct an income tax, called the withholding tax, from the wages of each employee. The amount deducted depends upon the amount of the employee's wages, whether married or single, and the number of exemptions claimed. One exemption may be claimed by each employee, one for a spouse if married, and one for each dependent. Each exemption reduces the amount of the tax.

Under the Federal Insurance Contributions Act, the employer may also be required to deduct an *FICA tax* or *social security tax*. Assume this tax to be 5.85% of the first $12,600 of the employee's earnings for the calendar year. Any amount earned in excess of $12,600 is not taxed.

The employer finds the amount of each tax to be deducted by using tables supplied by the government. Shown below at the left is a portion of an income tax withholding table for a weekly payroll. At the right is a portion of the social security tax table.

INCOME TAX WITHHOLDING TABLE
If the payroll period is weekly

And the wages are—		And the number of exemptions claimed is—			
		0	1	2	3
At least	But less than	The amount of income tax withheld shall be—			
$100	$105	$14.10	$11.80	$ 9.50	$ 7.20
105	110	14.90	12.60	10.30	8.00
110	115	15.70	13.40	11.10	8.80
115	120	16.50	14.20	11.90	9.60
120	125	17.30	15.00	12.70	10.40
125	130	18.10	15.80	13.50	11.20
130	135	18.90	16.60	14.30	12.00
135	140	19.70	17.40	15.10	12.80
140	145	20.50	18.20	15.90	13.60
145	150	21.30	19.00	16.70	14.40

SOCIAL SECURITY AND HOSPITAL INSURANCE TAX TABLE — 5.85%

$ Wages less than	$ Tax	$ Wages less than	$ Tax	$ Wages less than	$ Tax	$ Wages less than	$ Tax	$ Wages less than	$ Tax	$ Wages less than	$ Tax
82.14	4.80	92.40	5.40	102.65	6.00	112.91	6.60	123.17	7.20	133.42	7.80
82.31	4.81	92.57	5.41	102.83	6.01	113.08	6.61	123.34	7.21	133.59	7.81
82.48	4.82	92.74	5.42	103.00	6.02	113.25	6.62	123.51	7.22	133.77	7.82
82.65	4.83	92.91	5.43	103.17	6.03	113.42	6.63	123.68	7.23	133.94	7.83
82.83	4.84	93.08	5.44	103.34	6.04	113.59	6.64	123.85	7.24	134.11	7.84
83.00	4.85	93.25	5.45	103.51	6.05	113.77	6.65	124.02	7.25	134.28	7.85
83.17	4.86	93.42	5.46	103.68	6.06	113.94	6.66	124.19	7.26	134.45	7.86
83.34	4.87	93.59	5.47	103.85	6.07	114.11	6.67	124.36	7.27	134.62	7.87
83.51	4.88	93.77	5.48	104.02	6.08	114.28	6.68	124.53	7.28	134.79	7.88
83.68	4.89	93.94	5.49	104.19	6.09	114.45	6.69	124.71	7.29	134.96	7.89

If Henry Kraft, for example, earns $133.43 in one week and is entitled to three exemptions, his withholding tax is found in the withholding table on the $130–$135 wages line in column 3. The amount is $12.00. The amount of his social security tax is found in the tax column of the social security tax table on the "wages less than" $133.59, line. The amount is $7.81.

In addition to taxes, there may be deductions for union dues, disability insurance, group life insurance, hospital care, and other items. The amount the employee receives, after all deductions have been made, is called *net wages*.

EXERCISE.   (Practical problems)

1. The form below shows the names of eight employees of the Cardrite Company, the exemptions they claim, and their total wages for last week. Using the withholding and social security tax tables given above, find the withholding tax and the FICA tax that should be deducted from each employee's wages and write each amount in the appropriate tax column in the form.

	NAME	EXEMP-TIONS	TOTAL WAGES	INCOME TAX	FICA TAX
a	Jackson, A. M.	3	$123.28		
b	Johns, R. B.	0	$114.31		
c	Knox, V. E.	1	$133.80		
d	Lee, R. E.	2	$104.15		

	NAME	EXEMP-TIONS	TOTAL WAGES	INCOME TAX	FICA TAX
e	Marks, P. S.	3	$124.52		
f	Meeker, H. H.	1	$113.81		
g	Smart, V. J.	3	$112.96		
h	White, A. M.	2	$102.67		

[45]

2. Using the tax tables on page 45, complete the following table by entering (a) the income tax for each employee, (b) the FICA tax at 5.85% (c) total deductions, (d) net wages, and (e) the totals of all the money columns.

Use the column totals to prove your work. The sum of the income tax and FICA totals should equal the total deductions. The total wages minus the total deductions should equal the total net wages.

	NAME	EXEMPTIONS	TOTAL WAGES	DEDUCTIONS			NET WAGES
				INCOME TAX	FICA TAX	TOTAL	
a	Boyce, C. L.	0	$123.70				
b	Dean, J. M.	3	133.46				
c	Giles, R. J.	2	113.62				
d	Kern, F. R.	1	104.12				
e	Novak, L. S.	3	134.76				
	Totals						

3. Alice is employed on the basis of a 40-hour week at $2.84 an hour with time and a half for overtime. Last week she worked 45 hours. From her total earnings, the employer deducted the FICA tax at the rate of 5.85% and the income tax on the basis of 1 exemption claimed by Alice. In addition, the employer deducted $3.20 for group insurance and $3.10 for hospital care.

Using the above information and the tax tables on page 45, complete the form at the right for Alice by filling in the blanks.

Regular-time earnings $_____

Overtime earnings   _____

Total earnings $_____

Deductions:

   FICA tax $_____

   Income tax   _____

   Group insurance   _____

   Hospital care   _____

   Total deductions   _____

Net earnings $_____

DRILL 57. (Finding what part one number is greater or smaller than another number)

If you wish to find what part 36 is greater than 32, the difference, 4, represents the part and 32 represents the whole. Hence the fraction $\frac{4}{32}$, or $\frac{1}{8}$, shows by what part 36 is greater than 32.

If you wish to find what part 32 is smaller than 36, 4 represents the part and 36 the whole. Hence the fraction $\frac{4}{36}$, or $\frac{1}{9}$, shows by what part 32 is smaller than 36.

In each of the following, show in the blank the fraction that correctly completes the statement.

1. 30 is _____ smaller than 40

2. 40 is _____ greater than 36

3. 45 = 40 increased by _____ of itself

4. 30 increased by _____ of itself = 45

5. 60 decreased by _____ of itself = 40

6. 25 increased by _____ of itself = 35

7. 55 = 40 increased by _____ of itself

8. 75 decreased by _____ of itself = 30

9. 30 is _____ less than 50

10. 50 is _____ more than 30

11. 30 = 48 decreased by _____ of itself

12. 35 is _____ less than 45

SECTION 15. Special Wage Problems

Businesses that employ a large number of workers usually have a time clock and timecards for keeping a record of the time worked and the amounts earned by the employees.

EXERCISE. (Practical problems)

1. Below is the timecard of George Murray for the week ending March 19. Mr. Murray's regular work day is from 8 A.M. to 12 noon and from 1 P.M. to 5 P.M. The time at which he arrives and leaves each day is recorded on the card. A summary of the total hours worked each day is made at the right. If Mr. Murray arrives from one to fifteen minutes late or leaves from one to fifteen minutes early, he is credited for a full day less one quarter hour.

You are to complete the summary at the bottom of the timecard by showing (a) the regular hours and earnings, (b) the overtime hours, rate, and earnings, and (c) the total hours and total earnings. For over-

time work, Mr. Murray receives one and a half times the regular hourly rate.

2. Jane Brown works in the factory of the Winger Toy Company. The shop hours are from 8 A.M. to 12 noon and from 1P.M. to 5P.M. on the first five days of the week. Her rate of pay is $3.25 an hour, and his payroll number is 108.

At the right below is Miss Brown's timecard for the week ending May 21.* Complete this card, using the completed card in Problem 1 as a guide. For overtime, Miss Brown receives one and a half times her regular hourly rate.

PAYROLL NO. 76						
NAME George Murray						
WEEK ENDING March 19, 19--						

MORNING		AFTERNOON		OVERTIME		
IN	OUT	IN	OUT	IN	OUT	
M 7:56	12:01	12:55	5:04			8
TU 7:58	12:03	12:58	5:01			8
W 8:09	12:04	12:59	5:02			7¼
TH 7:54	12:03	1:12	5:01			7¼
FR 7:55	12:01	12:59	5:03	5:57	8:00	10

	HOURS	RATE	EARNINGS
REGULAR		4.10	
OVERTIME			
TOTALS			

PAYROLL NO. 108						
NAME Jane Brown						
WEEK ENDING May 21, 19--						

MORNING		AFTERNOON		OVERTIME		
IN	OUT	IN	OUT	IN	OUT	
M 7:53	12:04	12:58	5:03			
TU 7:58	12:03	1:00	5:05			
W 7:57	12:05	12:59	5:01			
TH 7:55	12:01	12:55	5:04			
FR 7:59	12:02	12:57	5:03			
SA				7:57	12:02	

	HOURS	RATE	EARNINGS
REGULAR			
OVERTIME			
TOTALS			

*Working hours are calculated in quarter-hour units so that if the employee arrives a few minutes before 8 A.M. or 1 P.M., or leaves a few minutes after 12 noon or 5 P.M., these few extra minutes are not taken into consideration.

● **3.** During one week, Henry Lake's overtime earnings amounted to $16.80. This was $\frac{1}{8}$ of his total earnings. His total earnings were $_____ .

● **4.** Ruth Dillon's total earnings for the second week in July were $144.90, which was $\frac{1}{6}$ more than her earnings for the first week. Her earnings for the first week were $_____ .

● **5.** Elmer Park's total earnings for the fourth week in June were $122.10. This was $\frac{1}{7}$ less than his earnings for the third week. His earnings for the third week were $_____ .

●DRILL **58.**   (Finding the whole when a part is known)

In an earlier section you learned that when the product and one factor of the product are known, the other factor can be found by dividing the product by the known factor. For example, if you pay $1.05 for $\frac{7}{8}$ lb. of meat, you know that

$$\tfrac{7}{8} \times \text{the price per pound} = \$1.05$$

$1.05 is the product, and $\frac{7}{8}$ is one of the factors of that product. The price per pound, which is the unknown factor, can be found by dividing the product, $1.05, by the known factor, $\frac{7}{8}$. Thus,

$$\tfrac{7}{8} \times \text{the price per pound} = \$1.05$$

$$\text{The price per pound} = \$1.05 \div \tfrac{7}{8} = \$1.20$$

Likewise, if $\frac{3}{4}$ of a certain number is 18, and you wish to find what that number is, you know that $\frac{3}{4} \times$ the original number = 18. Your solution would therefore be:

$$\tfrac{3}{4} \times \text{the original number} = 18$$

$$\text{The original number} = 18 \div \tfrac{3}{4} = 24$$

If 48 is known to be $\frac{1}{5}$ less than a certain unknown number, the unknown number is the whole and is therefore $\frac{5}{5}$ of itself. Since $\frac{5}{5}-\frac{1}{5}=\frac{4}{5}$, it follows that $\frac{4}{5} \times$ the unknown number = 48. Hence, the unknown number = $48 \div \frac{4}{5} = 60$.

Similarly, if 72 is known to be $\frac{1}{5}$ more than an unknown number, the unknown number is $\frac{5}{5}$ of itself. Since $\frac{5}{5}+\frac{1}{5}=\frac{6}{5}$, it follows that $\frac{6}{5} \times$ the unknown number = 72. Hence, the unknown number = $72 \div \frac{6}{5} = 60$.

In each of the following, show in the blank space the number that correctly completes the statement.

1. $\frac{3}{4} \times$ _____ = 48

2. $\frac{2}{3}$ of _____ = 54

3. 420 is $\frac{1}{6}$ greater than _____

4. _____ decreased by $\frac{1}{3}$ of itself = 150

5. $\frac{5}{4} \times$ _____ = 120

6. _____ less $\frac{2}{5}$ of itself = 180

7. 36 = $\frac{4}{3}$ of _____

8. _____ plus $\frac{1}{5}$ of itself = 150

9. 48 is $\frac{1}{4}$ smaller than _____

10. $\frac{3}{8}$ of _____ = 72

11. 90 is equal to _____ plus $\frac{2}{3}$ of itself

12. $\frac{8}{5}$ of _____ = 80

13. 336 = _____ minus $\frac{1}{8}$ of itself

14. 60 = $\frac{5}{6}$ of _____

SECTION 16. Personal Cash Record Summaries

In Section 1 you saw that a personal cash payments record may have special columns for classifying the payments. The monthly totals of this type of record are usually carried to a monthly summary sheet like the one shown below in Problem 1. The figures in the summary sheet provide helpful information for budgeting or planning expenditures for the next year.

EXERCISE. (Practical problems)

1. Shown below is the monthly summary for Anna Taylor, a secretary, for last year. Do the following:

   a Add each of the eight columns and write the total on the line labeled "Totals."

   b Check your work by adding horizontally the totals of the six Classification of Payments columns. The sum should equal the total of the Payments column.

MONTHLY SUMMARY

MONTH	RECEIPTS	PAYMENTS	CLASSIFICATION OF PAYMENTS					
			FOOD	CLOTHING	RENT	TRANSPORTATION	EDUCATION	SAVINGS
January	500 00	498 15	102 40	25 45	120 00	138 20	72 10	40 00
February	500 00	481 54	110 16	15 78	120 00	132 40	68 20	35 00
March	500 00	497 45	94 45	88 20	120 00	123 30	56 50	15 00
April	500 00	473 96	94 36	14 90	120 00	128 10	71 60	45 00
May	500 00	484 38	125 83	28 65	120 00	112 60	71 30	26 00
June	500 00	471 02	101 24	11 88	120 00	114 50	63 40	60 00
July	500 00	493 26	106 00	33 96	120 00	108 20	125 10	00 00
August	500 00	497 24	93 75	9 39	120 00	111 40	132 70	30 00
September	510 00	480 58	107 28	24 50	120 00	116 50	84 30	28 00
October	515 00	493 78	98 90	68 48	120 00	124 20	62 20	20 00
November	515 00	480 56	100 16	21 00	120 00	136 30	73 10	30 00
December	515 00	490 41	92 64	37 77	120 00	140 40	84 60	15 00
Totals (a)								

(b)

2. Dave Gold receives a monthly take-home pay of $600. His expenditures last month are shown at the right. Find what fractional part of the total take-home pay was spent for each item and write the fraction in the appropriate blank.

Food.....$180 or ____   Transportation $108 or ___

Clothing..$ 90 or ____   Medical ......$ 72 or ___

Housing .$120 or ____   Savings.......$ 30 or ____

3. Maria Cortez estimates that her total cash income for the coming year will be $6,600. She plans to budget the income as shown at the right. Show in the blank spaces the amount to be budgeted for each item.

Food .... $\frac{1}{4}$ or $_____   Transportation $\frac{9}{40}$ or $_____

Clothing . $\frac{1}{6}$ or $_____   Entertainment $\frac{3}{40}$ or $_____

Housing . $\frac{1}{5}$ or $_____   Savings.......$\frac{1}{12}$ or $_____

DRILL 59. (Expressing common fractions and decimal fractions)

Where dollars and cents were used in the preceding problems, you were dealing with decimal fractions or decimals. As you know, a decimal is just another way of expressing a fractional number which has a denominator of 10, 100, or 1,000, etc. The location of the decimal point in the decimal fraction is found by dividing the numerator of the fraction by the denominator. For example, the fraction $\frac{3}{10}$ is written as the decimal .3, since $3 \div 10 = .3$. Similarly, $\frac{7}{100}$ is written as .07, since $7 \div 100 = .07$.

You often need to change common fractions to decimal fractions and decimal fractions to common fractions. In the columns provided, express the following numbers as both common and decimal fractions.

	COMMON FRACTION	DECIMAL FRACTION
1. Eight tenths		
2. Thirty-two hundredths		
3. Four tenths		
4. Fifteen hundredths		
5. Seven hundredths		
6. Seven thousandths		
7. Seventeen thousandths		
8. One hundred thirty-five thousandths		
9. Eighty-four hundredths		
10. Fifty-eight thousandths		

DRILL 60. (Changing a common fraction to a decimal)

Frequently you will need to change a common fraction to a decimal. This is done by dividing the numerator by the denominator. For example, $\frac{5}{8} = 5 \div 8 = .625$. In cases where the numerator is not evenly divisible by the denominator, the decimal may be carried to a specified number of places of exact value or to the nearest tenth, hundredth, or thousandth, etc. Thus, the decimal equal to $\frac{2}{7}$ is $2 \div 7 = .28\frac{4}{7}$, carried to two places of exact value. To the nearest thousandth, $\frac{2}{7} = 2 \div 7 = .2857 = .286$.

1. Complete each of the following by showing the decimal equal to the fraction to two places of exact value.

a $\frac{5}{9} =$ _____ b $\frac{8}{11} =$ _____ c $\frac{11}{12} =$ _____ d $\frac{7}{15} =$ _____ e $\frac{13}{16} =$ _____

2. Complete each of the following by showing the decimal equal to the fraction to the nearest thousandth.

a $\frac{9}{11} =$ _____ b $\frac{5}{12} =$ _____ c $\frac{3}{13} =$ _____ d $\frac{5}{14} =$ _____ e $\frac{13}{15} =$ _____

Section 16.

DRILL **61.** (Multiplication by .1, .01, and .001)

When multiplying by .1, .01, .001, etc., the product is obtained by moving the decimal point in the multiplicand to the left as many places as there are decimal places in the multiplier, prefixing zeros if necessary.

Examples: .09 × .1 = .009

$28.70 × .01 = $.29

58 × .001 = .058

Write rapidly the products of the following multiplications.

1. 21.4 × .1 = _____
2. 8.3 × .01 = _____
3. 437 × .001 = _____
4. 76.4 × .01 = _____

5. 8.33 × .1 = _____
6. 281 × .001 = _____
7. 62.4 × .1 = _____
8. 4.19 × .01 = _____

9. $425 × .01 = _____
10. $640 × .001 = _____
11. $49.70 × .1 = _____
12. $1,890 × .01 = _____

DRILL **62.** (Changing a decimal to a common fraction)

A decimal is changed to a common fraction by expressing it as a common fraction with a denominator of 10, 100, or 1,000, etc., and reducing the result to lowest terms. Thus, $.015 = \frac{15}{1000} = \frac{3}{200}$.

● If the numerator of the fraction is a mixed number, as in $\frac{18\frac{3}{4}}{100}$, multiply the numerator and denominator by the denominator of the fraction in the numerator, and reduce the result to lowest terms. Thus, $.18\frac{3}{4} = \frac{18\frac{3}{4}}{100} = \frac{18\frac{3}{4} \times 4}{100 \times 4} = \frac{75}{400} = \frac{3}{16}$.

In each of the following problems, change the decimal to a common fraction reduced to lowest terms and write the fraction in the blank provided.

1. .16 = _____
2. .34 = _____

3. .155 = _____
4. .072 = _____

5. .525 = _____
6. .56 = _____

●7. $.14\frac{2}{3}$ = _____
●8. $.26\frac{2}{3}$ = _____

● 9. $.218\frac{3}{4}$ = _____
●10. $.203\frac{1}{8}$ = _____

●DRILL **63.** (Division by .1, .01, and .001)

When dividing a number by .1, .01, .001, etc., the quotient is found by moving the decimal point to the right in the dividend as many places as there are decimal places in the divisor, attaching zeros if necessary.

Examples: 750 ÷ .1 = 7,500

.0315 ÷ .01 = 3.15

$4.35 ÷ .001 = $4,350

Write rapidly the correct answers to the following problems.

1. 42.5 ÷ .1 = _____
2. 9.4 ÷ .01 = _____
3. 72.3 ÷ .001 = _____
4. 21.8 ÷ .01 = _____

5. 7.56 ÷ .1 = _____
6. .375 ÷ .001 = _____
7. 65.47 ÷ .1 = _____
8. 3.78 ÷ .01 = _____

9. $8.24 ÷ .001 = _____
10. $6.00 ÷ .1 = _____
11. $ .86 ÷ .01 = _____
12. $5.18 ÷ .001 = _____

Name_____

SECTION 17. Personal Budget Problems

Either in business or in managing your personal affairs, you must plan for the future. One way to protect income and to spend wisely is to prepare a budget of income and expenditures.

The chart below shows the planned distribution of the income of a man expressed in terms of percents of his income. For example, the chart shows that 12%, or 12 percent, of the income is appropriated for clothing. "Percent" means "per hundred." Thus, "12%" means "12 per 100" and indicates the ratio of 12 to 100. This ratio may be expressed by the fraction $\frac{12}{100}$ which, in turn, may be expressed by the decimal .12. Thus, 12%, $\frac{12}{100}$, and .12 are numerals representing the same number, and we may write $12\% = \frac{12}{100} = .12$. When we say that the portion appropriated for clothing is 12% of the income, we mean that the amount is $\frac{12}{100}$ or .12 times the income. Ordinarily we use the decimal form in the computation. Hence, if the income is $5,000, the amount appropriated for clothing is .12 × $5,000, or $600.

Since $12\% = \frac{12}{100}$, and since $\frac{12}{100}$ reduced to lowest terms is $\frac{3}{25}$, we may write $12\% = \frac{3}{25}$ or $\frac{3}{25} = 12\%$. This means that 12% expresses the ratio, or relationship, of 3 to 25 and that 3 is 12% of 25. Hence, to find what percent one number is of another, we write the ratio of the numbers as a fraction; we then divide the numerator by the denominator and express the resulting decimal as a percent. For example,

(a) 3 is what percent of 25?

$$\frac{3}{25} = 3 \div 25 = .12 = 12\%$$

(b) 9 is what percent of 12?

$$\frac{9}{12} = \frac{3}{4} = 3 \div 4 = .75 = 75\%$$

EXERCISE. (Practical problems)

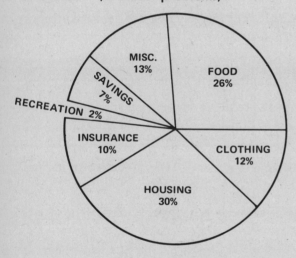

1. George Bard's net earnings are $800 a month. He has estimated his expenditures as shown on the chart at the left. Show in the spaces provided below the amount expended for each item given on the chart.

Food................$_____
Clothing.............$_____
Housing.............$_____
Insurance............$_____
Recreation..........$_____
Savings..............$_____
Miscellaneous........$_____

2. Sally Grey receives $120 monthly from her father for college expenses. Her budget for the current month is shown below. Find what percent of the total allowance for the month is budgeted for each item. Write the answers in the appropriate blanks.

For books and lunches $36 or _____%

For clothing $30 or _____%

For recreation $18 or _____%

For housing $24 or _____%

For savings (remainder of the allowance) $12 or _____%

Section 17.

DRILL 64. (Changing a decimal or whole number to a percent)

Many times you will need to change a decimal or whole number to a percent. This is done by moving the decimal point two places to the right and attaching a percent sign. For example, $.12\frac{1}{2} = 12\frac{1}{2}\%$; $1.16\frac{2}{3} = 116\frac{2}{3}\%$; $3 = 300\%$. Using this process, express each of the following as a percent.

1. $.06 =$ _____	4. $.8 \ =$ _____	7. $.21\frac{1}{2} =$ _____	10. $4.00 =$ _____
2. $.49 =$ _____	5. $.356 =$ _____	8. $.14\frac{5}{8} =$ _____	11. $3 \ =$ _____
3. $.5 \ =$ _____	6. $.082 =$ _____	9. $3.25 \ =$ _____	12. $8 \ =$ _____

DRILL 65. (Changing a fraction to a percent)

A fraction is changed to a percent by first changing it to a decimal and then changing that decimal to a percent. For example, $\frac{3}{7} = 3 \div 7 = .42\frac{6}{7} = 42\frac{6}{7}\%$, with the decimal carried to two places of exact value. To the nearest tenth of a percent, $\frac{3}{7} = 3 \div 7 = .4285 = .429 = 42.9\%$.

1. In each of the following, show the percent that is equal to the fraction. To obtain the percent, find the two-place decimal of exact value equal to the fraction; then change that decimal to a percent.

     a $\frac{4}{7} =$ _____   b $\frac{6}{11} =$ _____   c $\frac{8}{15} =$ _____   d $\frac{7}{16} =$ _____   e $\frac{17}{40} =$ _____

2. Show to the nearest tenth of a percent the percent that is equal to each of the following.

     a $\frac{6}{7} =$ _____   b $\frac{5}{11} =$ _____   c $\frac{17}{30} =$ _____   d $\frac{11}{14} =$ _____   e $\frac{7}{24} =$ _____

DRILL 66. (Finding what percent one number is of another)

To find what percent one number is of another, divide the one by the other and then express the quotient as a percent. For example, in finding what percent 5 is of 12, $5 \div 12 = .41\frac{2}{3} = 41\frac{2}{3}\%$.

Write in the percent as indicated in each of the following. In performing the division, carry the quotient to two places of exact value in cases where the division is not even at the second decimal place.

1. 84 is _____% of 240	6. \$12.60 is _____% of \$80
2. 130 is _____% of 325	7. \$315 is _____% of \$3,750
3. \$10.40 is _____% of \$130	8. \$146.25 is _____% of \$45
4. \$13.50 is _____% of \$4.50	9. \$4.55 is _____% of \$28
5. \$15.75 is _____% of \$3.50	10. \$15 is _____% of \$3.75

DRILL 67. (Changing a percent to a decimal)

To change a percent to a decimal, move the decimal point two places to the left and drop the percent sign. Thus, $6.5\% = .065$; $12\frac{1}{2}\% = .12\frac{1}{2}$ or $.125$. Using this process, express each of the following as a decimal.

1. $32\% =$ _____	4. $145\% =$ _____	7. $16.3\% =$ _____	10. $7\frac{3}{4}\% =$ _____
2. $8\frac{1}{3}\% =$ _____	5. $150\% =$ _____	8. $1.4\% =$ _____	11. $\frac{5}{6}\% =$ _____
3. $\frac{2}{3}\% =$ _____	6. $200\% =$ _____	9. $.6\% =$ _____	12. $.35\% =$ _____

DRILL 68.   (Finding a percent of a number)

To find the percent of the number in each of the following, multiply the number by the decimal that is equal to the given percent. If the answer contains a fraction of a cent, write it to the nearest cent.

1. 64% of $325   = $ _____   5. 120% of $13.42 = $ _____

2. 24.4% of $350 = $ _____   6. 300% of $3.75 = $ _____

3. 6.5% of $535 = $ _____   7. 6⅓% of $250   = $ _____

4. 215% of $22   = $ _____   8. 5⅛% of $175   = $ _____

DRILL 69.   (Multiplication by aliquot parts of 100%)

You have used aliquot parts of $1 for saving time in multiplication.   The same method can be applied in multiplying by a percent that is an aliquot part of 100%. For example, 66⅔% is ⅔ of 100%. For example, to find 66⅔% of $27, you may multiply $27 by ⅔. The product, $18, is found more quickly this way than by multiplying $27 by .66⅔. The following problems are to give you practice in multiplying by aliquot parts of 100%. Write the answers to the problems rapidly making each computation mentally wherever possible.

1. 33⅓% of $210   = $ _____   6. 87½% of $400 = $ _____   11. 62½% of $328   = $ _____

2. 62½% of $240   = $ _____   7. 75% of $440 = $ _____   12. 37½% of $3,240 = $ _____

3. 16⅔% of $270   = $ _____   8. 66⅔% of $183 = $ _____   13. 16⅔% of $495   = $ _____

4. 25% of $1,120 = $ _____   9. 33⅓% of $765 = $ _____   14. 20% of $245   = $ _____

5. 12½% of $656   = $ _____   10. 40% of $600 = $ _____   15. 12½% of $250   = $ _____

DRILL 70.   (Changing a percent to a common fraction)

A percent may be changed to a common fraction by expressing it as a fraction with a denominator of 100 and then reducing the fraction to lowest terms. Thus, $12\% = \frac{12}{100} = \frac{3}{25}$.

● Similarly, $8\frac{3}{4}\% = \frac{8\frac{3}{4}}{100} = \frac{35}{400} = \frac{7}{80}$.

● If the percent contains a decimal, change the percent to the decimal form and then the decimal to a fraction. For example, $7.5\% = .075 = \frac{75}{1,000} = \frac{3}{40}$.

Change each of the following percents to a common fraction reduced to lowest terms.

1. 22% = _____   5. 72% = _____   ● 9. 7.2% = _____

2. 32% = _____   6. 65% = _____   ●10. 3⅓% = _____

3. 45% = _____   ●7. 5.5% = _____   ●11. 2½% = _____

4. 60% = _____   ●8. 2.8% = _____   ●12. 18¾% = _____

UNIT FIVE   Commissions

SECTION 18.   Figuring Commissions

Many salespersons are paid either a commission on sales or a salary and a commission. The commission is usually a percent of the total sales or a percent of the sales in excess of a specified quota. For example, Evan Green is a traveling salesman. He receives a salary of $600 a month and a commission of 15% on his monthly sales in excess of $4,000. His last month's sales were $7,200. His commission for the month was .15 × ($7,200 − $4,000) = .15 × $3,200 = $480. His total earnings for the month were $600 + $480 = $1,080.

EXERCISE.   (Practical problems)

1. On a busy day an auto salesman, working on a straight commission basis, sold 3 used cars at $1,700 each. His commission was 6%. His earnings were $_____.

2. Sue Wilson receives a weekly salary of $105 plus a commission of 1% on all sales. Her sales for the last four weeks are shown at the right. Show (a) her commission for each week, (b) her total earnings for each week, (c) her total sales, total commission, total salary, and total earnings for the four weeks.

WEEK	SALES	COMMISSION	SALARY	TOTAL EARNINGS
1	$1,175		$105	
2	1,570		105	
3	1,290		105	
4	1,382		105	
Total				

3. Harold Cornell sells two types of vacuum cleaners on a straight commission basis. On one retailing for $89 he receives a commission of 20%. On the other, selling for $114, he receives 25%. Last week he sold 5 of the $89 cleaners and 3 of the $114 cleaners. His total earnings for the week were $_____.

4. Harriet Sawyer, a salesclerk, receives a salary of $175 a week plus $\frac{3}{4}$% commission on weekly sales in excess of $12,500. As her sales last week totaled $18,560, her total earnings for the week were $_____.

5. The Ashford Store pays its salesclerks weekly on a salary plus commission basis, paying 2% commission on sales above a specified weekly quota. The sales of four of the clerks for last week are shown below. You are to show for each clerk (a) the amount of the commission and (b) the total earnings for the week.

SALESCLERK	SALES	QUOTA	COMMISSION	SALARY	TOTAL EARNINGS
Myrtle Cooper	$1,420	$1,100		$100.00	
Elvira Handel	1,390	1,250		105.00	
Tom Pearson	1,410	1,200		102.50	
Florence Wilcox	1,325	1,175		101.50	

DRILL 71. (Finding 1%, 10%, 100%, or 1,000% of a number)

You will often find it necessary to multiply a number by 1%, 10%, 100%, or 1,000%. To do this, move the decimal point in the multiplicand as if the multiplication was by .01, .1, 1, or 10. The decimal or whole number equivalents of the percents are .01, .1, 1, and 10, respectively.

Examples:

$$1\% \text{ of } 235 = 235 \times .01 = 2.35$$
$$10\% \text{ of } 235 = 235 \times .1 = 23.5$$
$$100\% \text{ of } 235 = 235 \times 1 = 235$$
$$1,000\% \text{ of } 235 = 235 \times 10 = 2,350$$

Write rapidly the correct answers to the following problems. In cases where the result contains a fraction of a cent, give the answer to the nearest cent.

1.   1% of $29   = $_____

2.   10% of $64   = $_____

3.   100% of $38   = $_____

4. 1,000% of $31   = $_____

5.   10% of $47   = $_____

6.   1% of $76   = $_____

7. 1,000% of $6.50 = $_____

8.   10% of $2.25 = $_____

9.   1% of $450   = $_____

10.   100% of $3.47   = $_____

11. 1,000% of $.95   = $_____

12.   1% of $13.83   = $_____

13.   100% of $14.75   = $_____

14.   10% of $33.79   = $_____

15.   1% of $51.30   = $_____

16. 1,000% of $3.60   = $_____

17.   10% of $124.85   = $_____

18.   1% of $307.47 = $_____

DRILL 72. (Fractional parts of 1%)

In some problems a number is to be multiplied by a fractional part of 1%, such as $\frac{1}{2}\%$, $\frac{2}{3}\%$, or $\frac{3}{4}\%$. The multiplication is done by first multiplying the number by 1%. This is done by moving the decimal point two places to the left. The result is then multiplied by the fraction. For example, $\frac{3}{4}\%$ of $480 = \frac{3}{4} \times \$4.80 = \$3.60$. Complete the following problems.

1. $\frac{1}{2}\%$ of $540   = _____ × $_____ = $_____

2. $\frac{1}{3}\%$ of $255   = _____ × $_____ = $_____

3. $\frac{1}{8}\%$ of $624   = _____ × $_____ = $_____

4. $\frac{1}{4}\%$ of $1,380 = _____ × $_____ = $_____

5. $\frac{1}{5}\%$ of $1,860 = _____ × $_____ = $_____

6. $\frac{1}{10}\%$ of $1,480 = _____ × $_____ = $_____

7. $\frac{2}{3}\%$ of $690   = _____ × $_____ = $_____

8. $\frac{3}{4}\%$ of $1,240 = _____ × $_____ = $_____

9. $\frac{1}{10}\%$ of $540   = _____ × $_____ = $_____

10. $\frac{3}{8}\%$ of $2,400 = _____ × $_____ = $_____

11. $\frac{2}{5}\%$ of $6,500 = _____ × $_____ = $_____

12. $\frac{1}{3}\%$ of $1,935 = _____ × $_____ = $_____

13. $\frac{1}{8}\%$ of $3,400 = _____ × $_____ = $_____

14. $\frac{3}{5}\%$ of $2,550 = _____ × $_____ = $_____

15. $\frac{2}{3}\%$ of $2,100 = _____ × $_____ = $_____

16. $\frac{1}{4}\%$ of $2,240 = _____ × $_____ = $_____

17. $\frac{1}{2}\%$ of $7,900 = _____ × $_____ = $_____

18. $\frac{3}{4}\%$ of $180   = _____ × $_____ = $_____

[56]

SECTION 19. Graduated Commissions

Sometimes a salesperson may receive graduated commissions in which the rate of commission increases as the sales increase.

EXERCISE. (Practical problems)

1. Helen Morgan sells sets of encyclopedias. Her monthly commission is to be figured on the number of sets sold. She earns $18 each for the first 25 sets; $22 for each of the second 25 sets; and $26 each for those over 50 sold. She sold 48 sets in September and 61 in October. Her total commission for the two months was $_____.

2. The Maxwell Company pays its salespersons 5% commission on all sales and an additional 3% commission on all monthly sales in excess of $8,000. In April, Alton Drew, one of the salespersons, sold goods amounting to $14,000. His commission for the month was $_____.

3. In May, Alton Drew, in Problem 2, sold goods amounting to $12,350. (a) His May commission was $_____. (b) This was _____% less than his April commission.

4. Kathy Dix, a saleswoman, receives a salary of $500 a month, a 1% commission on all sales, and an additional 2% on monthly sales in excess of $6,500. For the month of June her sales amounted to $9,800 and for July, $8,250. Her total income was (a) $_____ in June and (b) $_____ in July.

5. Ray Duncan, a salesman, has offers of employment from two firms. The Cory Company offers him a salary of $550 a month, a commission of 2% on total monthly sales, and an additional 3% on monthly sales in excess of $7,000. The Gould Company offers him a commission of 6% on the first $2,000 of monthly sales, 8% on the next $2,000 of monthly sales, and 10% on all monthly sales in excess of $4,000. On sales averaging $12,000 a month, he would earn (a) $_____ more per month by accepting the position with the (b) _____ Company.

DRILL 73. (Finding the percent that one number is greater or smaller than another)

To find the percent by which one number *exceeds* another number, divide the difference by the *smaller* number. To find the percent by which one number is *less* than another number, divide the difference by the *larger* number. For example:

(a) 60 is what percent more than 50?
    60 − 50 = 10, difference
    10 ÷ 50 = .20 = 20% more

(b) 50 is what percent less than 60?
    60 − 50 = 10, difference
    10 ÷ 60 = .16⅔ = 16⅔% less

Write in the correct percent as indicated in each problem below. Use the space below for calculations.

1. 120 is _____ % more than 90

2. 90 is _____ % less than 120

3. 40 is _____ % more than 20

4. 90 is _____ % more than 30

5. 100 is _____ % less than 150

6. 240 is _____ % more than 200

7. 25 is _____ % less than 40

8. 35 is _____ % less than 50

9. 200 is _____ % more than 50

10. 300 is _____ % less than 375

11. 450 is _____ % more than 250

12. 250 is _____ % more than 150

13. 10 is _____ % less than 12

14. 125 is _____ % more than 25

DRILL 74. (Finding the number that is a given percent greater or smaller than a known number)

An expression such as "20% greater than 40" means 20% of 40 *added* to 40. Therefore, the number that is 20% greater than 40 = 40 + 20% of 40 = 40 + 8 = 48. Similarly, the expression "20% smaller than 40" means 20% of 40 subtracted from 40. Hence the number that is 20% smaller than 40 = 40 − 20% of 40 = 40 − 8 = 32.

In each of the following problems, write the answer in the blank provided.

1. _____ is 10% more than 80.

2. 60 plus 5% of itself = _____

3. _____ is 10% less than 90.

4. 70 minus 20% of itself = _____

5. $350 increased by 42% = _____

6. _____ = $368 decreased by 12½%

7. $750 decreased by 16⅔% = _____

8. ⅓% more than $450 = _____

9. _____ = $750 decreased by 30%

10. $4,500 increased by ⅕% = _____

11. ½% less than $800 = _____

12. _____ is 6.5% less than $800.

13. 135% more than $80 = _____

14. $1,600 decreased by ¾% = _____

SECTION 20. Commission Rates

The percent or rate of commission is always based on the sales. The rate may therefore be figured by dividing the amount of the commission by the amount of the sales. For example, if Leo Phelps receives $270 commission on sales amounting to $9,000, the commission rate is $270 ÷ $9,000 = .03 = 3%.

● In some situations, the rate of commission and the amount of commission are known, and the problem is one of finding the amount of the sales. For example, a salesman is offered a position that pays 8% commission. He wishes to find out how many dollars' worth of goods he must sell a month so that his monthly commission may be $750. This means that 8% × the sales = $750. The sales is the unknown factor of the product, $750, and can be determined by dividing $750 by 8%. $750 ÷ 8% = $750 ÷ .08 = $9,375. Hence, at 8% commission, he must sell $9,375 worth of goods in order to earn a commission of $750.

EXERCISE. (Practical problems)

1. On sales amounting to $8,300 a salesperson receives $581 commission. The rate of commission is _____%.

2. During February, Mary Bray, a salesclerk, sold goods amounting to $9,300. Her total earnings for the month were $822, which included her guaranteed salary of $450 a month. (a) Her commission for the month amounted to $_____. (b) The commission rate was _____%.

3. Robert Alpin's total sales last month were $10,200, and his commission was $231. As he receives commission only on monthly sales in excess of $6,000, his rate of commission is _____%.

● 4. Fred Landis, a salesman, is paid on a straight 6% commission basis. If he wishes to earn $195 commission next week, his sales for the week will have to be $_____.

● 5. Jean Mack is paid a monthly salary of $500 and a commission of 2% on all sales. Her total sales for the present month will have to be $_____ in order that her total income for the month may be $850.

●DRILL 75. (Finding a number when a given percent of it is known)

You will sometimes meet various personal and business problems similar to Problem 4 in the preceding exercise. A given percent of a number is known and you need to find what that number is. In such cases the problem is one of finding the unknown factor when the other factor and the product are known. For example, you may know that 15% of a certain number is 75. 75 is the product, and 15% is one of the factors of 75. The other factor of 75 is the unknown number. Since the unknown number is one of the factors of 75, it can be found by dividing 75 by the known factor, 15%. The solution would be:

$$15\% \times \text{the unknown number} = 75$$
$$\text{The unknown number} = 75 \div 15\%$$
$$= 75 \div .15 = 500$$

Find the missing amount in each of the following problems and write it in the blank provided.

1. 45% × _____ = $1,260

4. $33\frac{1}{3}$% × _____ = $4.75

2. 56% of _____ = $3.64

5. $324 is 75% of _____

3. $154 is 55% of _____

6. 145% × _____ = $17.40

DRILL 76. (Review of percent relationships)

The following drill provides additional practice in solving problems involving percent relationships.

1. 35% of $28 = _____

7. _____ is 15% less than $51

2. $6 is _____ % of $7.50

8. $400 = _____ % of $250

3. $71 is _____ % more than $50

9. $3.75 = 25% of _____

4. 341 is _____ % less than $440

● 10. $66\frac{2}{3}$% of _____ = $33

5. 115% of $24 = _____

● 11. $62\frac{1}{2}$% × _____ = $9.20

6. $550 is _____ % more than $250

● 12. $385 = 140% of _____

SECTION 21. Agents' Commissions

A person who acts as an agent, such as a real estate agent or a collection agent, usually receives a commission. The commission of a real estate agent is based on the sale price of the property sold. If a real estate agent who charges 6% sells a house and lot at $30,000, the commission is 6% × $30,000, or $1,800. If there are no other expenses connected with the sale of the property, the net proceeds received by the principal are $30,000 − $1,800 or $28,200.

The commission of a collection agent is based on the amount collected. If a collection agent who charges 30% commission collects a bill of $500 for a client, the commission is 30% × $500, or $150. If there are no other expenses to be deducted, the amount remitted to the client is $500 − $150, or $350.

● Sometimes the net proceeds and the commission rate are known, but you want to find the sale price or the amount collected. For example, the owner of a piece of property wants to receive $4,650 on its sale after allowing the real estate agent 7% commission. That is, 93% × the sale price = $4,650. The sale price of the property should therefore be $4,650 ÷ 93%, or $5,000.

EXERCISE. (Practical problems)

1. Roger Lyon, a real estate agent, sold a house and lot for Dan Jennings for $39,000. He charged 6% for commission and $185 for other expenses connected with the sale of the property. (a) The amount of Mr. Lyon's commission was $_____. (b) Mr. Jennings' net proceeds from the sale of the property amounted to $_____.

2. Hazel Reid, a collection agent, collected a bill of $925 for the Bethel Corporation. She deducted 35% for her commission. (a) Her commission amounted to $_____. (b) The amount she remitted to the corporation was $_____.

3. Leon Blake, a collection agent, collected 80% of a debt of $775 for B. R. Melick. He charged 30% for making the collection. The amount he remitted to B. R. Melick was $_____.

● 4. Jon Marston, wishes to sell his house and lot at a price that will bring him $32,900 after deducting the real estate agent's commission of 6%. The sale price of the property should be $_____.

● 5. Helen Garret, a real estate agent, sold a piece of property for $26,250, which was 5% more than the owner was asking for it. The owner's asking price for the property was $_____.

Often, a given number is known to be a stated percent greater or smaller than another number. This is a problem in finding the unknown factor when the other factor and the product are known. For example, 198 is 10% more than some number. In other words, the unknown number increased by 10% of itself equals 198. To find the unknown number you would use the following process:

$$100\% \times \text{the number} = \text{the number}$$
$$\underline{+10\% \times \text{the number} = \text{the increase}}$$
$$110\% \times \text{the number} = 198$$
$$\text{The number} = 198 \div 110\% = 180$$

On the other hand, if 162 is 10% less than a certain number, you know that the unknown number decreased by 10% of itself equals 162. Your solution for finding the unknown number would be:

$$100\% \times \text{the number} = \text{the number}$$
$$\underline{-10\% \times \text{the number} = \text{the decrease}}$$
$$90\% \times \text{the number} = 162$$
$$\text{The number} = 162 \div 90\% = 180$$

Find the missing number in each of the following and write it in the blank provided.

1. 198 is 10% greater than _____

2. 252 is 10% smaller than _____

3. _____ increased by 15% of itself = 690

4. _____ decreased by 15% of itself = 340

5. $19.50 = _____ increased by 30% of itself

6. $162 is 35% more than _____

7. $59.50 = _____ decreased by 30% of itself

8. 40% more than _____ = $490

9. $1,375 is 45% less than _____

10. _____ less 20% of itself = $140

11. $675 is 25% greater than _____

12. $425 is 16⅔% less than _____

UNIT SIX   Borrowing Money

SECTION 22.   Borrowing Money on a Note

When a person borrows money, a promissory note is usually given to the lender as evidence of the loan. John Hunter, a fruit farmer, lost his peach crop due to a spring snowfall and he must borrow $1,200 for a three-month period from the Jackson National Bank. He makes out the note below for the $1,200 at 6% interest. Mr. Hunter has good standing in the community, and the bank lets him have his money on his personal note.

```
$ 1,200.00 _____                    _____ April 17, 19 --

Three months _____ AFTER DATE  I  PROMISE TO PAY TO

THE ORDER OF  Jackson National Bank _____

One thousand two hundred and  no/100  _____ DOLLARS

PAYABLE AT  Jackson National Bank _____

VALUE RECEIVED WITH INTEREST AT  6  %

NO. 28   DUE  July, 17, 19-  _____     John Hunter _____
```

You will notice that the time of this note is less than one year. An interest rate, however, unless otherwise specified, shows what percent of the loan is charged for interest for a full year. If money is borrowed for only a part of a year, interest must be calculated for a full year and then multiplied by the fraction representing the part. In the above note, for example, the interest is found by multiplying a full year's interest by $\frac{1}{4}$, as three months are $\frac{3}{12}$, or $\frac{1}{4}$, of a year.

EXERCISE.   (Practical problems)

1. At the end of three months Mr. Hunter pays the Jackson National Bank the face of the above note plus the interest. He gives the bank a check for the amount of $_____.

2. Stan Turner, a farmer, needed some money to carry him through the harvest period. His local bank let him have $500 for a period of 6 months with interest at $6\frac{1}{2}\%$. Mr. Turner paid the note promptly on its maturity date, giving the bank a check for $_____ in payment.

3. To her university, Jean Peters paid back a year loan of $750, plus interest of $37.50. The interest was _____% of the principal.

DRILL 78. (Finding interest for years or parts of a year)

As you know, an interest rate, unless otherwise specified, is the rate for one year. Hence, the interest for one year is found by multiplying the principal by the rate. For example, the interest on $500 at 6% for 1 year = $500 × .06 = $30. Interest for any other period of time is found by multiplying the interest for one year by the time in years. In other words, interest = principal × rate × time in years. Thus, the interest on $500 at 6% for $2\frac{1}{2}$ years = $500 × .06 × $2\frac{1}{2}$ = $75.

For convenience in calculating interest when the time is in days or months, the commercial year is considered to contain 360 days, or 12 months of 30 days. If the time of a loan is 60 days, then this period is 60/360 or $\frac{1}{6}$ of a year. 30 days would be $\frac{1}{12}$ of a year, and 90 days, $\frac{1}{4}$ of a year. Similarly, 6 months would be $\frac{6}{12}$ or $\frac{1}{2}$ of a year, and 4 months would be $\frac{1}{3}$ of a year. Hence, the interest on $450 at 5% for 4 months, for example, would be $450 × .05 × $\frac{1}{3}$ = $7.50.

In the following problems the principal, rate, and time are given. Find the interest by multiplying principal × rate × time, with the time expressed in years or a fraction of a year.

	PRINCIPAL	RATE	TIME	AMT. OF INTEREST		PRINCIPAL	RATE	TIME	AMT. OF INTEREST
1.	$ 350	6%	3 yr.	_____	7.	$5,000	5%	120 da.	_____
2.	800	5%	$1\frac{1}{2}$ yr.	_____	8.	1,100	7%	90 da.	_____
3.	500	7%	6 mo.	_____	9.	2,000	8%	8 mo.	_____
4.	600	8%	$\frac{1}{2}$ yr.	_____	10.	800	7%	180 da.	_____
5.	250	4%	2 yr.	_____	11.	2,000	6%	240 da.	_____
6.	300	6%	4 mo.	_____	12.	8,000	5%	9 mo.	_____

DRILL 79. (Finding the rate of interest)

In any interest problem, the interest for one year divided by the principal gives the rate of interest. Thus, if you pay $20 interest for a loan of $500 for one year, the rate of interest you pay is equal to $20 ÷ $500 = .04 = 4%. If the interest is known for a period other than one year, first find what the interest would be for one year and then divide that amount by the principal. For example, if you pay $10 interest for a loan of $400 for 6 months ($\frac{1}{2}$ year), this is equivalent to $10 ÷ $\frac{1}{2}$, or $20, for one year. The rate of interest you pay is equal to $20 ÷ $400 = .05 = 5%.

In the following problems the principal, time, and amount of interest are given. Find the rate of interest by dividing the interest for one year by the principal.

	PRINCIPAL	TIME	AMT. OF INTEREST	RATE		PRINCIPAL	TIME	AMT. OF INTEREST	RATE
1.	$1,200	3 mo.	$18	_____	3.	$ 900	4 mo.	15	_____
2.	400	6 mo.	14	_____	4.	1,800	2 mo.	21	_____

DRILL **79.** (continued)

	PRINCIPAL	TIME	AMT. OF INTEREST	RATE		PRINCIPAL	TIME	AMT. OF INTEREST	RATE
5.	$ 240	1 mo.	$ 1.20	____	9.	$2,500	2 yr.	$300	____
6.	2,000	9 mo.	120	____	10.	3,000	4 yr.	720	____
7.	4,500	8 mo.	150	____	11.	8,000	1½ yr.	840	____
8.	1,500	3 yr.	315	____	12.	4,200	2½ yr.	840	____

DRILL **80.** (Finding exact interest)

Most businesses use the commercial year to compute interest because it is easier. However, the federal government often uses a 365-day year when it computes interest on a loan from a federal agency. When 365 days are used to compute interest, it is called *exact* or *accurate* interest.

The formula for computing exact interest is the same as the formula for figuring interest with a commercial year, except that you use 365 days instead of 360 days.

For example, the exact interest on $1,000 for 146 days at 6% would be:

PRINCIPAL	X	RATE	X	TIME	=	INTEREST
$1,000	x	6%	x	146 days		$= \$60 \times \dfrac{146}{365} = \$60 \times \dfrac{2}{5} = \$24$

In each of the problems below, find the exact interest to the nearest cent and write that amount in the blank space provided. NOTE: In this book, the 360-day year is used for interest problems unless otherwise specified.

	PRINCIPAL	RATE	TIME	INTEREST		PRINCIPAL	RATE	TIME	INTEREST
1.	$ 200	6%	73 days	$_____	5.	$29,200	4%	302 days	$_____
2.	8,000	5%	219 days	$_____	6.	900	6%	200 days	$_____
3.	2,500	8%	292 days	$_____	7.	4,200	8%	112 days	$_____
4.	1,095	7%	88 days	$_____	8.	14,600	7%	64 days	$_____

SECTION 23. Borrowing Money on a Note (concluded)

The time specified in a note fixes the date of maturity, or the date on which the note is due for payment. The date of maturity is found by counting forward, from the date of the note, the stated number of months or days. When the time is stated in months, the date of maturity is the same date in the month of maturity as the date on the note, if the month of maturity has such a date. If it does not, the date of maturity is the last date in the month of maturity. For example, if the date of a note is January 31 and the time is two months, the date of maturity is January 31 + 2 mo. = March 31. If the time were three months, the date of maturity would be January 31 + 3 mo. = April 30.

When the time is in days, the date of maturity is found by the method illustrated at the right. The illustration shows the computation of the date of maturity of a 60-day note dated March 25. The date of maturity is found to be May 24.

	60 days
− Days left in March	6
	54
− Days in April	30
Days in May	24

EXERCISE. (Practical problems)

1. On June 30, Pat Riley borrowed $800 from the Oneida National Bank, giving the bank her four-month note for the amount. The note was dated June 30, and the interest rate was 6%. (a) The date of maturity of the note was _____. (b) On that date Ms. Riley paid the note, giving the bank her check for $_____.

2. Frank Blye was short of ready cash when his taxes came due on October 15. It was therefore necessary for him to borrow $540 from the bank to pay his taxes. To obtain the loan, he gave the bank his 60-day note for $540, dated October 15, and bearing interest at $6\frac{1}{2}$%. (a) The note came due for payment on _____ (b) Mr. Blye paid the note promptly on its maturity date, giving the bank a check for $_____ in payment.

3. The Citizens Bank & Trust Co. has on hand the five notes listed below, representing loans to the persons named in the "Maker" column. Show for each note (a) the date of maturity of the note and (b) the amount due at maturity.

	MAKER	FACE OF NOTE	DATE OF NOTE	TIME	INT. RATE	MATURITY DATE	AMOUNT DUE AT MATURITY
a	Cathy Bridges	$450	July 31	4 mo.	6%		
b	Herman Chase	680	June 27	60 da.	7%		
c	Ernest DuBois	600	May 30	5 mo.	5%		
d	Donald King	400	April 4	90 da.	$7\frac{1}{2}$%		
e	Lee Ling	720	July 18	60 da.	$6\frac{1}{2}$%		
f	Carol Krone	300	Nov. 10	30 da.	4%		
g	Thomas O'Hara	400	Jan. 3	45 da.	8%		

DRILL **81.** (Finding interest by the 60-day method)

Sixty days, or 2 months, is $\frac{60}{360}$, or $\frac{1}{6}$ of a 360-day year. When the interest rate is 6% for a year, then the rate for 60 days is $\frac{1}{6}$ of 6% or 1% (.01). To find the interest on any principal at 6% for 60 days, simply multiply the principal by 1% (.01). You do this by moving the decimal point 2 places to the left. For example: $545 at 6% for 60 days = $545 × .01 = $5.45 *interest*.

Six days is $\frac{1}{10}$ of 60 days, and the interest for 6 days would be .001 of the principal. To find the interest for 6 days at 6%, move the decimal point 3 places to the left. For example: $1,080 at 6% for 6 days = $1,080 × .001 = $1.08 *interest*.

Similarly, 600 days is 10 times 60 days, and the interest is .1 of the principal. To find the interest for 600 days at 6%, move the decimal point one place to the left in the principal. Also, 6,000 days is 100 times 60 days, so that the interest is equal to the principal.

When the time is a multiple of 6, 60, 600, or 6,000 days, multiply the interest for 6, 60, 600, or 6,000 days by the appropriate factor. For example, the interest on $400 at 6% for 6 days is $.40. The interest for 12 days is 2 × $.40 = $.80; for 18 days, 3 × $.40; for 24 days, 4 × $.40; and so on.

If the time is a fractional part of 6, 60, 600, or 6,000 days, multiply the interest for 6, 60, 600, or 6,000 days by the fraction representing the part. For example, the interest on $900 at 6% for 6 days is $.90. The interest for 1 day is $\frac{1}{6}$×$.90, or $.15; for 2 days, $\frac{1}{3}$×$.90; for 3 days, $\frac{1}{2}$×$.90; and so on.

By using the 60-day method, you should be able to find mentally the amount of interest in each of the following problems. Place your answers in the blanks provided. The interest rate in each case is 6%.

	PRINCIPAL	TIME	INTEREST		PRINCIPAL	TIME	INTEREST
1.	$ 450	6 days	$_____	10.	$ 250	240 days	$_____
2.	570	60 days	$_____	11.	320	180 days	$_____
3.	350	600 days	$_____	12.	2,400	1 day	$_____
4.	175	2 mo.	$_____	13.	1,800	2 days	$_____
5.	265	6,000 days	$_____	14.	2,400	3 days	$_____
6.	1,000	12 days	$_____	15.	1,260	10 days	$_____
7.	500	18 days	$_____	16.	1,600	15 days	$_____
8.	300	24 days	$_____	17.	900	20 days	$_____
9.	800	120 days	$_____	18.	450	30 days	$_____

SECTION 24. Borrowing from a Bank

When a person borrows money at a bank, a note must be signed that is either interest bearing or non-interest-bearing. If it is interest bearing, the interest will be paid by the borrower at the maturity of the note. If the note does not bear interest, the bank will deduct interest in advance, at an agreed rate, at the time the loan is made. Interest deducted in advance in this manner is called *discount*, and the note that the borrower gives the bank is said to be *discounted*. On the date the loan is made, the bank gives the borrower the face of the note less the discount.

Example: To pay for some emergency repairs on his home, Bill Burke discounts at the Monroe County State Bank his 60-day non-interest-bearing note for $350. The bank's discount rate is 6%. Find the discount and the proceeds (the amount actually received by the borrower).

Solution

Face of note	$350.00
Discount, 6% on $350 for 60 days	3.50
Proceeds	$346.50

EXERCISE. (Practical problems)

1. (a) From the following data, write a promissory note, using the blank below. Face of note, $1,865; date June 18; time, 60 days; made payable to First National Bank of Auburn; payable at First National Bank of Auburn; interest, none; number, 39; maker, Mary Spenser.

$_____   _____ 19_____

_____ AFTER DATE _____ PROMISE TO PAY TO

THE ORDER OF _____

_____ DOLLARS

PAYABLE AT _____

VALUE RECEIVED WITH INTEREST AT _____ %

NO. _____ DUE _____   _____

(b) Mary Spenser discounts the above note at her bank on June 18, the discount rate being 6%. The bank credits her account for the proceeds, which amount to $_____.

2. On August 12, Oscar Hill found that he had overdrawn his checking account at the bank by $213.15. He immediately discounted at the bank his 30-day non-interest-bearing note for $550 and had the proceeds credited to his account. The bank's discount rate was 6%. (a) The proceeds amounted to $_____. (b) After the proceeds were credited to his account, the balance of his account was $_____.

DRILL 82. (Finding interest by the 1-day method)

The interest at 6% for any number of days can be found in the manner shown at the right, as follows:

1. Find the interest for 6 days.

2. Divide by 6, which gives the interest for 1 day.

3. Multiply by the number of days given in the problem.

Example: Find the interest on $480 for 14 days at 6%.

1. $.48 = int. for 6 da.

2. $.48 ÷ 6 = $.08 int. for 1 da.

3. 14 × $.08 = $1.12 int. for 14 da.

If the interest for 6 days is not exactly divisible by 6, multiply it by the number of days in the problem and divide that product by 6. For example, the interest on $407 for 14 days at 6% would be (14 × $.407) ÷ 6. This is equal to $5.698 ÷ 6, which is $.949 or $.95.

Calculate the interest in each of the problems below. Make the calculations on a separate piece of paper, but place your final answer in the blank space at the right of the problem.

	PRINCIPAL	RATE	TIME	INTEREST
1.	$ 480	6%	70 days	
2.	840	6%	25 days	
3.	660	6%	53 days	

	PRINCIPAL	RATE	TIME	INTEREST
4.	$ 500	6%	90 days	
5.	950	6%	55 days	
6.	1,075	6%	41 days	

●DRILL 83. (Combinations involving parts of 6 days or 60 days)

Adding the interest for 1, 2, or 3 days to the interest for 6 days gives the interest for 7, 8, or 9 days. Also, adding the interest for 7, 8, or 9 days to the interest for 60 days gives the interest for 67, 68, or 69 days. This process is indicated by the first illustration at the right. Calculations are carried correct to four decimal places and the final result rounded to the nearest cent.

Similarly, adding the interest for 10, 15, 20, or 30 days to the interest for 60 days gives the interest for 70, 75, 80, or 90 days. This process is demonstrated at the right.

(a) Calculate interest at 6% on $1,385 for 67 days:

$13|8500 = int. for 60 da.

6) 1|3850 = int. for 6 da.

2308 = int. for 1 da. (⅙ of 6 da.)

$15|4658 = int. for 67 da.

Ans. $15.47

(b) Calculate interest at 6% on $575.50 for 70 days:

6) $5|7550 = int. for 60 da.

9592 = int. for 10 da. (⅙ of 60 da.)

$6|7142 = int. for 70 da.

Ans. $6.71

Calculate the interest in each of the problems below as shown in the examples above. Make the calculations on a separate piece of paper, but place your final answer in the blank space at the right of the problem.

	PRINCIPAL	RATE	TIME	INTEREST
1.	$1,845	6%	7 days	
2.	1,670	6%	8 days	
3.	1,575	6%	9 days	
4.	890	6%	67 days	
5.	865	6%	68 days	

	PRINCIPAL	RATE	TIME	INTEREST
6.	$ 795.00	6%	69 days	
7.	825.00	6%	70 days	
8.	1,045.00	6%	75 days	
9.	1,435.00	6%	80 days	
10.	512.50	6%	90 days	

SECTION 25. Borrowing on Collateral

Many banks require the borrower to pledge some form of property, referred to as *collateral*, as a guarantee that the loan will be paid at maturity. Common forms of collateral are bonds, stocks, and life insurance policies. A description of the property is written on the face of the note that the borrower signs, and the note is referred to as a *collateral note*.

Collateral notes are often made payable "on demand" rather than at the end of a stated period of time. A note payable on demand is called a *demand note*. Interest is usually payable monthly or quarterly. When a demand note is paid, the amount due is the face of the note plus interest on the face for the number of days from the date of the note, or date of last interest payment, to the date of settlement. The method of figuring the number of days is illustrated at the right. This shows the calculation of the number of days from March 10 to May 27.

Calculation of the number of days from March 10 to May 27:

$$\begin{array}{r} 31 \\ -10 \\ \hline 21 \text{ days left in March} \\ 30 \text{ days in April} \\ 27 \text{ days in May} \\ \hline 78 \text{ days total} \end{array}$$

A mortgage on real estate owned by the borrower is often given as security for a loan of a relatively large sum for a long period of time. Usually, the mortgage agreement provides that the interest shall be paid at stated periods, usually quarterly. It may also provide that a specified additional amount shall be paid on each interest date to apply against the principal.

EXERCISE. (Practical problems)

1. On September 8, Robert Blake borrows $1,500 from the Bank of Monroeville at 6% on the demand note shown below, depositing 25 shares of Eastman Kodak Co. common stock as collateral security. On November 27 of the same year he makes full payment of the note and the interest.

DEMAND NOTE

$ 1,500.00 _____ _____ September 8 ___ 19--

On demand ____ I ____ promise to pay to ____ Bank of Monroeville ____

or order, at the Banking House of said Bank in current funds One thousand five hundred DOLLARS

with interest at the rate of ____ 6% ____ per annum, for value received, having deposited with said Bank as

collateral security ____ 25 shares Eastman Kodak Co., common ____

which I hereby authorize said Bank or its President or Cashier to sell without notice at public or private sale at the option of said Bank or of its President or Cashier, in case of the nonperformance of this promise applying the net proceeds the payment of this note, including interest, and accounting to me the surplus, if any. In case of deficiency I promise to pay to said Bank the amount thereof forthwith after such sale with legal interest, and it is hereby AGREED and UNDERSTOOD that if recourse is had to the collaterals, any excess of collaterals upon this note shall be applicable to any other note or claim held by said Bank against me, and in case of any exchange of, or addition to the collaterals above named, the provisions of this note shall extend to such new or additional collaterals. And if this note is placed in the hands of an attorney at law for collection, or has to be sued on, I agree to pay ten per cent attorney's fees and all expenses incurred in its collection, same to be taxed up in judgment. If collaterals are sold the said Bank is authorized to bid on same as any outside party.

No. ____ 9 ____

Robert Blake

By _____

(a) Interest on the note is charged for _____ days. (b) The amount of the interest is $_____.

(c) The amount Mr. Blake must pay on November 27 in full settlement of the note and interest is $_____.

Section 25. (concluded)

2. On April 1, John Mason places an $8,000 mortgage at 6% on his home. The mortgage agreement requires quarterly payment of interest ($\frac{1}{4}$ of the interest for one year), together with a payment of $100 on the principal. (a) The amount of interest due on July 1, the end of the first quarter, will be $_____. (b) The total amount Mr. Mason must pay on July 1 will be $_____. (c) The amount of principal in force during the second quarter will be $_____. (d) The interest due on October 1, the end of the second quarter, will be $_____. (e) The total amount Mr. Mason must pay on October 1, the end of the second quarter, will be $_____.

3. During August and September the Fidelity Trust Company received payment in settlement of each of the twelve demand notes listed below. For each note, find the number of days from the date of the note to the date of payment. Make your calculations on a separate piece of paper, but write your answer at the right of each problem in the column headed "Time."

	MAKER	DATE OF NOTE	DATE PAID	TIME (DAYS)
a	Martin Glynn	July 21	Aug. 27	
b	James Cole	July 23	Sept. 10	
c	Gene Miner	June 25	Aug. 18	
d	Donald Ried	May 31	Aug. 7	
e	Mary Burgess	Nov. 16	Jan. 24	
f	Doris Reeves	Oct. 3	Feb. 15	

	MAKER	DATE OF NOTE	DATE PAID	TIME (DAYS)
g	Henry Paley	June 25	Sept. 21	
h	Leon Marks	June 12	Aug. 30	
i	Norman Jeffers	May 3	Aug. 2	
j	Earl Simon	June 16	Sept. 13	
k	Billie Peters	April 23	June 4	
l	Lynn Martin	Sept. 12	Jan. 21	

DRILL 84. (Finding interest by the 1-day method)

The following drill provides additional practice in finding interest by the 1-day method. Make the calculations on a separate piece of paper, but place the final answers in the appropriate spaces provided below.

	PRINCIPAL	RATE	TIME	INTEREST		PRINCIPAL	RATE	TIME	INTEREST
1.	$ 725	6%	17 days		9.	$1,310.00	6%	38 days	
2.	875	6%	21 days		10.	911.40	6%	43 days	
3.	710	6%	26 days		11.	1,125.50	6%	27 days	
4.	1,220	6%	37 days		12.	1,511.10	6%	29 days	
5.	670	6%	22 days		13.	800.00	6%	19 days	
6.	847	6%	33 days		14.	925.00	6%	23 days	
7.	650	6%	25 days		15.	627.00	6%	34 days	
8.	745	6%	35 days		16.	795.00	6%	41 days	

SECTION 26. Borrowing from a Credit Union or Finance Company

Many persons borrow from a credit union or a consumer finance company.

On a loan from a credit union, the borrower receives the face amount of the loan and repays it in equal installments, usually monthly, plus interest on the unpaid balance. The amount the borrower receives is called the *amount financed*. The interest he pays is called the *finance charge*.

END OF	UNPAID BALANCE	FINANCE CHARGE AT 1%	PAYMENT ON PRINCIPAL	TOTAL PAYMENT
1st mo.	$180	$1.80	$ 60.00	$ 61.80
2d mo.	120	1.20	60.00	61.20
3d mo.	60	.60	60.00	60.60
		$3.60	$180.00	$183.60

For example, Tina George borrows $180 from a credit union in which she is a member. She agrees to repay the loan in three monthly payments of $60 each plus a finance charge of 1% a month on the unpaid balance. A schedule of the unpaid balances, finance charges, and monthly payments is shown above.

Most finance companies and many credit unions have worked out repayment schedules so that the monthly payments are equal amounts. In one company, for example, a loan of $100 may be repaid in six monthly installments of $18.15 each, including the finance charge. The amount repaid to the company is 6 × $18.15, or $108.90. The total finance charge is $108.90 − $100.00, or $8.90.

EXERCISE. (Practical problems)

1. Joe Fazio borrows $200 from his credit union, agreeing to repay the loan in five equal monthly payments plus a finance charge of 1% a month on the unpaid balance. Complete the following schedule to show (a) the unpaid balance, the finance charge, the payment on principal, and the total payment for each month, and (b) the total finance charge, total payment on principal, and total payments for the five months.

END OF	UNPAID BALANCE	FINANCE CHARGE AT 1%	PAYMENT ON PRINCIPAL	TOTAL PAYMENT
1st month				
2d month				
3d month				
4th month				
5th month				

2. Frank Cross wishes to borrow $300 for six months. He can obtain the loan from a credit union in which he is a member by agreeing to repay it in 6 equal monthly payments plus interest at 1% per month on the unpaid balance. He can also obtain the loan from a personal finance company and repay it in 6 monthly payments of $54.45 each, including the finance charge. (a) If he borrows from the credit union, the finance charge for the 6 months will be $_____. (b) If he borrows from the finance company, the total finance charge will be $_____. (c) By borrowing from the credit union he will save $_____.

SECTION 27. Borrowing from Other Agencies

An installment loan can also be obtained from the personal loan department of a commercial bank or from an industrial bank.

The methods of these banks vary. At some, the borrower receives the face of the loan and repays the combined total of the face and the finance charge. For example, on a loan of $300 at 6% for twelve months, the finance charge would be $300 × .06, or $18. The borrower would receive $300 and would repay $318 in twelve monthly payments of $26.50 each ($318 ÷ 12 = $26.50). In complying with the laws on installment loans, the lender has to figure the finance charge per $100 (FC/100) of the amount financed. For this loan, the finance charge is $18, and the amount financed is $300. The finance charge per $100 of amount financed is ($18 × 100) ÷ $300, which is $1,800 ÷ $300, or $6.

At other banks, the loan is made on the discount basis, and the borrower receives the proceeds. In a case like the loan above, the proceeds would be $300 − $18, or $282. The borrower would receive $282 and would repay $300 in twelve monthly payments of $25 each. The finance charge per $100 of amount financed would be ($18 × 100) ÷ 282, which is $1,800 ÷ 282, or $6.38 to the nearest cent.

The true rate of interest on an installment loan is considerably higher than the stated rate, because the borrower does not have the use of the original principal throughout the entire life of the loan. The true rate, or *annual percentage rate*, as it is called, depends upon the finance charge per $100 of amount financed and the number of payments. The rate is determined by means of tables, a portion of which is shown below.

Assuming that the finance charge per $100 of amount financed is $6 and that the loan is to be repaid in 12 monthly payments, read across on the 12-payment line to the value nearest $6. This is $6.06 in the 11% column. The annual percentage rate, or true rate, on this loan is therefore 11%.

When the finance charge per $100 falls half way between two adjacent columns, use the higher

ANNUAL PERCENTAGE RATE TABLE FOR MONTHLY PAYMENT PLANS

No. of Payments	ANNUAL PERCENTAGE RATE										
	$10\frac{3}{4}$%	11%	$11\frac{1}{4}$%	$11\frac{1}{2}$%	$11\frac{3}{4}$%	12%	$12\frac{1}{4}$%	$12\frac{1}{2}$%	$12\frac{3}{4}$%	13%	$13\frac{1}{4}$%
	FINANCE CHARGE PER $100 OF AMOUNT FINANCED										
6	3.16	3.23	3.31	3.38	3.45	3.53	3.60	3.68	3.75	3.83	3.90
12	5.92	6.06	6.20	6.34	6.48	6.62	6.76	6.90	7.04	7.18	7.32
18	8.73	8.93	9.14	9.35	9.56	9.77	9.98	10.19	10.40	10.61	10.82
24	11.58	11.86	12.14	12.42	12.70	12.98	13.26	13.54	13.82	14.10	14.38
30	14.48	14.83	15.19	15.54	15.89	16.24	16.60	16.95	17.31	17.66	18.02

percentage rate. For example, on the 12-payment line, $6.27 is half way between $6.20 and $6.34. Since $6.34 is in the $11\frac{1}{2}$% column, $11\frac{1}{2}$% would be selected as the rate represented by $6.27.

EXERCISE. (Practical problems)

1. You borrow $480 for 6 months from the personal loan department of a local commercial bank, agreeing to pay interest at the rate of 7% a year on the face of the loan and to repay the combined total of the principal and interest in 6 equal monthly installments. (a) The amount financed is $_____. (b) The amount of the finance charge is $_____. (c) The total amount to be repaid to the bank is $_____. (d) Your monthly payments to the bank will be $_____ each. (e) The finance charge per $100 of amount financed (FC/100) is $_____. (f) The annual percentage rate on the loan is _____%.

2. Today, Roger Judd obtains a loan at the personal loan department of a commercial bank by signing a note for $600, which is to be repaid in 12 equal monthly installments. The bank deducts in advance 12 months' interest at the rate of $6\frac{1}{2}$% a year and gives Mr. Judd the proceeds. (a) The amount of the finance charge is $_____. (b) The amount Mr. Judd receives, which is the amount financed, is $_____. (c) The amount he must pay the bank each month is $_____. (d) The finance charge per $100 of amount financed (FC/100) is $_____ to the nearest cent. (e) The annual percentage rate on the loan is _____%.

3. A loan of $500 is repaid in 30 monthly installments of $19.50 each. (a) The total amount repaid on the loan is $_____. (b) The finance charge on the loan is $_____. (c) The amount financed is $_____. (d) The finance charge per $100 of amount financed (FC/100) is $_____. The annual percentage rate on this loan is _____%.

4. For each installment loan in the table at the right, show (a) the total amount repaid, (b) the amount of the finance charge, (c) the finance charge per $100 of amount financed (FC/100), and (d) the annual percentage rate.

| | AMOUNT FINANCED | MONTHLY PAYMENTS | | | FINANCE CHARGE | FC/100 | ANNUAL PERCENTAGE RATE |
		NUMBER	EACH	TOTAL			
a	$600	24	$28.50				
b	$400	30	$15.55				
c	$540	18	$33.10				
d	$451	12	$40.00				

DRILL 85. (Finding interest by the 1-day method)

The following drill provides additional practice in finding interest by the 1-day method. Make the calculations on a separate piece of paper, but place the final answers in the appropriate spaces provided below.

	PRINCIPAL	RATE	TIME	INTEREST		PRINCIPAL	RATE	TIME	INTEREST
1.	$ 920	6%	35 da.	_____	4.	$2,110	6%	64 da.	_____
2.	1,450	6%	46 da.	_____	5.	850	6%	73 da.	_____
3.	835	6%	51 da.	_____	6.	1,225	6%	92 da.	_____

● DRILL 86. (Interchanging the principal and time)

When the principal is $6, $60, $600, or $6,000, or a multiple or aliquot part of any of these amounts, and the time is in days, finding the interest can be simplified by interchanging the principal and the time. For example, if you wish to find the interest at 6% on $120 for 56 days, interchange the principal and time, and find the interest on $56 for 120 days. Since the interest for 60 days is $.56, the interest for 120 days is 2 × $.56, or $1.12. Thus, the interest at 6% on $120 for 56 days is $1.12.

Similarly, to find the interest at 6% on $700 for 73 days, find the interest on $73 for 700 days. The solution would be as shown at the right.

6) $ 7|3000 = int. for 600 da.
       1|2167 = int. for 100 da. (⅙ of 600 da.)
    $ 8|5167 = int. for 700 da.
           Ans. $8.52

Calculate the interest in each of the problems below, using the method of interchanging the principal and time. Make the calculations on a separate piece of paper, but place your final answer in the blank at the right of each problem.

	PRINCIPAL	RATE	TIME	INTEREST		PRINCIPAL	RATE	TIME	INTEREST
1.	$ 60	6%	71 da.	_____	7.	$1,200	6%	57 da.	_____
2.	70	6%	107 da.	_____	8.	1,800	6%	73 da.	_____
3.	75	6%	93 da.	_____	9.	6,000	6%	35 da.	_____
4.	600	6%	85 da.	_____	10.	1,000	6%	29 da.	_____
5.	100	6%	113 da.	_____	11.	7,000	6%	43 da.	_____
6.	700	6%	110 da.	_____	12.	3,300	6%	55 da.	_____

SECTION 28. Installment Buying

When an article is purchased on the installment plan, the buyer usually pays a certain amount down and an agreed amount at regular intervals until the full purchase price is paid. In setting the price to an installment buyer, the seller usually adds a finance charge to the cash price to cover the extra costs involved in an installment sale. If there are no additional charges, the finance charge is the amount by which the installment price exceeds the cash price.

Example: A stereo phonograph marked to sell at $320 may be purchased on the installment plan for $80 down and $12 a month for 24 months. The finance charge may be found as shown below.

FINDING THE FINANCE CHARGE

Down payment	= $80
Installments, 24 × 12	= 288
Installment price	= $368
Cash price	= 320
Finance charge	= $48

When a person buys an article on the installment plan, he is in effect borrowing from the merchant.

The amount borrowed is the cash price less the down payment. This amount represents the amount financed. If no down payment is required, the amount financed is the same as the cash price.

In the case of the stereo phonograph in the example at the left, the amount financed is $240, which is the cash price, $320, less the down payment, $80. The finance charge, $48, may be thought of as the interest the buyer pays for the use of $240 of the merchant's money.

FINDING THE ANNUAL PERCENTAGE RATE

The rate of interest or annual percentage rate represented by the finance charge is found by means of tables in the same manner as the annual percentage rate on an installment loan. A portion of the tables is shown below.

In the case of the stereo phonograph referred to above and at the left, the finance charge is $48 and the amount financed is $240. The finance charge per $100 of amount financed is ($48 × 100) ÷ $240, which is $4,800 ÷ $240 or $20.

On the 24-payment line in the table, the nearest value to $20 is $20.11 in the $18\frac{1}{4}\%$ column. The annual percentage rate paid by the buyer is therefore $18\frac{1}{4}\%$.

ANNUAL PERCENTAGE RATE TABLE FOR MONTHLY PAYMENT PLANS

No. of Payments	ANNUAL PERCENTAGE RATE										
	$15\frac{3}{4}\%$	16%	$16\frac{1}{4}\%$	$16\frac{1}{2}\%$	$16\frac{3}{4}\%$	17%	$17\frac{1}{4}\%$	$17\frac{1}{2}\%$	$17\frac{3}{4}\%$	18%	$18\frac{1}{4}\%$
	FINANCE CHARGE PER $100 OF AMOUNT FINANCED										
6	4.64	4.72	4.79	4.87	4.94	5.02	5.09	5.17	5.24	5.32	5.39
12	8.74	8.88	9.02	9.16	9.30	9.45	9.59	9.73	9.87	10.02	10.16
18	12.93	13.14	13.35	13.57	13.78	13.99	14.21	14.42	14.64	14.85	15.07
24	17.22	17.51	17.80	18.09	18.37	18.66	18.95	19.24	19.53	19.82	20.11
30	21.62	21.99	22.35	22.72	23.08	23.45	23.81	24.18	24.55	24.92	25.29

EXERCISE. (Practical problems)

1. The cash price of a 10-speed bicycle is $139. It may be purchased on the installment plan for a down payment of $25 and 12 payments of $10 each. (a) The installment price of the bicycle is $_____. (b) The finance charge amounts to $_____. (c) The amount financed is $_____.

2. Your father buys a used car costing $2,275 and is allowed $625 on the trade-in of his old car. The balance plus a finance charge of $186 is to be paid in 24 equal monthly installments, each of which will amount to $_____.

3. An electric range may be purchased for $330 cash or on the installment plan by paying $30 down and 24 monthly installments of $14.75 each. (a) The installment price of the range is $_____. (b) The finance charge is $_____. (c) The amount financed is $_____. (d) The finance charge per $100 of amount financed is $_____. (e) The annual percentage rate is_____%.

4. For each of the following installment purchases, show (a) the total monthly payments, (b) the installment price, (c) the finance charge, (d) the amount financed, (e) the finance charge per $100 of amount financed (FC/100), and (f) the annual percentage rate.

		CASH PRICE	DOWN PAYMENT	MONTHLY PAYMENTS			INSTALL-MENT PRICE	FINANCE CHARGE	AMOUNT FINANCED	FC/100	ANNUAL PERCENTAGE RATE
				NUMBER	EACH	TOTAL					
a	Slide projector	$130	$20	18	$7						
b	Radio-stereo	$250	$30	30	$9						
c	Typewriter	$140	None	24	$7						
d	Clarinet	$ 98	$10	12	$8						

DRILL 87.   (Finding interest at rates other than 6%)

To find interest when the rate is other than 6%, first find the interest at 6% and then convert that result to interest at the desired rate. In some cases this may be done by taking an appropriate aliquot part of the interest at 6%, as shown at the right.

Find the interest on $2,100 for 20 days at $4\frac{1}{2}$%:

3) $21.00 = int. for 60 da. @ 6%
4) $ 7.00 = int. for 20 da. @ 6%
   1.75 = int. for 20 da. @ $1\frac{1}{2}$%
$ 5.25 = int. for 20 da. @ $4\frac{1}{2}$%

In cases where an aliquot part cannot be used conveniently, multiply the interest at 6% by the given rate and divide the product by 6. For example, as shown above, the interest on $2,100 for 20 days at 6% is $7. Now assume an interest rate of $2\frac{1}{2}$%. To find the interest at $2\frac{1}{2}$%, multiply $7 by $2\frac{1}{2}$ and divide the product by 6. Thus, $2\frac{1}{2}$ × $7 = $17.50. $17.50 ÷ 6 = $2.92.

Calculate the interest in each of the problems below. Make all calculations on a separate piece of paper, but place your answer in the appropriate blank at the right of each problem.

	PRINCIPAL	RATE	TIME	INTEREST
1.	$550	3%	70 days	
2.	630	2%	75 days	
3.	700	4%	80 days	
4.	625	8%	66 days	

	PRINCIPAL	RATE	TIME	INTEREST
5.	$725	5%	90 days	
6.	850	7%	40 days	
7.	500	$4\frac{1}{2}$%	70 days	
8.	800	$7\frac{1}{2}$%	80 days	

UNIT SEVEN   Saving and Investing

SECTION 29. Using Savings Accounts

The most common means of saving money is an account in a savings bank. Savings amounting to only a few dollars monthly may be deposited in a savings account, where it will earn interest. The interest is added to the depositor's account at regular intervals, usually either quarterly or semiannually. Interest rates are always quoted as annual rates. The rate for a quarterly period is one fourth of the annual rate. The rate for a semiannual period is one half of the annual rate. For example, you may deposit $400 in a bank that pays 5% interest and adds interest to your account every three months, or quarterly. The rate for one quarter is therefore $5\% \div 4$, or $1\frac{1}{4}\%$. On April 1, at the end of the first quarter, $5 interest ($1\frac{1}{4}\%$ of $400) is added to your account, giving you a balance of $405.

EXERCISE. (Practical problems)

1. The bankbook record at the right shows Frank Stanton's bank balance on January 2. You are to complete the record by filling in the spaces marked with a star (*).

The Milton Savings Bank pays interest at the rate of 5% a year and adds the interest to the depositor's balance on January 2 and the first of April, July, and October. No interest is allowed on fractional parts of a dollar.

MILTON SAVINGS BANK
In Account with *Frank Stanton*

DATE		WITH-DRAWAL	DEPOSIT	INTEREST	BALANCE
19-- Jan.	2		724 40		724 40
Apr.	1			*	*
July	1			*	*
Oct.	1			*	*
Jan.	2			*	*

HOLLIS SAVINGS BANK
In Account with *Linda Hodges*

DATE		WITH-DRAWAL	DEPOSIT	INTEREST	BALANCE
19-- Apr.	1			6 76	548 60
Apr.	10		130 —		*
May	15	85 —			*
June	20		74 60		*
July	1			*	*
Aug.	12		60 —		*
Sept.	4	75 —			*
Sept.	25		40 —		*
Oct.	1			*	*

● **2.** The bankbook record at the left shows Linda Hodge's bank balance on April 1 and her deposits and withdrawals through October 1. You are to complete the record by filling in the blanks marked with a star (*).

The Hollis Savings Bank pays interest at the rate of 5% a year and adds interest to the depositor's account on the second of January and the first of April, July, and October. Interest is allowed on only the smallest balance on deposit during the interest period. No interest is allowed on fractional parts of a dollar.

DRILL 88. (Compound interest tables)

Money in a savings bank earns what is called compound interest. At the end of each interest period, interest is added to the previous balance. The sum becomes the new principal on which interest is figured for the next period. When interest is added regularly in this manner it is said to be compounded.

Banks and other financial institutions use tables in making compound interest calculations. The table below shows the amount to which $1 will grow if placed at interest for various rates and interest periods. For example, if interest is compounded annually for 10 years (10 periods) at 5%, the table shows that the accumulated principal, or compound amount, is $1.628895. For an original principal of $200, it would be 200 × $1.628895, which is $325.78.

● If the interest is compounded semiannually, use one half of the rate and twice the number of annual periods; if quarterly, use one fourth of the rate and four times the number of annual periods.

Example: The Home Savings Bank pays 5% interest compounded quarterly. If you deposit $500, what will be your principal amount at the end of 3 years?

5% interest compounded quarterly = $1\frac{1}{4}$% quarterly rate.

3 years = 12 compounding periods.

$1 at $1\frac{1}{4}$% for 12 periods = $1.160755 (see table).

500 × $1.160755 = $580.38 accumulated principal or compound amount.

Use the above table in completing the problems at the left. Show in the blank column the compound amount to which each principal will grow at the end of the specified number of periods. Perform your calculations in the space provided below.

Periods	1%	1¼%	1½%	2%	3%	4%	5%	6%	Periods
1	1.010000	1.012500	1.015000	1.020000	1.030000	1.040000	1.050000	1.060000	1
2	1.020100	1.025156	1.030225	1.040400	1.060900	1.081600	1.102500	1.123600	2
3	1.030301	1.037971	1.045678	1.061208	1.092727	1.124864	1.157625	1.191016	3
4	1.040604	1.050945	1.061364	1.082432	1.125509	1.169859	1.215506	1.262477	4
5	1.051010	1.064082	1.077284	1.104081	1.159274	1.216653	1.276282	1.338226	5
6	1.061520	1.077383	1.093443	1.126162	1.194052	1.265319	1.340096	1.418519	6
7	1.072135	1.090850	1.109845	1.148686	1.229874	1.315932	1.407100	1.503630	7
8	1.082857	1.104486	1.126493	1.171659	1.266770	1.368569	1.477455	1.593848	8
9	1.093685	1.118292	1.143390	1.195093	1.304773	1.423312	1.551328	1.689479	9
10	1.104622	1.132271	1.160541	1.218994	1.343916	1.480244	1.628895	1.790848	10
11	1.115668	1.146424	1.177949	1.243374	1.384234	1.539454	1.710339	1.898299	11
12	1.126825	1.160755	1.195618	1.268242	1.425761	1.601032	1.795856	2.012197	12
13	1.138093	1.175264	1.213552	1.293607	1.468534	1.665074	1.885649	2.132928	13
14	1.149474	1.189955	1.231756	1.319479	1.512590	1.731676	1.979932	2.260904	14
15	1.160969	1.204829	1.250232	1.345868	1.557967	1.800944	2.078928	2.396558	15
16	1.172579	1.219890	1.268986	1.372786	1.604706	1.872981	2.182875	2.540352	16
17	1.184304	1.235138	1.288020	1.400241	1.652848	1.947901	2.292018	2.692773	17
18	1.196147	1.250577	1.307341	1.428246	1.702433	2.025817	2.406619	2.854339	18
19	1.208109	1.266210	1.326951	1.456811	1.753506	2.106849	2.526950	3.025600	19
20	1.220190	1.282037	1.346855	1.485947	1.806111	2.191123	2.653298	3.207136	20
21	1.232392	1.298063	1.367058	1.515666	1.860295	2.278768	2.785963	3.399564	21
22	1.244716	1.314288	1.387564	1.545980	1.916103	2.369919	2.925261	3.603537	22
23	1.257163	1.330717	1.408377	1.576899	1.973587	2.464716	3.071524	3.819750	23
24	1.269735	1.347351	1.429503	1.608437	2.032794	2.563304	3.225100	4.048935	24
25	1.282432	1.364193	1.450945	1.640606	2.093778	2.665836	3.386355	4.291781	25

NO.	BEGINNING PRINCIPAL	RATE	TIME	COMPOUNDING PERIOD	COMPOUND AMOUNT
1.	$ 800	5%	10 years	annually	
2.	600	6%	20 years	annually	
3.	2,000	3%	18 years	annually	
4.	1,200	4%	25 years	annually	
● 5.	400	5%	6 years	quarterly	
● 6.	600	4%	4 years	quarterly	
● 7.	500	6%	5 years	quarterly	
● 8.	3,000	4%	12 years	semiannually	
● 9.	1,100	6%	8 years	semiannually	

[78]

SECTION 30. Buying Life Insurance

In the case of a person's death, life insurance protects the dependents from financial loss. It also provides a method of saving. Most types of life insurance have a cash value that may be withdrawn if the insured stops the insurance.

Premium rates depend upon the age of the insured and the kind of policy. Rates also vary with different companies. The upper table at the right is a sample of annual premiums for $1,000 of insurance under three different kinds of insurance policies. Premiums for larger amounts are found by multiplying the rate for $1,000 by the appropriate factor. For example, the annual rate for a $2,000 straight life policy at age 26 would be 2 × $13.04, or $26.08.

Premiums may be paid semiannually or quarterly instead of annually. In the company whose rates are shown in the table, the semiannual premium is figured by multiplying the total annual premium by .51. The quarterly premium is found by multiplying the total annual premium by .26.

All policies of the kinds referred to above contain tables of cash surrender values showing the amount of money the policyholder may receive if the policy is canceled. The lower table at the right shows cash values per $1,000 for policies taken out at age 26.

Some companies charge higher premiums than others, but they return part of the premiums to the policyholders as dividends. The policyholder may deduct the dividend from the premium due or leave it with the company for the purchase of additional insurance or to draw interest. The dividend may be taken in cash.

ANNUAL PREMIUM FOR $1,000 INSURANCE			
AGE	KIND OF POLICY		
	STRAIGHT LIFE	20-PAYMENT LIFE	20-YEAR ENDOWMENT
26	$13.04	$21.92	$42.69
27	13.47	22.49	42.75
28	13.92	23.08	42.82
29	14.41	23.70	42.90

CASH SURRENDER VALUE FOR $1,000 INSURANCE AGE 26			
END OF YEAR	STRAIGHT LIFE	20-PAYMENT LIFE	20-YEAR ENDOWMENT
3	$ 4	$ 27	$ 79
5	27	69	164
10	90	185	401
15	170	318	677

EXERCISE. (Practical problems)

In solving the problems in this exercise, use the rates in the tables shown above.

1. Jerry Panos, who is 28 years old, takes out a 20-payment life policy for $5,000. (a) At his age, the annual premium on a 20-payment life policy for $1,000 is $_____. (b) For a $5,000 policy, the annual premium is $_____.

2. Warren Bolton, age 26, takes out a straight life policy for $1,000 and elects to pay the premiums quarterly. (a) If paid annually, the cost of the annual premium would be $_____. (b) The cost of the quarterly premium is $_____. (c) The annual cost of the premiums at the quarterly rate is $_____. (d) He could save $_____ each year by paying the premium annually rather than quarterly.

3. At age 29, David Reber takes out a 20-year endowment policy for $6,000, paying the premium quarterly. (a) If paid annually, the total annual premium on the policy would be $_____ . (b) If paid quarterly, the cost of each quarterly premium is $_____ ; and the total annual cost is $_____ . (c) He would save $_____ each year by paying the premium annually instead of quarterly.

4. Bert Darwin, age 29, figures that from his income he can save $25 a month for investment in life insurance. Expressed in even thousands of dollars, he can pay the annual premium on $_____ of 20-payment life insurance with one year's savings.

5. Lucas Tapia took out a 20-payment life policy for $7,000 at age 26. At the end of the fifteenth year he turned in the policy for its cash surrender value and received $_____ from the insurance company.

6. Alice Larsen has a 20-year endowment policy for $8,000 at the annual premium rate of $48.31 per $1,000. Today she receives notice that the next annual premium will be due next month and that she will be entitled to a dividend of $56.32. If she uses the dividend to reduce the premiums, she will send the insurance company a check for $_____ when she makes the premium payment.

7. Pete Thomas took out a straight life policy for $6,000 at the annual premium rate of $22.33 per $1,000 and paid the premiums for a period of 10 years. Over this period, the policy earned dividends totaling $247.80, and Mr. Thomas used them to reduce the premiums. His total net payments to the insurance company amounted to $_____ .

8. At the end of the tenth year, Pete Thomas (Problem 7) turned in his policy for its cash surrender value of $118 per $1,000, and received $_____ for it.

9. The total net payments to the insurance company minus the cash surrender value of the policy gives the net cost of the insurance protection. (a) In the case of Pete Thomas (Problems 7 and 8), the net cost of the protection for 10 years was $_____ . (b) The average annual net cost was $_____ . (c) This was equivalent to an annual net cost of $_____ per $1,000.

SECTION 31. Investing in Bonds

A bond is a form of long-term, interest-bearing note. It is issued by a government or corporation for the purpose of borrowing money. The market price of a bond is quoted as a percent of the par value. If Western Union bonds are quoted at $81\frac{1}{4}$, and the par value of each bond is $1,000, the market price of one bond is $81\frac{1}{4}\%$ of $1,000, or $812.50. An investor usually makes a purchase of bonds through a bond broker or stockbroker, who charges a commission for the service. The investor's total investment in a purchase of bonds equals the market price of the bonds plus the cost of the commission.

Example: Pauline Cline buys through a bond broker ten $1,000 Cities Service bonds at $74\frac{1}{8}$ plus $5.00 commission per bond. Find the amount of her investment.

$.74\frac{1}{8} \times \$1,000 = \$741.25$ market price of 1 bond
$10 \times \$741.25 = \$7,412.50$ market price of 10 bonds
$10 \times \$5.00 = \underline{50.00}$ commission on 10 bonds
$\overline{\$7,462.50}$ total investment

EXERCISE. (Practical problems)

1. Edwin Sherman buys nine Ford Motor $1,000 bonds at $97\frac{3}{4}$, plus $5 commission per bond. (a) The market price of the nine bonds is $_____. (b) The total commission is $_____. (c) Sherman's total investment in the nine bonds is $_____.

2. An investor buys eight $500 bonds at $103\frac{1}{2}$ plus $5 commission per bond. (a) Total market price of the eight bonds is $_____. (b) The total cost of the commission is $_____. (c) The total investment in the bonds is $_____.

3. In each of the following problems, show (a) the total market price of the bonds, (b) the commission, and (c) the total investment.

	NUMBER OF BONDS	PAR VALUE PER BOND	MARKET PRICE PER BOND	COMMISSION PER BOND	TOTAL MARKET PRICE	TOTAL COMMISSION	TOTAL INVESTMENT
a	5	$1,000	$103\frac{1}{4}$	$5.00			
b	8	$1,000	$92\frac{5}{8}$	$5.00			
c	7	$1,000	$78\frac{3}{8}$	$5.00			
d	6	$ 500	$84\frac{3}{4}$	$5.00			
e	4	$ 500	$112\frac{1}{4}$	$5.00			

SECTION 32. Investing in Bonds (concluded)

Bond interest is usually paid semiannually at a specified annual rate based on the par value. If you own a $1,000 bond that bears 8% interest, payable semiannually, each semiannual interest payment is 4% of $1,000, or $40. Your annual income from the bond is 8% of $1,000, or $80.

An investor's rate of income on the investment, is found by dividing the annual income by the amount invested. For example, if you pay $1,200, including commission, for a $1,000, 6% bond, your annual income is $60 (6% of $1,000), and the amount invested is $1,200. The rate of income you get on this investment is therefore $60 ÷ $1,200, which is .05, or 5%.

EXERCISE. (Practical problems)

1. Sally Decker owns 40 General Chemical $1,000 bonds, bearing 7% interest, payable April 1 and October 1. Her semiannual income from the bonds is $_____.

2. Albert Duran owns 15 Jetco $8\frac{1}{2}\%$, $1,000 bonds. His annual income from the 15 bonds is $_____.

3. David Berg buys a $1,000, 6% bond at 62, including the broker's commission. (a) His annual income from the bond is $_____. (b) His total investment in the bond is $_____. (c) His rate of income on the investment is _____%, figured to the nearest tenth of a percent.

4. Kay Enos is considering the purchase of Western Utility $8\frac{3}{4}\%$, $1,000 bonds, quoted at $106\frac{3}{4}$, plus $2.50 commission per bond. If she makes the purchase, her rate of income on the investment, computed to the nearest tenth of a percent, will be _____%.

● **5.** (a) In Problem 4, if Ms. Enos desires an annual income of $700 from her investment, the number of Western Utility bonds she will have to buy is _____. (b) Her total investment in the bonds will be $_____.

SECTION 33. Investing in Stocks

Shares of stock are issued and sold by a corporation to obtain capital for operating the business. Investors purchase the shares expecting to receive dividends from the corporation or sell the shares at a higher price.

Most purchases of stocks by investors are made through stockbrokers, who charge a commission for their services. For brokers dealing on the New York Stock Exchange, the commission is based on the market value of a round lot (100 shares), as shown below.

MARKET VALUE	COMMISSION
Under $100	As mutually agreed
$ 100 to $ 800	$2\% + \$ 6.40$
$ 800 to $2,500	$1\frac{3}{10}\% + \$ 12$
$2,500 and above	$\frac{9}{10}\% + \$ 22$

Example: Find the commission on 300 shares of stock purchased at 35 ($35 per share).

$100 \times \$35 = \$3,500$ market value of 100 shares

$\frac{9}{10}\%$ of $3,500 = \$31.50$

Plus $\qquad$ 22.00

Commission per 100 shares = $53.50

$3 \times \$53.50 = \$160.50$ commission on 300 shares

If an odd-lot (less than 100 shares) is purchased, the commission is $2 less than the amount computed by using the rates given in the table.

Example: Find the commission on 40 shares of stock purchased at $39\frac{3}{4}$ ($39\frac{3}{4}$ per share).

$40 \times \$39\frac{3}{4} = \$1,590$ market value of 40 shares

$1\frac{3}{10}\%$ of $1,590 = \$20.67$

Plus $\qquad$ 12.00

$\qquad$ $32.67

Less $\qquad$ 2.00

Commission on 40 shares = $30.67

EXERCISE. (Practical problems)

1. Using the commission rates shown above, find the commission charges on each of the following stock purchases. Make the necessary calculations in the space provided below, but enter your answer on the correct line in the "Commission" column.

	NO. OF SHARES	MARKET PRICE	COMMISSION
a	100	$38\frac{1}{2}$	
b	100	$9\frac{3}{4}$	
c	300	47	
d	200	$64\frac{3}{4}$	

	NO. OF SHARES	MARKET PRICE	COMMISSION
e	40	27	
f	70	32	
g	80	55	
h	90	$62\frac{1}{2}$	

2. Alfred Hart purchased 45 shares of Computer Devices stock at 33. The broker calculated his commission on the basis of the rates shown on page 83. The total cost of the shares was $_____ .

3. Karen Jones placed an order with her broker to buy 200 shares of Cook Scientific stock at $18\frac{3}{8}$. The broker bought the stock at that price and charged $33.54 per 100 shares of commission. Ms. Jones' total investment in the stock amounted to $_____ .

4. Gerald Tice owns 100 shares of National Nickel Company stock, par value $50 per share. It pays a quarterly dividend of $1\frac{1}{4}\%$. (a) He receives from the company each quarter a dividend check for $_____ . (b) This amounts to an annual income of $_____ .

5. On an investment in 150 shares of Western Freightways stock, you receive a regular quarterly dividend of 35¢ a share. At that rate, your annual income from the investment amounts to $_____ .

6. In Problem 5, the total cost of the 150 shares, including commission, was $4,105. The rate of income on your investment, figured to the nearest tenth of a percent, is _____ %.

7. Standard Instrument stock pays a quarterly dividend of 75¢ a share. George Wilson purchases 40 shares of the stock at 85, paying $53 for commission. On a total investment of (a) $_____ , Mr. Wilson receives an annual income amounting to (b) $_____ , which is equivalent to a rate of income of (c) _____ %, figured to the nearest tenth of a percent.

● **8.** Fairchild Electronics stock pays a quarterly dividend of $62\frac{1}{2}$¢ a share and can be purchased at 50. If you want an annual income of $1,000 from an investment in the stock, the number of shares you must buy is (a) _____ , and the total cost of the purchase, including commission charges of $240, will be (b) $_____ .

● **9.** In Problem 8, your rate of income on the investment, figured to the nearest tenth percent, will be _____ %.

[84]

SECTION 34. Investing in Stocks (concluded)

When a person sells stock, a commission must be paid to the broker. This commission is figured in the same manner as when stock is purchased. In some states both transfer taxes and fees on the shares sold must be paid. The amount which the seller receives is called the net proceeds. This amount is the market value of the shares less the commission and taxes.

EXERCISE. (Practical problems)

1. Irvin Holt placed 60 shares of Colonial Markets stock with his broker to sell for him at $42\frac{5}{8}$. The broker sold the shares at that price and charged $43.02 for commission and $3.06 for taxes. The net proceeds Mr. Holt received from his broker were $_____.

2. Pauline Craft purchased 40 shares of Allied Industries stock at $48\frac{1}{4}$, paying $42.87 for the broker's commission. Four weeks later she sold the shares at $53\frac{1}{2}$, paying $2.05 for taxes and fees and $45.97 for the commission. (a) The total cost of the stock was $_____. (b) The net proceeds from the sale were $_____. (c) Ms. Craft's profit on the purchase and sale was $_____.

3. Colin Knapp purchased 100 shares of stock at a total cost of $2,883.25. He received two quarterly dividends of $42\frac{1}{2}$¢ each and then sold the stock, receiving net proceeds of $3,210.68. (a) The total dividends he received were $_____. (b) His profit on the purchase and sale of the stock was $_____. (c) His total gain from owning and selling the stock was $_____.

4. Leo Kelly bought 25 shares of stock at a total cost of $1,898.75. He kept the stock for two years. During that time he received regular semiannual dividends of $1.75 per share. He then sold the stock and received the net proceeds, $1,751.22. (a) The total dividends he received were $_____. (b) His loss on the purchase and sale of the stock was $_____. (c) His net gain from owning and selling the stock was $_____.

● 5. Carla North purchased 200 shares of stock at $19\frac{3}{4}$ and paid $69.55 for the broker's commission. She received three quarterly dividends of $17\frac{1}{2}$¢ each per share and then sold the stock at $18\frac{7}{8}$, paying $78.06 for commission and taxes. Ms. North received (a) $_____ in dividends, lost (b) $_____ on the purchase and sale of the stock, and suffered a net loss of (c) $_____ on the entire transaction.

SECTION 35. Investing in Real Estate

The annual net income from an investment in real estate is the gross rental income less the expenses. The expenses should include all payments for such items as taxes, insurance, repairs, interest on any mortgage, and an allowance for depreciation. The owner's rate of income on the investment is found by dividing the annual net income by the amount of the cash investment in the property.

EXERCISE. (Practical problems)

1. Gale Foy bought a house and a lot as an investment for $30,000, paying $20,000 in cash and giving a 7% mortgage for the remainder. The house is valued at $26,000 and the lot at $4,000. During the first year, she rented the house for the full year at $400 a month. In addition to the interest on the mortgage, she paid $1,011 for taxes, $159 for insurance, $350 for repairs, and allowed 2% of the value of the house for depreciation. (a) Her gross rental income for the year was $_____. (b) Her total expenses amounted to $_____. (c) Her net income was $_____.

2. In Problem 1, Ms. Foy's rate of income on her cash investment was _____%.

3. Ed Wilson is planning to buy, as an investment, an apartment house, which rents for $775 a month. He can buy the building by paying $50,000 in cash and giving $7\frac{1}{2}$% mortgage for $20,000. In addition to interest on the mortgage, the expenses connected with owning the property, including depreciation, average $4,250 a year. Assuming that the rent and expenses remain the same, Mr. Wilson will obtain from the property an annual net income of (a) $_____, which is equivalent to a rate of income of (b) _____% on his cash investment.

4. Arnold Wolf owns a building and rents it to a tenant. He bought the building for $75,000, paying the full purchase price in cash. The total expense connected with the ownership of the property averages $4,500 a year. Mr. Wolf wants a net income of 8% on his investment. In order to cover expenses and provide the desired net income, he must receive from the tenant a gross rental income of (a) $_____ a year, or (b) $_____ a month.

● 5. A house that rents for $250 a month is offered for sale at $25,000. The expenses for taxes, insurance, upkeep, and depreciation are estimated to average $1,200 a year. Jane Fine is considering buying the house as an investment, paying the full purchase price in cash. If she desires a net annual of income 8% on her investment, the highest price she can afford to offer for the house is $_____.

UNIT EIGHT   Home Expenses

SECTION 36. Owning a Home

The expense of home ownership consists of the expense for taxes, insurance, repairs, depreciation, interest on the mortgage, and interest on the owner's cash investment in the property. Before buying a home, you should compare the expense of ownership with the expense of renting or leasing. This comparison will let you determine whether it will be financially better for you to own a home or rent.

EXERCISE.   (Practical problems)

1. Gordon Ruskin pays $275 a month for an apartment. He has a chance to buy a certain home for $28,000, which he considers a real bargain. He has this $28,000 in an investment yielding 5%. He estimates that the annual expense of operating the home will be: taxes, $800; insurance $90; depreciation, $600; upkeep, $300. (a) Mr. Ruskin is paying a yearly apartment rent of $_____. (b) The yearly expense of owning the home will be $_____. (c) On the basis of comparative costs, should he buy it? _____.

2. Since Mr. Ruskin, in Problem 1, has been a tenant over a long period of years, his landlord agrees to reduce his rent 5%. (a) This will reduce Mr. Ruskin's rent to $_____. (b) Considering this reduction, should Mr. Ruskin buy the house on the basis of comparative costs?_____ (c) What is the difference in annual expense, between owning the home and paying the reduced rent? $_____

3. On January 2, Joel Burton paid $25,000 for the house in which he had been living. He had been paying rent at $240 a month. To obtain funds for the purchase, he withdrew $5,000 from a savings account which was paying 5% annually, and gave a 7% mortgage for the balance of the purchase price. In addition to the loss of savings bank interest and the cost of the interest on the mortgage, other expenses during the first year of ownership were: taxes, $600; insurance, $85; repairs, $150; miscellaneous expenses, $75; depreciation estimated at $300. During the first year, he saved $_____ by owning the house instead of renting it.

4. Your father is considering the advisability of buying a house and lot for $30,000. As a down payment, he can pay $10,000 which he now has invested at 5% interest. The remainder of the purchase price can be borrowed from a local bank at 8%. Taxes on the house and lot will be $2\frac{3}{4}$%. Depreciation on the house, valued at $25,000, will be 2% a year. Insurance on the house will be $\frac{1}{2}$% and maintenance on the house $1\frac{1}{2}$%. At the request of your father, you calculate the yearly expense of owning this home will amount to $_____.

SECTION 37. Taxes on the Home

Taxes on real estate are fixed at a certain rate on the assessed value of the property. The assessed value is usually less than the actual market value of the property, being as little as 25% or 30% of the market value in some cases. The rate is often expressed as a certain number of dollars for each $100 or $1,000 of assessed value. Sometimes the rate is expressed in terms of mills (tenths of a cent) per dollar. A rate of 32 mills, for example, is equal to 3.2 cents or $.032 on each dollar. At 32 mills per dollar, the tax bill on property assessed at $3,000 would be 3,000 × $.032, or $96.

EXERCISE. (Practical problems)

1. Elmer Dean owns a home in the village of Wayland valued at $25,000. This property is assessed at full value. At the local tax rate of 25 mills, Mr. Dean will pay a real estate tax of $_____.

2. The tax rate for the present year in East Vernon is $4.1322 on each $100 of assessed value. Franz Korby owns a home in East Vernon which is valued at $30,000 and assessed at 70%. The tax on Mr. Korby's home this year amounts to $_____.

3. In each of the following problems, show (a) the assessed value and (b) the tax bill.

	VALUE OF PROPERTY	ASSESSED VALUE		TAX RATE	TAX BILL
		PERCENT OF MARKET VALUE	AMOUNT		
a	$25,500	60%		44 mills	
b	32,000	75%		$2.3121 on each $100	
c	29,000	80%		$31.201 on each $1,000	
d	24,800	50%		$.051312 on each $1	
e	38,000	100%		$3.04224 on each $100	
f	27,500	40%		$71.584 on each $1,000	

SECTION 38. Insuring the Home

Protection against loss resulting from damage to one's property by fire or other causes can be obtained from an insurance company. The basic premium rates are rates for a one-year policy and are usually expressed as a certain number of cents for each $100 of insured value. Under an ordinary policy the insurance company bears the full amount of any loss up to the face of the policy.

EXERCISE. (Practical problems)

1. Walter Denton owns a house valued at $21,500 and household goods valued at $6,500. He insures the house for its full value at the rate of $.26 per $100 and the household goods for their full value at $.33 per $100. Mr. Denton pays (a) $_____ for a one-year policy on the house, (b) $_____ for a one-year policy on the household goods, and a total of (c) $_____ for both policies.

2. Reduced rates are sometimes charged for policies written for more than one year. For example, the rate of a 3-year policy is sometimes 2.7 times the rate of a one-year policy. If the annual rate on certain property is $.25 per $100, the 3-year rate is $.68 (2.7 × $.25).

E. J. Dorr wished to insure his house for $27,500 under a 3-year policy. The annual rate is $.28 per $100. (a) The total premium he will pay for a 3-year policy is $_____. (b) He will save $_____ annually by taking out a 3-year policy instead of a 1-year policy every year.

3. Suzy Hart owns a house valued at $30,000 which she wished to insure for 80% of its value under a 3-year policy. The annual rate is $.34 per $100; the 3-year rate is 2.7 times the annual rate. The total premiums she will pay for a 3-year policy is $_____.

4. Harvey Morris owns a house valued at $25,000. He insures the house for 80% of its value under a 3-year policy. The annual rate is $.24 per $100; the 3-year rate is 2.7 times the annual rate. (a) The total premium for a 3-year policy is $_____. (b) The average annual cost of the premium is $_____.

5. When property is insured for less than one year, the premium is determined by applying the short-rate table. A portion of this table is shown at the right. If the annual premium for insuring your home is $50, but you wish to insure the property for only 4 months, the cost of the insurance, as shown in the table, will be 44% of the annual premium (44% of $50), or $22.

POLICY TERM	% OF ANNUAL PREMIUM	POLICY TERM	% OF ANNUAL PREMIUM
2 mo.	27	7 mo.	67
3 mo.	35	8 mo.	74
4 mo.	44	9 mo.	80
5 mo.	52	10 mo.	87
6 mo.	60	11 mo.	94

In each of the following problems, show (a) the annual premium and (b) the cost of the short-term policy. In calculating the cost of the policy, use the short-rate table given above.

	DESCRIPTION	FACE OF POLICY	ANNUAL RATE PER $100	ANNUAL PREMIUM	POLICY TERM	COST OF POLICY
a	Household Goods	$ 6,000	$ .36		3 mo.	
b	Brick Dwelling	26,000	.27		7 mo.	
c	Frame Dwelling	28,500	.35		5 mo.	
d	Household Goods	7,500	.32		9 mo.	
e	Frame Dwelling	28,500	.26		8 mo.	
f	Brick Dwelling	45,000	.24		10 mo.	

6. If property is insured with more than one company, the loss is distributed among the companies in proportion to the amount of insurance carried by each. For example, a house is insured with Company A for $15,000 and Company B for $9,000, a total coverage of $24,000. Company A holds $\frac{5}{8}$ of the total and Company B, $\frac{3}{8}$. If fire damage of $16,000 occurs, Company A will be required to pay $10,000 ($\frac{5}{8}$ of $16,000) and Company B, $6,000 ($\frac{3}{8}$ of $16,000).

An apartment house is insured for $52,000 with the Hampton Insurance Company and for $28,000 with the Beneficial Insurance Company. A fire occurs, causing a loss of $12,400, which is to be divided between the two companies. You are to show in the proper spaces below (a) the fractional relationship of each company's policy to the total insurance, (b) the fraction in lowest terms, (c) the loss to be divided, and (d) each company's share of the loss.

	FRACTIONAL RELATION- SHIP TO TOTAL	FRACTION IN LOWEST TERMS	TOTAL LOSS	COMPANY'S SHARE OF LOSS
Hampton	$\dfrac{52,000}{\rule{1cm}{0.4pt}}$ or	$\times$	$ _____	= $ _____
Beneficial	$\dfrac{28,000}{\rule{1cm}{0.4pt}}$ or	$\times$	$ _____	= $ _____

Section 38. (concluded)

7. A business block is insured for $36,000 with Franklin Mutual, $48,000 with Lincoln Casualty, and $60,000 with Madison Indemnity. The building is damaged by fire, causing a loss of $33,600. Each company's share of the loss is as follows: (a) Franklin Mutual, $_____; (b) Lincoln Casualty, $_____; (c) Madison Indemnity, $_____.

● 8. Lower rates are allowed on policies having a coinsurance clause. If a building valued at $50,000 is insured under an 80% coinsurance-clause policy, it must be insured for at least $40,000 (80% of $50,000) in order to hold the company liable for the full amount of any loss up to the face of the policy. If it is insured for only $30,000, for example, which is $\frac{3}{4}$ of $40,000, and a fire loss occurs amounting to $6,000, the company will pay only $\frac{3}{4}$ of the loss, or $4,500 ($\frac{3}{4}$ of $6,000).

A building having a value of $22,500 is insured for $16,000 under a policy containing an 80% coinsurance clause. A fire loss of $3,150 occurs. (a) Reduced to lowest terms, the portion of the loss borne by the insurance company is represented by the fraction _____. (b) The owner will collect $_____ from the insurance company.

● 9. In each of the following problems, show the amount that the fire insurance company will pay in settlement of the fire loss.

	DESCRIPTION	VALUE	INSURED FOR	COINSURANCE CLAUSE	FIRE LOSS	COMPANY WILL PAY
a	Frame dwelling	$30,000	$20,000	80%	$ 2,700	
b	Brick apartment	75,000	55,000	80%	9,000	
c	Brick dwelling	25,000	15,000	80%	1,900	
d	Frame dwelling	20,000	16,000	90%	2,250	
e	Brick dwelling	30,000	24,000	80%	3,400	

SECTION 39. Checking Electric and Gas Bills

Users of electricity or gas are usually billed every month or every two months by the electric or gas company. The electric bill is based on the number of kilowatt-hours used during the month. The gas bill is based on the cubic feet of gas used during the month. There is usually a certain minimum charge below which an electric or gas bill cannot fall.

EXERCISE.   (Practical problems)

1. The monthly bills of the Consumers Electric Company are based on the rate schedule at the right. If Harry Page uses 189 kilowatt-hours of electricity during April, his bill will amount to $_____.

First 20 KWH or less	$2.00
Next 50 KWH	3.5¢ per KWH
Next 130 KWH	3.0¢ per KWH
Over 200 KWH	2.0¢ per KWH

2. Murray Carter's electric bill for the month of June shows a May 31 meter reading of 504 KWH and a June 30 reading of 917 KWH. (a) During June he has used _____ KWH of electricity. (b) According to the rate schedule in Problem 1, Mr. Carter's electric bill for June will be $_____.

3. The monthly electric rates of the Deerfield Power & Light Company are shown in the table at the right.

The electric meter of Frederick Harrington, one of the company's customers, had a reading of 8,993 KWH on October 31 and a reading of 9,708 on November 30. (a) During the month of November, Mr. Harrington used _____ KWH of electricity. (b) His bill for November was $_____.

First 12 KWH or less	$2.25
Next 50 KWH	5.0¢ per KWH
Next 138 KWH	3.5¢ per KWH
Over 200 KWH	2.0¢ per KWH

Section 39. (concluded)

4. The monthly rates of the Hadley Gas Company are given below.

SCHEDULE OF GAS RATES	
First 400 cu. ft. or less........$2.50	Next 4,000 cu. ft........... $.20 per 100 cu. ft.
	All over 6,000 cu. ft.......... .12 per 100 cu. ft.
Next 1,600 cu. ft......... .25 per 100 cu. ft.	

The readings on gas bills are shown in terms of 100 cubic feet. A reading of "348" represents 34,800 cubic feet. Henry Howe's gas bill for July shows a June 30 meter reading of "476" and a July 31 meter reading of "513". (a) He has used _____ cu. ft. of gas during July. (b) According to the schedule of rates given above, his bill will be $_____.

5. The monthly gas rates of the Municipal Gas & Electric Company are shown at the right.

The April 30 and May 31 meter readings of three customers of the company are given in the table below. In the table, show (a) the number of cubic feet of gas used and (b) the amount of the bill.

First 300 cu. ft. or less	$2.00
Next 1,700 cu. ft.	30¢ per 100 cu. ft.
Next 5,000 cu. ft.	22¢ per 100 cu. ft.
Over 7,000 cu. ft.	16¢ per 100 cu. ft.

CUSTOMERS	METER READINGS		CUBIC FEET USED	AMOUNT OF BILL
	APRIL 30	MAY 31		
Greg Cady	545	588		
Grace Haller	862	929		
Matt Watson	492	610		

SECTION 40. Checking Water Bills

Most homes and businesses are supplied with water by private water companies or publicly owned water systems. The rates vary with the amount of water used and, in some instances, with the size of the inlet pipe.

EXERCISE. (Practical problems)

1. The Northridge Municipal Water District charges the quarterly water rates shown below.

> First   1,200 cu. ft.............$7.50 minimum charge
> Next   3,600 cu. ft.............50¢ per 100 cu. ft.
> Next 15,000 cu. ft.............30¢ per 100 cu. ft.
> Thereafter ....20¢ per 100 cu. ft.

Brenda Holt used 2,848 cu. ft. of water during the second quarter of last year and 5,438 cu. ft. during the third quarter. Her water bill was (a) $_____ for the second quarter and (b) $_____ for the third.

2. Water rates in the city of Winthrop are shown at the right. During the third quarter of last year, Otto Reese, a resident of Winthrop, used 3,431 cubic feet of water. His water bill for the quarter was $_____.

> First   1,200 cu. ft., 60¢ per 100 cu. ft.
> Next   3,600 cu. ft., 50¢ per 100 cu. ft.
> Next 15,000 cu. ft., 30¢ per 100 cu. ft.
> Over 19,800 cu. ft., 20¢ per 100 cu. ft.

3. Fred Kent's water bill shows that his meter reading on June 30 was 62,297 cu. ft. as compared with 56,973 cu. ft. on March 31. (a) During the March 31–June 30 quarter he has used _____ cu. ft. of water. (b) According to the water rates in Problem 2, his water bill for the quarter will be $_____.

5. The Riverside Water District charges the quarterly water rates shown at the right. In one quarterly period, Mr. Franklin Williamson used 59,800 gallons of water. Mr. Williamson's bill for the quarter was $_____.

> First 9,000 gallons, $.70 per 1,000 gallons
> Next 21,000 gallons, .50 per 1,000 gallons
> Over 30,000 gallons, .40 per 1,000 gallons

SECTION 41. Checking Telephone Bills

A residential telephone subscriber usually has a choice between an individual line and the less expensive party line. There may also be a choice between unlimited and limited local service. Limited service has a lower monthly rate, but the subscriber is limited to a specified number of calls a month. An extra charge must be paid for each additional call.

There is a federal excise tax on all telephone charges. There may also be a state or local tax.

EXERCISE.   (Practical problems)

1. Robert Scofield pays $9.20 a month for unlimited local telephone service, plus the federal 9% tax and a local 5% tax. The total monthly cost of the local service is $_____.

2. On his telephone bill for last month, Ogden Arnold was charged $10.50 for his regular local service and $8.70 for toll calls, both exclusive of the 9% federal tax and a 6% local tax. After the taxes were added, the total charge for the local service was (a) $_____, the total charge for the toll calls was (b) $_____, and the total amount of the bill was (c) $_____.

3. Delio Junco pays $5.80 a month for telephone service limited to 75 local calls and $.05½ for each additional call. In April, he made 87 local calls and no toll calls. After the federal 9% tax and a local 3% were added, the total cost of the local service at the monthly rate was (a) $_____, the total cost of the additional calls was (b) $_____, and the total telephone bill for the month was (c) $_____.

4. For a two-party line, Vera Tucker can select unlimited local service at $5.40 a month or limited service at $4.20 a month for a maximum of 60 calls, with a charge of $.05½ for each additional call. These rates are subject to the 9% federal tax but no local tax. If she averages 90 calls a month she will save $_____ a month by selecting the unlimited service.

5. Jack Kinney made a long-distance telephone call to Chicago and talked for ten minutes. The charge was $1.40 for the first three minutes and $.45 for each additional minute. In addition, there was an 8% federal tax and a 4% local tax. (a) The telephone company's charge for the call was $_____. (b) The total cost of the call, including the taxes, was $_____.

SECTION 42. Shopping Wisely

Money often can be saved by buying large quantities instead of small quantities and by buying during special sales. The percent saved is found by dividing the amount saved by the higher of the two prices or costs.

EXERCISE. (Practical problems)

1. The price of a 1-pound bag of a certain brand of coffee is 99¢; the price of a 3-pound bag is $2.79. You would save _____¢ by buying one 3-pound bag instead of three 1-pound bags.

2. At a stock reduction sale, Otis Vadney purchased a sportcoat that was reduced from $55 to $46.50, two shirts that were reduced from $6.95 to $5.45 each, three neckties that were reduced from $3.50 to $2.35 each, and a dozen handkerchiefs that were reduced from $7.50 to $4.95 a dozen. By purchasing during the sale he saved $_____ on the total purchase.

3. During a midseason sale, a power lawn mower is advertised at 20% off the regular price of $65.95. At the reduced price you would pay (a) $_____ for the mower and would save (b) $_____.

4. In the Star Food Store, Brand A tuna fish is priced at $1.15 for two $6\frac{1}{2}$ oz. cans. Brand B is priced at 51¢ for one 7 oz. can. (a) At the rate of two $6\frac{1}{2}$ oz. cans for $1.15 the price per ounce of Brand A is _____¢, to the nearest tenth of a cent. (b) At the rate of one 7 oz. can for 51¢, the price per ounce of Brand B is _____¢, to the nearest tenth of a cent. (c) The less expensive brand is Brand _____.

5. During a close-out sale, Adele Russo purchased a pair of bowling shoes that were reduced from $18 a pair to $14.95. By purchasing the shoes at the sale price, she saved _____%, to the nearest whole percent.

6. Ice cream is priced at 75¢ a quart or $1.25 a half gallon. By purchasing it by the half gallon instead of by the quart, you save _____%, to the nearest whole percent.

SECTION 42. Shopping Wisely (concluded)

A person can often choose between buying and renting. When this choice occurs, there may be a considerable difference between the cost of buying and the cost of renting. Before making a decision, one should be sure that all costs related to each choice have been compared.

EXERCISE. (Practical problems)

1. Sam Sumner can rent a chain saw to cut firewood for $5 a day or for $1 per hour. If he rents the saw and keeps it for two days and three extra hours, he would be charged $_____.

2. Jane Wilson wanted to see if she would enjoy skiing before investing in expensive equipment. She decided to take a train to the nearest ski area where she would rent equipment for one day and take ski lessons. A round-trip train ticket cost $17.50. Rental of the equipment was $8 a day and lessons were $6.50 per hour. All taxes were included. If Jane took two hours of lessons, how much did her day of skiing cost? $_____.

3. Jack Morgan changed jobs and had to move from one city to another city 100 miles away. Rather than hire a moving company, he decided to rent a truck and move his furniture himself. He paid $40 per day and 15¢ a mile to rent the truck. He made the round trip in one day and returned the truck to the agency from which he had rented it. How much did he pay? $_____. The Webster Moving Company would have moved Mr. Morgan's furniture for $100. How much did he save by renting the truck? $_____.

4. Early in the fall, a man offered to snowplow Trent Butler's driveway. He promised to snowplow every day in the winter that there was more than three inches of snow. He would charge $10 each time he plowed. Mr. Butler had been considering the purchase of a snowblower. He estimated that it would cost $550 to own and operate and would last for five years. The weather bureau told Mr. Butler that there were usually about ten snowfalls of more than three inches per year. Should Mr. Butler buy the snowblower or hire the man? _____. How much would he save per year by his decision? $_____.

UNIT NINE   Transportation

SECTION 43.   Owning an Automobile

The expense of owning and operating a car includes the cost of such items as license fees, insurance, garage rent, gasoline, oil, tires, repairs and upkeep, interest on the original cost of the car, and depreciation. The total depreciation of the car is the difference between the original cost and the amount received for it when it is traded in or discarded. The total depreciation divided by the number of years the car has been owned gives the average annual depreciation. The average annual depreciation is often expressed as a percent of the original cost. This percent is called the rate of depreciation.

EXERCISE.   (Practical problems)

1. Juanita Ferrer bought a new car for $4,500. She used the car five years and then traded it in for $900. (a) The total depreciation for the five-year period was $_____. (b) The average annual depreciation was $_____.

2. In Problem 1 the average annual depreciation is _____% of the original cost of the car.

3. Tim Unger purchases an automobile for $3,250. He estimates that he will use the car for seven years and then trade it in for $520. (a) The estimated annual depreciation is $_____. (b) The estimated rate of depreciation is _____ %.

4. Ronald Slagen purchased a new car for $2,925. His car expenses for the first year were: gasoline and oil, $418.75; repairs and upkeep, $87.75; insurance, $221.50; license plates, $20.50; interest at 6% on the original cost; and depreciation estimated at 18%. The total car expense for the year was $_____.

5. In Problem 4 Mr. Slagen drove the car 15,500 miles during the year. The average annual car expense per mile was _____¢, computed to the nearest tenth of a cent.

SECTION 44. Insuring the Automobile

The common types of automobile insurance are: *bodily injury*, covering bodily injury to others; *property damage*, covering damage to the property of others; *comprehensive damage*, covering damage to one's own car, except by collision or upset; *collision*, covering damage to one's own car by collision or upset.

Premium rates for auto insurance vary widely in different areas. High rates are usually charged in thickly populated areas and low rates in areas that are thinly populated.

Within a given area, premiums for bodily injury and property damage are the same for all makes of cars and are determined by how the car is used. There are several classes of car use. Three common classes are shown in the first table at the right.

Annual premiums for bodily injury and property damage insurance for Classes 1A, 1B, and 1C in a medium-rate area are shown in the second table. Higher rates are charged where a car is used for business purposes.

The rates for bodily injury are for the basic limits, $10/20,000, a maximum of $10,000 for injury to one person and $20,000 when more than one person is injured. The rates for property damage are for the basic limit, $5,000. Premiums for higher limits can be found by multiplying the premium for the basic limit by the percents shown in the third table.

Premiums for comprehensive and collision insurance depend upon the use, the price range, and age of the car. The fourth table shows the premiums that apply to certain Chevrolet, Dodge, Ford, and Plymouth 4-door sedans used for pleasure driving only (class 1A)

CLASS	DESCRIPTION
1A	Cars used for pleasure driving only.
1B	Cars customarily used in driving to or from work less than 10 miles one way.
1C	Cars customarily used in driving to or from work more than 10 miles one way.

BODILY INJURY AND PROPERTY DAMAGE

TYPE OF INSURANCE	LIMITS	CLASS OF USE		
		1A	1B	1C
Bodily Injury	$10/20,000	$57.00	$63.00	$74.00
Property Damage	$5,000	35.00	39.00	45.00

RATES FOR HIGHER LIMITS

BODILY INJURY		PROPERTY DAMAGE	
MAXIMUM LIMITS	PERCENT OF $5/10,000 PREMIUM	MAXIMUM LIMITS	PERCENT OF $5,000 PREMIUM
$20/40,000	110%	$10,000	105%
$25/50,000	113%	$25,000	108%
$50/100,000	121%	$50,000	112%

COMPREHENSIVE DAMAGE AND COLLISION CLASS 1A

TYPE OF INSURANCE	AGE OF CAR IN YEARS			
	−1	1+ −3	3+ −5	5+
Comprehensive	$ 34.00	$26.00	$19.00	$15.00
Collision ($50-Ded)	$122.00	$92.00	$79.00	$67.00

EXERCISE. (Practical problems)

In solving the problems in this exercise, use the tables given above.

1. How three autos are used is shown below. Each car is insured for the basic limits of $10/20,000 for bodily injury and $5,000 for property damage. In the appropriate columns, you are to show (a) the class of use for each car, (b) the annual premium for bodily injury insurance, and (c) the annual premium for property damage.

	DESCRIPTION OF USE	CLASS OF USE	ANNUAL PREMIUM	
			BODILY INJURY	PROPERTY DAMAGE
a	Used for driving to work; 22 miles one way.			
b	Used for pleasure driving only.			
c	Used for driving to work; 8 miles one way.			

2. Under a "$50-deductible" collision policy, the owner must pay the first $50 for repairs and replacements resulting from a collision or upset and the insurance company pays only the amount over $50. On October 5, Allen Coran purchased collision insurance, with $50 deductible, for his 2-year old Ford. The car is used only for pleasure. Two months later, his car was damaged in a collision, and the repair bill amounted to $627.18. (a) The premium he paid on October 5 was $_____. (b) He collected $_____ from the insurance company in settlement of the repair bill.

3. Comprehensive damage and collision insurance, with $50 deductible, is to be purchased for each of the cars below. You are to show for each car (a) the annual premium for comprehensive damage and (b) the annual premium for $50-deductible collision.

	MAKE	AGE OF CAR	CLASS OF USE	ANNUAL PREMIUM	
				COMPRE-HENSIVE	COLLISION $50 DEDUCTIBLE
a	Plymouth	6 months	1A		
b	Ford	4½ years	1A		
c	Dodge	5 years	1A		
d	Chevrolet	2 years	1A		

4. On her new Volkswagen, Sally Page wants to carry $25/50,000 of bodily injury insurance and $10,000 of property damage insurance. The car is used for pleasure driving only. (a) For the bodily injury insurance she will have to pay $_____. (b) The property damage insurance will cost $_____.

5. Miss Page, in Problem 4, also wished to carry comprehensive damage and $50-deductible collision insurance. (a) The comprehensive damage insurance will cost $_____. (b) The collision insurance will cost $_____.

6. A 2-year old Ford, which is in class 1A, is insured with the following coverage: bodily injury, $20/40,000 limits; property damage, $25,000 limit; comprehensive damage; collision, $50-deductible. The total cost of the premium amounts to $_____.

SECTION 45. Figuring Travel Expenses

Many employees are required to travel as part of their jobs. For example, salespersons, engineers, and executives often must travel to customers or to branch plants located far from the home office.

When you travel for your employer, you are usually required to fill out a travel expense voucher as a record of the money you spent on the trip. The travel expense voucher for John Mirandez is shown below. John is a sales manager for the Ferris Corporation, which builds and sells radios, television sets, and other small appliances. The travel expense voucher shows that John flew from Chicago, where the home office is located, to Denver to visit a branch plant. John used taxis to get to and from the airports in Chicago and Denver. He stayed at the Brown Palace Hotel in Denver for two nights, and spent money on meals, telephone calls, and tips. John included taxi fares under "transportation" and telephone calls and tips under "miscellaneous."

Travel Expense Voucher

FERRIS CORPORATION

Account Title __Sales__   Account No. __65-18-A__

Purpose of trip
To inspect Denver plant

Name __John Mirandez__
Address __18 Spruce St.__
City __Chicago__
State __Illinois__
Zip Code __60658__

Signature of Traveler _____   Date __10/3/--__

DATE	DEPARTED FROM	TIME	AUTO MILEAGE	TRANS-PORTATION COSTS		LODGING		MEALS		MISC.		TOTAL	
9/30	Chicago	2:15 p.m.	——	163	27	21	90	7	12	3	00	195	29
10/1			——			21	90	15	10	4	20	41	20
10/2	Denver	9:00 a.m.	——	7	50			6	25	2	00	15	75
	TOTALS			170	77	43	80	28	47	9	20	252	24

TRAVEL EXPENSE VOUCHER FOR JOHN MIRANDEZ

Even if you don't travel yourself, you may need to prepare travel expense vouchers for your boss as a secretary or audit travel expense vouchers as a bookkeeper.

EXERCISE. (Practical problems)

1. George Polaski is a salesman for the R & I Steel Co. in Montreal, Canada. He just returned from a three-day trip to the company's plant in Pittsburgh. Mr. Polaski's expenses were: February 2: roundtrip airfare, $127; taxis, $8.75; hotel, $21.67; meals, $7.65; telephone, $5.78; tips, $3.50; February 3: taxis, $2.50; hotel, $21.67; meals, $14.75; tips, $2.25; February 4: taxis, $8.75; meals, $6.75; telephone, $2.35; tips, $5.75. Complete the travel voucher below for Mr. Polaski.

Signature of Traveler _____ Date _____

DATE	DEPARTED FROM	TIME	AUTO MILEAGE	TRANS—PORTATION COSTS	LODGING	MEALS	MISC.	TOTAL
	TOTALS							

2. R. Hull is a salesman for the Mohican Rug Co. in Albany, New York. He has just returned from a two-day trip to a customer in Cleveland, Ohio. Mr. Hull's expenses were: May 4: roundtrip train fare, $110.26; taxis, $4.75; hotel, $18.75; meals, $9.75; tips, $4.75; May 5: taxis, $2.25; hotel, $18.75; meals, $22.75; tips, $3.75; May 6: taxis, $5.75; meals, $10.50; tips, $4.50. Complete Mr. Hull's travel voucher.

Signature of Traveler _____ Date _____

DATE	DEPARTED FROM	TIME	AUTO MILEAGE	TRANS—PORTATION COSTS	LODGING	MEALS	MISC.	TOTAL
	TOTALS							

Section 45. (concluded)

3. Sally Winters, who lives in Atlanta, is planning to visit her uncle in Dallas, Texas. If she flies to Dallas, she will need to take a limousine to the airport ($4.25 one way) and to purchase an airline roundtrip ticket ($140 including tax). Her uncle will pick her up at the Dallas airport, and she will stay at her uncle's house.

If Sally drives her car to Dallas, the trip will take two full days and cover 805 miles of highway, one-way. She estimates that her car costs her 12¢ per mile to operate. Sally will have to buy meals on the road and stay overnight at a motel along the way.

Compute the amount of money Sally will have to spend to travel to Dallas by car and by plane by filling in the blanks below:

ESTIMATED COST BY AIR:

		ESTIMATED COST BY CAR:	
Airline roundtrip ticket	$_____	Car mileage at 12¢ per mile	$_____
Limousine to/from Atlanta Airport	$_____	Meals for four days @ $12	$_____
		Motel for two nights @ $18	$_____
Total cost by air	$_____	Total cost by car	$_____

4. Donald Ferrar lives in Pittsburgh and wants to visit his grandfather in Grand Rapids, Michigan. The distance for the trip one-way is 410 miles. If Donald drives his car, he estimates the trip will take about 8 hours. He estimates that lunch and supper will have to be purchased on the road and that these will run about $2 and $5, respectively. He will leave in the morning, so he does not plan to stay at a motel.

If Donald flies to Grand Rapids, the roundtrip airfare is $66. The flight takes 1½ hours. He would need to drive his car to the airport, a distance of 35 miles, and park it in the airport parking lot for the three days he would be gone. The parking lot charges $3.25 per day for parking. He figures his car costs him 12¢ per mile to drive. His grandfather will pick him up at the Grand Rapids Airport, and he would stay at his grandfather's house.

(a) Donald should estimate he will need to spend $_____ to go by car.

(b) Donald should plan to spend $_____ to go by plane.

(c) It will cost Donald the least money to go by _____. He will save $_____.

[103]

SECTION 46. Shipping Goods

Common methods used to ship goods are parcel post, express, and freight. For small packages, parcel post is usually the most economical. For larger packages, either parcel post or express may be used. Large, bulky shipments are usually sent by freight.

EXERCISE. (Practical problems)

1. Parcel-post rates vary with distance and weight as shown by the table below. Using the table, find what it will cost to send a package weighing 6 pounds to your mother who is 850 miles away. It will cost $_____.

Weight 1 pound and not exceeding pounds	Zones				
	Local	1 and 2	3	4	5
		Up to 150 miles	150 to 300 miles	300 to 600 miles	600 to 1,000 miles
2....	$0.60	$0.65	$0.70	$0.75	$0.80
3....	.60	.75	.80	.85	.95
4....	.65	.80	.85	.95	1.10
5....	.70	.85	.90	1.05	1.20
6....	.70	.95	1.00	1.15	1.35
7....	.75	1.05	1.10	1.25	1.50
8....	.75	1.10	1.15	1.35	1.60
9....	.80	1.15	1.20	1.45	1.75
10....	.80	1.20	1.30	1.55	1.90

TABLE OF PARCEL-POST RATES

2. The package in Problem 1 is valued at $35. You decide to insure it and find that the insurance rates are:

VALUATION	INSURANCE FEE
Up to $ 15.00	20¢
$ 15.01 to 50.00	30¢
50.01 to 100.00	40¢
100.01 to 150.00	50¢
150.01 to 200.00	60¢

The insurance fee on the package will therefore be $_____.

3. In addition to insuring the package, you ask the post office for a return receipt from your mother. This costs an additional 15¢ fee. The combined cost of insurance and return receipt is $_____.

4. If you send a 3-lb., parcel-post package to someone in the fourth zone, insuring it for $85 and requesting a return receipt, it will cost $_____ to send the package.

5. Alton Duffy wishes to send an express shipment weighing 125 pounds from St. Louis to Dallas. The express rate is $28.60 a hundred pounds. The express charge is $_____. (Calculate the rate on fractional parts of 100 pounds on a proportionate basis.)

6. Freight rates are usually based on 100 pounds, with fractional parts of 100 pounds being charged on a proportionate basis. For each of the following freight shipments show the amount of the freight charges.

NO.	WEIGHT OF SHIPMENT	RATE ON 100 LB.	FREIGHT CHARGES
1	825 lb.	$3.71	
2	1,340 lb.	2.94	
3	567 lb.	6.13	
4	2,120 lb.	2.27	

Name‗‗‗‗‗‗‗‗‗‗‗‗‗‗‗‗‗‗‗‗‗‗‗‗‗‗

UNIT TEN   Taxes

SECTION 47.   Property Tax Rates

Most of the money needed by villages, towns, and cities is obtained by taxes collected from the property owners of the local tax districts. The tax rate is found by dividing the amount to be collected by the total value of property on the assessment rolls. For example, if a town needs $160,000 for operating expenses and has on its rolls property assessed at $10,000,000, the decimal tax rate is $160,000 ÷ $10,000,000 = .016. The decimal rate, .016, may be expressed as $.016 per $1 of assessed valuation, 1.6¢ per $1, 16 mills per $1, $1.60 per $100, or $16 per $1,000.

EXERCISE.   (Practical problems)

1. A certain school district has property with an assessed valuation of $27,000,000. The school budget for the coming year shows that $1,500,000 will be needed for operating the schools. Of this amount it is estimated that $96,750 will be received from the state and federal government. (a) The amount to be raised by taxes on the local property owners is $‗‗‗‗‗‗‗. (b) The tax rate, expressed as a decimal, will be‗‗‗‗‗‗. (Carry the decimal correct to five places.)

2. Ronald Evers owns a house and lot assessed at $27,500 in the school district in Problem 1. The tax on Mr. Evers' property will amount to $‗‗‗‗‗‗‗.

3. The decimal rate that you found in Problem 1 may be expressed as $‗‗‗‗‗‗ per $100 of assessed valuation.

4. Convert the following decimal tax rates (a) to dollars per $100, (b) to dollars per $1,000, (c) to cents per $1, (d) to mills per $1.

| | DECIMAL RATE | EQUIVALENT RATE EXPRESSED AS | | | |
		DOLLARS PER $100	DOLLARS PER $1,000	CENTS PER $1	MILLS PER $1
4-a	.064	$	$	¢	mills
4-b	.0295	$	$	¢	mills
4-c	.0085	$	$	¢	mills
4-d	.03721	$	$	¢	mills
4-e	.00943	$	$	¢	mills
4-f	.00062	$	$	¢	mills

Name_____

SECTION 48. Sales and Excise Taxes

Many states and some cities and counties levy a sales tax on the retail price of an article. This tax is usually collected from the purchaser by the retailer and forwarded to the proper tax official.

EXERCISE. (Practical problems)

1. You are a clerk in a local store and on March 14 make the sale shown on the sales slip below. Complete the sales slip. (Figure the sales tax to the nearest cent.)

2. Jan Pearson, 413 Yale Avenue, bought the items listed on the sales slip below from Lucille's Dress Boutique on November 2.

You are to complete the sales slip. (Figure the sales tax to the nearest cent.)

Bob Gibson's Photo Shop
18 Cameron Avenue

DATE *March 14* 19 --

SOLD TO *Janice Paine*
ADDRESS *12 Cheshire Drive*

CLERK	CASH	CHARGE	TAKE	SEND	UNIT PRICE	AMOUNT	
			DESCRIPTION				
6	rolls film				3.21		
8	rolls film				3.49		
3	pkg. flash bulbs				2.29		
	Sales tax 5%						

LUCILLE'S DRESS BOUTIQUE
800 BROADWAY GLENHAVEN

DATE *November 2* 19 --

SOLD TO *Jan Pearson*
ADDRESS *413 Yale Avenue*

CLERK	CASH	CHARGE	TAKE	SEND	UNIT PRICE	AMOUNT	
			DESCRIPTION				
1	pant suit				39.95		
3	scarves				4.25		
2	blouses				14.80		
	Sales tax 4%						

3. Find the total of each of the following purchases. (Figure the sales tax to the nearest cent.)

a

48 ft. @ 75¢ = _____
18 lb. @ $12\frac{1}{2}$¢ = _____
16 lb. @ $37\frac{1}{2}$¢ = _____
24 yd. @ $33\frac{1}{3}$¢ = _____
90 ft. @ $16\frac{2}{3}$¢ = _____
Net cost _____
Sales tax (6%) _____
Total cost _____

b

$5\frac{1}{2}$ yd. @ $3.50 = _____
$15\frac{1}{4}$ yd. @ 6.25 = _____
13 cwt. @ .75 = _____
24 sacks @ .89 = _____
25 bu. @ 75 = _____
Net cost _____
Sales tax (3%) _____
Total cost _____

● 4. The total amount you paid for a portable television set was $126.88, which included a sales tax of 4%. Before the tax was added, the retail price of the television set was $_____.

SECTION 49. Social Security Taxes and Benefits

The Federal Insurance Contributions Act (FICA) taxes employees, employers, and self-employed persons to provide money for retired and disabled workers and their dependents. This is also known as the *Social Security Tax*. An employer must deduct and send to the federal government a specified rate percent from each employee's taxable earnings (up to a designated maximum) each payday. Then the employer must contribute an equal amount.

The taxes of self-employed individuals are greater than the tax they would pay if they were employees. The estimated tax for the year is paid to the government in one amount when they file their income tax return in April, or it may be paid in four installments.

EXERCISE. (Practical problems)

1. Carol Bayer earns $642 a month as bookkeeper for the Acme Garage and is paid twice a month. From her salary, 5.85% is deducted for the FICA tax. The amount deducted for this tax from her semimonthly pay check is $_____.

2. An employee or self-employed person who earns more than $12,600 in one calendar year is taxed on the first $12,600 only. Last year, Ronald Eckert's salary as office manager for the Century Company was $14,820. At 5.85%, the total amount deducted from his salary for the FICA tax was $_____.

3. The total wages of four employees from January 1 to August 12 are shown in *Column 1* of the table given below. Their wages for the week ended August 19 are shown in *Column 2*. You are to show in *Column 3* the FICA tax that should be deducted from each employee's wages for the week ended August 19. The tax is 5.85% and is levied on only the first $12,600 of wages earned in the calendar year.

	NAME	COLUMN 1 TOTAL WAGES JAN. 1 TO AUG. 12	COLUMN 2 WAGES FOR WEEK ENDED AUG. 19	COLUMN 3 FICA TAX FOR WEEK ENDED AUG. 19
a	Jane Dennis	$6,490	$156	
b	Peter Cristo	$9,230	$180	
c	Eloise Turner	$12,480	$265	
d	Frank Russo	$12,540	$325	

4. The employer is taxed on the total taxable wages he has paid. The rate is the same as the rate for the employee. The Acme Garage, in Problem 1, paid taxable wages of $6,863.45 in April; and the rate was 5.85%. The FICA tax that the Acme Garage had to pay for April was $_____.

5. Alex Capello is a self-employed person, operating a men's tailoring shop. His net earnings last year from the business were $13,862.47, and the FICA tax rate was 8% on the first $12,600 of earnings. His self-employment tax for the year was $_____.

6. A worker who has met the employment requirements of the laws may retire at age 65 or older and receive monthly retirement payments for the rest of his life. The amount he is entitled to receive each month is called his *primary amount*. In most cases, the amount depends upon his average monthly earnings since 1950. The table at the right shows the primary amounts for average monthly earnings from $856 to $900.

George Howard retires at age 65. His average monthly earnings are $875. As shown in the table, his primary amount is $_____.

7. The workers listed in the table below retire at age 65. Complete the table by showing the primary amount for each.

	NAME	AVERAGE MONTHLY EARNINGS	PRIMARY AMOUNT
a	Toni Cristo	$867	
b	John Perry	$894	
c	Susan Mateer	$877	
d	Thomas Brown	$858	

PARTIAL TABLE OF PRIMARY BENEFITS

AVERAGE MONTHLY EARNINGS		PRIMARY AMOUNT
AT LEAST	BUT NOT MORE THAN	
$856	$860	$376.50
861	865	377.50
866	870	378.50
871	875	379.50
876	880	380.50
881	885	381.50
886	890	382.50
891	895	383.50
896	900	384.50

8. A worker may retire as soon as he reaches age 62. If he does, his monthly benefits will be 80% of what they would be if he were 65. For each month he waits after age 62, the reduction is less.

Lois Tonkin retires at age 62, and her average monthly earnings are $869. (a) If she were 65, her monthly benefits would be $_____. (b) Since she is only 62, her monthly benefits will be $_____.

9. A worker retiring at age 62 is entitled to monthly benefits equal to 80% of his primary rate. Elmer Gilday plans to retire at age 63, at which time his average monthly earnings will be $888. He will be entitled to monthly benefits amounting to $_____.

10. David Cohen retires at age 65. His average monthly earnings are $879. His wife is also 65 and is entitled to a monthly benefit equal to one-half of her husband's primary amount. (a) Mr. Cohen's primary amount is $_____. (b) His wife will be entitled to monthly benefits amounting to $_____. (c) Together, Mr. Cohen and his wife will receive a total of $_____ each month.

11. Emil Ludwig retires at age 65 with average monthly earnings amounting to $857. His wife is 62. If she were 65 she would be entitled to monthly benefits equal to one-half of her husband's primary amount. Instead of waiting until she becomes 65, she elects to begin receiving benefits at age 62 at 75% of what they would be if she were 65. (a) Mr. Ludwig's primary amount is $_____. (b) If Mrs. Ludwig were 65 she would be entitled to monthly benefits of $_____. (c) Since she elects to begin receiving payments at age 62, her monthly benefits will be $_____. (d) Together, Mr. and Mrs. Ludwig will receive a total of $_____ each month.

SECTION 50. Income Taxes

The federal government levies an income tax on the taxable incomes of nearly all persons. On or before April 15, each taxpayer must file an income tax return on the income earned for the preceding year.

The tax rate and amount of income exempted from the tax vary from time to time. To solve the problems in this section, assume that the tax rates and exemptions given below are in effect.

Schedule X. SINGLE TAXPAYERS not qualifying for rates in Schedules Y and Z.

If the taxable income is: *The tax is:*

Over— But not over— of excess over—
$4,000 — $6,000.............$690, plus 21% — $4,000
$6,000 — $8,000.............$1,110, plus 24% — $6,000
$8,000 — $10,000............$1,590, plus 25% — $8,000
$10,000 — $12,000...........$2,090, plus 27% — $10,000

Schedule Y. MARRIED TAXPAYERS FILING JOINT RETURNS and CERTAIN WIDOWS AND WIDOWERS

If the taxable income is: *The tax is:*

Over— But not over— of excess over—
$4,000 — $8,000.............$620, plus 19% — $4,000
$8,000 — $12,000............$1,380, plus 22% — $8,000
$12,000 — $16,000...........$2,260, plus 25% — $12,000
$16,000 — $20,000...........$3,260, plus 28% — $16,000

Schedule Z. UNMARRIED (or legally separated) TAXPAYERS WHO QUALIFY as HEADS OF HOUSEHOLD

If the taxable income is: *The tax is:*

Over— But not over— of excess over—
$4,000 — $6,000.............$660, plus 19% — $4,000
$6,000 — $8,000.............$1,040, plus 22% — $6,000
$8,000 — $10,000............$1,480, plus 23% — $8,000
$10,000 — $12,000...........$1,940, plus 25% — $10,000

Exemptions

One $750 exemption for the taxpayer
One $750 exemption for the taxpayer's spouse
One $750 exemption for each of the taxpayer's dependents

Example

David Gore is a married man with two dependent children. His income for one year consisted of the following: salary, $14,300; interest, $180. Allowable deductions were: contributions, $335; interest on mortgage, $680; taxes, $740; other deductions, $320. Mrs. Gore has no income, but she and Mr. Gore filed a joint return because of the lower rate. A joint return is one return that includes the income, deductions, and exemptions of both persons.

Tax Calculation

1. Gross Income ($14,300+$180). $14,480.00
2. Less Deductions ($335 + $680 $740 + $320)............... 2,075.00
3. Net Income................. $12,405.00
4. Less Exemptions (4 × $750)... 3,000.00
5. Taxable Income.............. $ 9,405.00
6. Tax Liability (Schedule Y)
   Tax on first $8,000 = $1,380.00
   22% of $1,405   309.10 $ 1,689.10

EXERCISE. (Practical problems)

In solving the following problems, use the exemptions and rates given above.

1. For each of the taxpayers listed below, show (a) the taxpayer's net income, (b) his total exemptions, (c) his taxable net income, and (d) his tax liability.

	NAME	STATUS	NO. OF EXEMPTIONS	GROSS INCOME	ALLOWABLE DEDUCTIONS	NET INCOME	TOTAL EXEMPTIONS	TAXABLE NET INCOME	TAX LIABILITY
a	Hilda Cole	Single	1	$ 7,840	$ 648				
b	Fred & Anna Yager	Married, filing a joint return	3	$21,757	$3,800				
c	Robert Neary	Single, head of a household	2	$13,473	$2,132				

2. Charles Halpern is a single man with a dependent mother and qualifies as a head of household. In filling out his income tax return, he reports the following income: wages, $10,279; interest on savings account, $121. He claims the following deductions: contributions to religious and charitable organizations, $258; interest paid on loan, $67; state income, gasoline, and sales taxes, $327; damage to automobile, not covered by insurance, $75; union dues, $78; other deductions, $85. What is his taxable income (a) using actual deductions $_____ ? (b) using the standard deduction (The standard deduction is 15% of gross income not to exceed $2,000.) $_____ ? (c) Which should he use _____ ?

3. Frank and Ruth Wyld, a married couple with three dependent children, report the following income items and deductions on their joint income tax return: salary, $11,648; other income, $132; contributions, $210; interest expense, $254; state income taxes, $195; real estate taxes, $488; other taxes, $140; other deductions, $127. You are to compute their tax liability if they file a joint return using the table on page 109. The amount is $_____ .

4. Hazel Savoie, an unmarried school teacher supporting a dependent mother and father, qualifies as the head of a household. For one year, her salary income is $10,500, and income from other sources amounts to $154. Her allowable deductions are as follows: contributions, $262; interest expense, $387; taxes, $835; other deductions, $63. The amount of her tax liability, using the table on page 109, is $_____ .

5. The income tax laws require the employer to furnish each employee a tax-withholding statement showing the wages earned during the year and the amount withheld by the employer. For various reasons, the amount withheld is seldom exactly equal to the employee's actual tax liability. The employee must therefore file with the Internal Revenue Service an income tax return showing all information needed for finding the actual tax liability, so that any underpayment may be collected or any overpayment refunded.

In filling out their joint income tax return, Mr. and Mrs. Richard Paton, who claim four exemptions, report the following income: salary, $12,880; interest, $92. They claim the following deductions; contributions, $240; interest, $424; taxes, $790; other deductions, $81. (a) Based on the exemptions and rates given on page 109, the amount of the Paton's actual tax liability is $_____ . (b) The tax-withholding statement furnished Mr. Paton by his employer shows that the income tax withheld from his salary during the year was $2,447.00. The Patons may therefore request a refund of $_____ .

UNIT ELEVEN   The Small Business

SECTION 51.   The Balance Sheet

At regular intervals the proprietor of a business takes an inventory of the things owned (assets) and the debts owed (liabilities) in order to find the amount of capital or proprietorship. The amount of the proprietorship is determined by subtracting the total liabilities from the total assets. The information about the assets, liabilities, and proprietorship is usually shown in a formal statement known as a balance sheet.

EXERCISE.   (Practical problems)

1. Joan Meeker, owner of Joan's Card Shop, has assets valued at $26,243 and liabilities amounting to $4,697. The amount of her proprietorship is $_____.

2. Grace Cole, owner of the In Boutique, takes an inventory of her assets and finds that she has the following items: cash amounting to $2,374, merchandise worth $27,353, store supplies worth $212, and store equipment valued at $4,785. An examination of her unpaid bills shows that she owes Gibson Brass Co. $1,700 and Lobar Sales Co. $659 for merchandise purchased from them on account. (a) The total of her assets is $_____. (b) The total of her liabilities is $_____. (c) The amount of her proprietorship is $_____.

3. Gene Wolfe, owner of an apparel store, has the following assets: cash, $3,864; merchandise inventory, $31,620; store supplies, $420; land and building, $24,700; store equipment, $8,620. He owes the Cohen Apparel Co. $1,343, Marcus Brothers $894, and Adams Textile Co. $1,188. (a) His total assets are $_____. (b) His total liabilities are $_____. (c) The amount of his proprietorship is $_____.

4. At the end of the year, Julio Alvaro, owner of a shoe store, prepares the following balance sheet. You are to complete this balance sheet by showing (a) the total assets, (b) the total liabilities, (c) the amount of Alvaro's capital, and (d) the total liabilities and proprietorship.

JULIO ALVARO SHOE STORE
BALANCE SHEET, DECEMBER 31, 19--

ASSETS			LIABILITIES		
Cash	3,143	77	National Shoe Manufacturing Co.	1,384	88
Merchandise Inventory	32,668	33	Metro Leather Goods Co.	517	64
Store Supplies	303	00	Union National Bank	795	00
Prepaid Insurance	194	75			
Store Equipment	7,927	00	Total Liabilities		
Office Equipment	1,120	00			
Other Assets	1,844	50	PROPRIETORSHIP		
			Julio Alvaro, Capital		
Total Assets			Total Liabilities and Proprietorship		

SECTION 52. The Income Statement

A retailer's net income is the amount by which the net sales exceed the cost of goods sold and the operating expenses. By net sales is meant the total sales for the period less customers' returns and any allowances given to customers because of merchandise that turned out to be imperfect or in damaged condition.

EXERCISE. (Practical problems)

1. For the month of March, the total sales of Tom's Shoppe were $22,637.42. The sales returns and allowances for the month totaled $2,421.57. The store's net sales for the month were $_____.

2. The cost of goods sold is found by subtracting the ending inventory from the sum of the beginning inventory and the cost of the purchases. The gross profit is found by subtracting the cost of goods sold from the net sales.

Example: Kay's Music Center wants to know the cost of the goods that have been sold during the year. Net sales for the year have been $98,000; purchases, $55,300. The inventory count taken at the beginning of the year showed goods on hand of $19,800. The count of stock at the end of the year shows an inventory of $18,300. In order to determine the cost of goods sold and the gross profit for the year, the bookkeeper sets up the figures shown at the right.

The Kandy Kane Shop gives you the following data on its operations for the past year: net sales, $107,200; inventory at beginning of year, $19,700; purchases during year, $69,800; inventory at end of year, $21,600. You are to set up this information in the space at the right, showing (a) cost of goods sold and (b) gross profit on sales.

Kay's Music Center

Net Sales......................		$98,000
Beginning Inventory............	$19,800	
Add Purchases..................	55,300	
Mdse. Available for Sale........	$75,100	
Less Ending Inventory..........	18,300	
Cost of Goods Sold.............		56,800
Gross Profit on Sales...........		$41,200

Kandy Kane Shop

Net Sales......................		$ ......
Beginning Inventory............	$	
Add Purchases..................	......	
Mdse. Available for Sale........	$	
Less Ending Inventory..........	......	
Cost of Goods Sold.............		......
Gross Profit on Sales...........		$ ......

3. For the quarter ending March 31 of the current year, the records of Lou's Grocery show the following: net sales, $42,574; purchases, $18,528; operating expenses, $12,829, merchandise inventory January 1, $6,143; merchandise inventory March 31, $4,894.

You are to set up this information in the space at the right, showing (a) the cost of goods sold, (b) the gross profit on sales, and (c) the net income.

Lou's Grocery

Net Sales......................		$ ......
Less Cost of Goods Sold Inventory, January 1........	$	
Add Purchases.................	......	
Mdse. Available for Sale......	$	
Less Inventory, March 31....	......	
Cost of Goods Sold........		......
Gross Profit on Sales........		$ ......
Less Operating Expenses.....		......
Net Income..................		$ ......

Section 52. (concluded)

4. The details of the income and expenses of a business are usually set forth in a formal report called an *income statement*. To save space, the cost of goods sold section is often shown in condensed form, as in the income statement given below, with the details of the cost supplied on a separate report. On the statement below, the net sales and cost of goods sold are shown for the three classes of merchandise handled by the store — shoes, handbags, and accessories.

You are to complete the following statement by showing (a) the total income, (b) the cost of goods sold, (c) the gross profit on sales, (d) the total operating expenses, and (e) the net income.

JULIO ALVARO SHOE STORE
INCOME STATEMENT
FOR THE MONTH ENDED DECEMBER 31, 19--

Income:

Net Sales — Shoes	$128,862	
Handbags	14,343	
Accessories	6,795	
Total Income		$ ......
Cost of Goods Sold:		
Shoes	$ 84,657	
Handbags	9,319	
Accessories	4,134	......
Gross Profit on Sales		$ ......
Operating Expenses:		
Employee Salaries	$ 19,534	
Owner Salary	10,500	
Rent	5,400	
Advertising	4,368	
Taxes	936	
Other Expenses	1,992	
Total Operating Expenses		......
Net Income		$ ......

5. As a rule, a businessperson makes a percentage analysis of the income statement to show what percent each major item is of the net sales. For example, in Problem 4, above, the net sales are $150,000 and the cost of goods sold is $98,110. To the nearest tenth of a percent, the cost of goods is 65.4% of the net sales ($98,110 ÷ $150,000 = .6540, or 65.4%).

Shown at the right is the condensed income statement of Kester's Gift Shop. You are to divide each item by the net sales and write the result, to the nearest tenth of a percent, in the blank space provided.

Kester's Gift Shop

Net Sales	$112,000	100.0%
Cost of Goods Sold	83,450	......
Gross Profit on Sales	28,550	......
Operating Expenses	13,720	......
Net Income	$14,830	......

SECTION 53. Figuring Payrolls

In many businesses, employees are paid by the hour. The time worked by each employee is often kept on a time card, like the one you used in Section 15. From the record on the time cards, a clerk prepares the weekly payroll register.

EXERCISE. (Practical problems)

1. The payroll register of Davis Plumbing Supplies is shown below. You are to complete it by entering (a) the total hours worked by each employee, (b) his total earnings, (c) his FICA tax, (d) his income tax, (e) his total deductions, (f) his net pay, and (g) the totals for all of the employees. Use the tables on page 115 to determine the FICA and income tax deductions.

PAYROLL REGISTER		WEEK ENDED October 5, 19--											
NAME	EX-EMP-TIONS	TIME RECORD					TOTAL HOURS	HOUR RATE	TOTAL EARN-INGS	DEDUCTIONS				NET PAY
		M	T	W	T	F				FICA	INCOME TAX	INS.	TOTAL	
Carter, R.	3	8	8	8	8	8		3.36				2.40		
Fahey, T.	1	8	8	7	7	8		3.25				1.60		
Ivers, F.	2	8	8	8	8	8		3.35				2.40		
Stein, D.	2	8	4	8	8	8		3.44				1.00		
Udell, H.	3	8	8	8	8	8		3.10				2.40		
							TOTALS							

2. When wages are paid in cash, the payroll clerk must obtain cash from the bank in the right denominations to pay each employee the exact amount of his wages. To do this, the clerk prepares a change sheet. The change sheet for the payroll in Problem 1 is shown at the right. In it have been entered the net pay and number of each denomination needed for the first employee, R. Carter. Make the necessary entries for the other employees and show the totals for all the employees.

CHANGE SHEET OCTOBER 5, 19--										
NAME	NET PAY	$20	$10	$5	$1	50¢	25¢	10¢	5¢	1¢
Carter, R.	112 14	5	1		2			1		4
Fahey, T.										
Ivers, F.										
Stein, D.										
Udell, H.										
Totals										

3. When the change sheet is completed, the totals of the change columns are transferred to a change memorandum, which is used to get the right number of each denomination at the bank.

The form at the right is the change memorandum for the change sheet in Problem 2. In it have been entered the number and amount of $20 bills needed. Complete the form by entering (a) the number needed of the other denominations, (b) the amount of each denomination, and (c) the total of the "Amount" column. This total should equal the total of the net pay column shown on the change sheet.

CHANGE MEMORANDUM		
DENOMI-NATION	NUMBER OF EACH DE-NOMINATION	AMOUNT
$20.00	24	480 00
10.00		
5.00		
1.00		
.50		
.25		
.10		
.05		
.01		
TOTAL		

Section 53. (continued)

INCOME TAX WITHHOLDING TABLE
If the payroll period is weekly

Wages are		And the number of exemptions claimed is —			
At least	But less than	0	1	2	3
		The amount of income tax withheld shall be—			
$100	$105	$14.10	$11.80	$.9.50	$.7.20
105	110	14.90	12.60	10.30	8.00
110	115	15.70	13.40	11.10	8.80
115	120	16.50	14.20	11.90	9.60
120	125	17.30	15.00	12.70	10.40
125	130	18.10	15.80	13.50	11.20
130	135	18.90	16.60	14.30	12.00
135	140	19.70	17.40	15.10	12.80
140	145	20.50	18.20	15.90	13.60
145	150	21.30	19.00	16.70	14.40

SOCIAL SECURITY AND HOSPITAL INSURANCE TAX TABLE — 5.85%

$ Wages less than	$ Tax	$ Wages less than	$ Tax	$ Wages less than	$ Tax	$ Wages less than	$ Tax	$ Wages less than	$ Tax	$ Wages less than	$ Tax
82.14	4.80	92.40	5.40	102.65	6.00	112.91	6.60	123.17	7.20	133.42	7.80
82.31	4.81	92.57	5.41	102.83	6.01	113.08	6.61	123.34	7.21	133.59	7.81
82.48	4.82	92.74	5.42	103.00	6.02	113.25	6.62	123.51	7.22	133.77	7.82
82.65	4.83	92.91	5.43	103.17	6.03	113.42	6.63	123.68	7.23	133.94	7.83
82.83	4.84	93.08	5.44	103.34	6.04	113.59	6.64	123.85	7.24	134.11	7.84
83.00	4.85	93.25	5.45	103.51	6.05	113.77	6.65	124.02	7.25	134.28	7.85
83.17	4.86	93.42	5.46	103.68	6.06	113.94	6.66	124.19	7.26	134.45	7.86
83.34	4.87	93.59	5.47	103.85	6.07	114.11	6.67	124.36	7.27	134.62	7.87
83.51	4.88	93.77	5.48	104.02	6.08	114.28	6.68	124.53	7.28	134.79	7.88
83.68	4.89	93.94	5.49	104.19	6.09	114.45	6.69	124.71	7.29	134.96	7.89

4. Complete the following payroll register, change sheet, and change memorandum. Use the tables given above to determine the FICA and income tax deductions.

PAYROLL REGISTER WEEK ENDED April 14, 19--														
NAME	EX-EMP-TIONS	TIME RECORD					TOTAL HOURS	HOUR RATE	TOTAL EARN-INGS	DEDUCTIONS				NET PAY
		M	T	W	T	F				FICA	INCOME TAX	OTHER	TOTAL	
Baker, D.	2	7	8	8	8	8		3.43				2.40		
Crane, F.	1	8	7½	8	8	8		3.14				1.60		
Maier, J.	3	8	6	8	8	8		3.55				3.20		
Pabas, S.	1	8	8	8	6½	8		3.20				1.60		
Turco, L.	3	8	8	8	8	8		3.36				2.10		
							TOTALS							

CHANGE SHEET APRIL 14, --										
NAME	NET PAY	$20	$10	$5	$1	50¢	25¢	10¢	5¢	1¢
Baker, D.										
Crane, F.										
Maier, J.										
Pabas, S.										
Turco, L.										
Totals										

CHANGE MEMORANDUM			
DENOMI-NATION	NUMBER OF EACH DE-NOMINATION	AMOUNT	
$20.00			
10.00			
5.00			
1.00			
.50			
.25			
.10			
.05			
.01			
	TOTAL		

5. Most employers keep a separate payroll record for each employee. This record is called the *individual earnings record* and is shown below. The information on the individual earnings record is used to determine when each employee has received $12,600 in gross pay for the year and is no longer subject to FICA taxes. The record is also used to prepare tax information forms which each business must file with the state and federal governments.

Shown below is the individual earnings record for Susan Burrows. During the week of January 18, Susan received a raise. Complete her earnings record for the weeks of the 18th and 25th using the tables for FICA and withholdings taxes found on p. 115.

NAME **Susan Ann Burrows** SOCIAL SECURITY NO. **173-30-1568**

ADDRESS **45-20 169th Street** EXEMPTIONS **2**

CITY **Flushing, New York**

WEEK ENDED	GROSS PAY	WITH-HOLDING TAX	FICA	GROUP INSURANCE	HEALTH INSURANCE	TOTAL DEDUC-TIONS	NET PAY	TAXABLE EARNINGS ACCUMU-LATED
1/4	124.00	12.70	7.25	2.15	5.60			
1/11	124.00	12.70	7.25	2.15	5.60			
1/18	134.00			2.15	5.60			
1/25				2.15	5.60			

6. Complete the individual earnings record for John Kline below. Use the tables for FICA and withholding taxes found on p. 115.

NAME **John Eldon Kline** SOCIAL SECURITY NO. **134-56-9860**

ADDRESS **16 Kent Drive** EXEMPTIONS **1**

CITY **Chicago, Illinois**

WEEK ENDED	GROSS PAY	DEDUCTIONS			TOTAL DEDUC-TIONS	NET PAY	TAXABLE EARNINGS ACCUMU-LATED
		WITH-HOLDING TAX	FICA	OTHER			
TOTALS FOR THIRD QUARTER	4,056.00	460.20	237.12	320.97	1,018.29	3,037.71	4,056.00
10/5	104.00			8.23			
10/12	104.00			8.23			
10/19	114.00			9.78			
10/26	114.00			9.78			

SECTION 54. Preparing and Using Charts

Any set of related numerical facts, or data, may be presented in the form of a chart or graph. The most common types of charts are: (1) the vertical bar chart, (2) the horizontal bar chart, (3) the line chart, (4) the rectangle chart, and (5) the circle chart.

EXERCISE. (Practical problems)

1. The vertical bar chart below shows the sales of Harold Sampson for each quarter of last year. You are to interpret this chart in dollars by entering at the right of the chart the dollar volume of sales for each quarter.

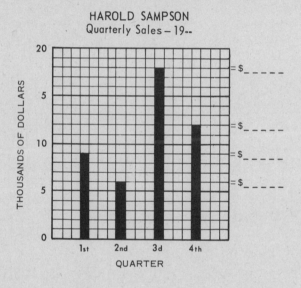

HAROLD SAMPSON
Quarterly Sales — 19--

3. The horizontal bar chart below shows the sales made by six salesmen for the week ending June 18 of the current year. You are to interpret this chart by showing at the right of the chart the amount of each salesman's sales.

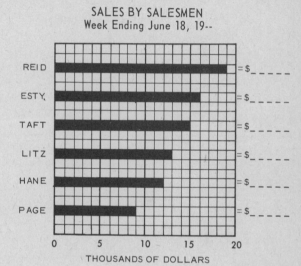

SALES BY SALESMEN
Week Ending June 18, 19--

2. The quarterly sales of Robert Hager for last year were: first quarter, $7,000; second quarter, $13,000; third quarter, $11,000; fourth quarter, $17,000. Using the chart paper below and with the chart above as a model, show these quarterly sales figures in the form of a vertical bar chart.

ROBERT HAGER
Quarterly Sales — 19--

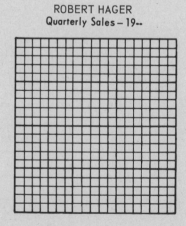

4. The sales of Pelton's Market for December of last year were: meat, $3,700; poultry, $2,400; eggs, $1,700; butter, $1,100; canned goods, $800. Using the chart paper below, show these facts by means of a horizontal bar chart. Let each horizontal division represent $200. The end of a bar representing an odd amount, such as $3,700, would be placed midway between $3,600 and $3,800.

DISTRIBUTION OF SALES
December, 19--

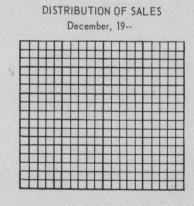

5. The monthly kilowatt-hours of electricity used by Janet Monroe last year were as follows:

Jan. 370	May 190	Sept. 170
Feb. 320	June 190	Oct. 260
Mar. 290	July 170	Nov. 250
Apr. 220	Aug. 150	Dec. 310

Using the chart paper at the right, show these facts by means of a vertical bar chart.

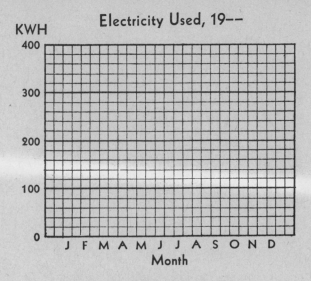

Electricity Used, 19--

6. The distances from Cincinnati, Ohio, to five other cities are as follows:

Los Angeles	1,900 mi.
Salt Lake City	1,500 mi.
Denver	1,100 mi.
Houston	900 mi.
Minneapolis	700 mi.

Using the chart paper at the right, make a horizontal bar chart to represent these facts.

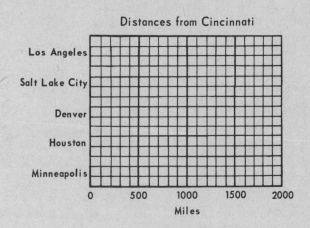

Distances from Cincinnati

7. The line chart at the right shows Paul Snyder's monthly gross profit and expenses for last year. You are to interpret this chart by completing the following statements.

a. His gross profit was smallest in the month of _____ .

b. His gross profit was greatest in the month of _____ .

c. In January, his gross profit was $_____, his expenses were $_____, and his net profit was $_____ .

d. He had a loss instead of a profit in the months of _____ and _____ .

e. He made the greatest net profit in the month of _____ . The amount of the net profit was $_____ .

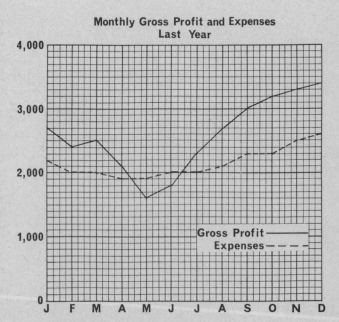

Monthly Gross Profit and Expenses Last Year

Section 54. (concluded)

8. The total income for David Risco, a commission salesman, for the first ten weeks of last year and this year are shown below.

WEEK	LAST YEAR	THIS YEAR	WEEK	LAST YEAR	THIS YEAR
1	$670	$700	6	$800	$780
2	710	750	7	790	760
3	740	790	8	760	790
4	760	820	9	780	840
5	770	810	10	820	870

From these figures you are to construct on the graph paper at the right a line chart showing (a) the income for this year, using a solid line; and (b) the income for last year, using a dotted line.

9. The owner of the Superway Store, wanting to show the types of sales transactions for last year, prepares the rectangle chart below. This type of chart is especially suited to showing information which, when added, makes up the whole. Sections of the chart represent parts of the whole. You will observe that the total sales are $310,000. You are to write in the appropriate blank spaces on the chart the amount of (a) the installment sales, (b) the C.O.D. sales, (c) the charge account sales, and (d) the cash sales.

10. On a vacation trip this summer, Lloyd Davis spent $420. Mr. Davis wants to prepare a chart showing the distribution of the expense. For this purpose, either a rectangle chart as shown in Problem 9 or a circle chart may be used. He decides to use a circle chart and prepares the chart below. The sections of the chart are based on the following figures taken from his expense record: food, $147; lodging, $126; transportation, $105; amusement, $33.60; miscellaneous expense, $8.40. You are to find the percent relationship of each of these items to the total expense and enter this percent in the correct section of the circle chart.

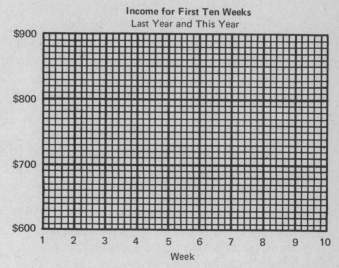

Income for First Ten Weeks
Last Year and This Year

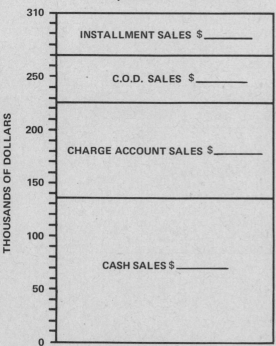

THE SUPERWAY STORE
Composition of Sales—19--

LLOYD DAVIS
Vacation Expense-

UNIT TWELVE   The Retailer: Buying

SECTION 55. Purchasing Merchandise

When a store owner finds that more merchandise is needed, an order is placed with a wholesaler or a manufacturer. Upon receipt of the order, the seller uses it as the basis for making out an invoice. This invoice is mailed to the buyer or included with the delivery of the merchandise.

EXERCISE.   (Practical problems)

1. Sam Speed's Auto Parts store keeps a record of its stock of goods on perpetual inventory cards. One of the cards for "shock absorbers" is shown at the right. The balance, or number of units in stock, is recorded at the beginning of the month in the column at the right. When a purchase or a sale is made during the month, the date, order number or sale number, and quantity are recorded in the proper columns. After each entry, the balance on hand is recorded in the "Balance" column.

The purchases and sales shown below occurred during May in addition to those already recorded on the card. You are (a) to record these purchases and sales on the card and (b) to record the balance on hand after each entry.

STOCK NO.	DESCRIPTION				MINIMUM
183	Shock Absorbers, 61-B31				15
	BOUGHT		SOLD		BALANCE
DATE	Order No.	Quantity	Sale No.	Quantity	No. of Units in Stock
May 1					19
5			843	3	16
6	A143	12			28

May 8 Sold	6 Sale No.	855		May 20 Sold	9 Sale No.	901
12 Sold	8 Sale No.	872		25 Sold	5 Sale No.	915
12 Bought	18 Order No.	A166		25 Bought	24 Order No.	A191
16 Sold	2 Sale No.	885		31 Sold	6 Sale No.	934

2. On April 4, the owner of Sam Speed's Auto Parts makes out the following purchase order to East Coast Auto Supply, Inc. The order shows the quantity and description of each article desired and the price previously paid for it. Complete the following purchase order by entering the order for 15 shock absorbers, No. 61-B48, @ $5.85 each, and 9 battery chargers, No. B22-416 @ $8.95 each.

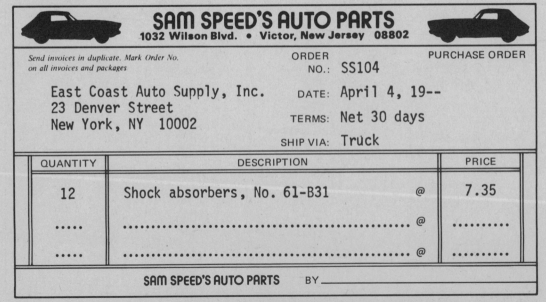

SAM SPEED'S AUTO PARTS
1032 Wilson Blvd. • Victor, New Jersey 08802

Send invoices in duplicate. Mark Order No. on all invoices and packages

ORDER NO.: SS104   PURCHASE ORDER

East Coast Auto Supply, Inc.
23 Denver Street
New York, NY 10002

DATE: April 4, 19--
TERMS: Net 30 days
SHIP VIA: Truck

QUANTITY	DESCRIPTION		PRICE
12	Shock absorbers, No. 61-B31	@	7.35
.....	....	@	....
.....	....	@	....

SAM SPEED'S AUTO PARTS   BY _____

[120]

Section 55. (continued)

3. From the purchase order, the billing clerk of East Coast Auto Supply, Inc., makes out the following invoice. You are to (a) make the extensions and (b) show the total of the invoice.

INVOICE

DATE April 6, 19--

EAST COAST AUTO SUPPLY, INC.
23 Denver St., New York, New York 10002

SOLD TO

Sam Speed's Auto Parts
1032 Wilson Blvd.
Victor, NJ 08802

OUR NO. PA2312
CUST. ORDER NO. SS104

TERMS Net 30 days

SHIPPED VIA Truck

QUANTITY	DESCRIPTION	UNIT PRICE	AMOUNT
12	Shock absorbers, No. 61-B31	7.35	....
15	Shock absorbers, No. 61-B48	5.85	....
9	Battery chargers, No. B22-416	8.95	....
			....

4. When merchandise is returned by the buyer, a credit memorandum is received from the seller. The following credit memorandum is received by Sam Speed's Auto Parts for goods returned to East Coast Auto Supply, Inc. You are to (a) make the extensions, and (b) show the total of the credit memorandum.

CREDIT MEMORANDUM

EAST COAST AUTO SUPPLY, INC.
23 Denver St., New York, New York 10002

April 12, 19--

Sam Speed's Auto Parts

1032 Wilson Blvd.

Victor, NJ 08802

WE CREDIT YOUR ACCOUNT AS FOLLOWS:

2 Shock absorbers, No. 61-B48 $5.85 ea.		....
4 Battery chargers, No. B22-416 8.95 ea.		....

Section 55. (concluded)

5. Sam Speed's Auto Parts store lists all purchases in a book called a purchases journal and all returns and allowances are listed in a purchases returns and allowances journal. All purchases made between April 1 and April 22 have been listed in the purchases journal below.

PURCHASES JOURNAL

DATE		NAME OF CREDITOR	POST REF.	TOTAL		TIRES AND TUBES		BATTERIES		PARTS AND SUPPLIES	
19-- April	4	East Coast Auto Supply		256	50					256	50
	7	Energee Battery Corp.		284	73			149	20	135	53
	10	Imperial Tire & Rubber Co.		392	62	268	05			124	57
	12	Premier Auto Products, Inc.		202	48					202	48
	18	A & K Specialty Mfg. Co.		87	15					87	15
	22	Energee Battery Corp.		183	59			102	16	81	43

(a) Since April 22, two additional purchases have been made: (1) April 25, from Imperial Tire & Rubber Co., $114.01; consisting of tires and tubes, $78.60, and parts and supplies, $35.41; (2) April 30, from Energee Battery Corp., $143.25; consisting of batteries, $119.45, and parts and supplies, $23.80. You are to record each of these purchases in the purchases journal. Use as a guide the entries that already appear in the journal. (b) Record the column totals on the bottom line. Prove the totals by comparing the total of the "Total" column with the sum of the three totals at the right. The two amounts should be the same.

6. Sam Speed's Auto Parts' purchases returns and allowances journal appears on April 27 as follows.

PURCHASES RETURNS AND ALLOWANCES JOURNAL

DATE		NAME OF CREDITOR	POST REF.	TOTAL		TIRES AND TUBES		BATTERIES		PARTS AND SUPPLIES	
19-- April	9	East Coast Auto Supply, Inc.		47	50					47	50
	11	Energee Battery Corp.		12	95			12	95		
	14	Imperial Tire & Rubber Co.		39	74	21	15			18	59

On April 27, Sam Speed's Auto Parts returns to the Energee Battery Corp. $46.75 of batteries and $3.48 of parts and supplies purchased on April 22 (see Problem 5), receiving a credit memorandum for $50.23. (a) You are to record this return in the purchases returns and allowances journal. (b) Record the totals on the bottom line, and prove the totals in the way you did in Problem 5.

[122]

DRILL 89. (Combinations of aliquot parts)

You learned in a previous section how to use aliquot parts when the price is an aliquot part of $1. Sometimes the price is a combination of an aliquot part and the base. For example, $1.10 is equal to $1 + $.10, or $1 + $\frac{1}{10}$ of $1; 1.12\frac{1}{2}$ is equal to $1 + $.12$\frac{1}{2}$, or $1 + $\frac{1}{8}$ of $1. Similarly, $1.25 is equal to $1 + $\frac{1}{4}$ of $1; $1.50 is equal to $1 + $\frac{1}{2}$ of $1; $2.50 is equal to $2 + $\frac{1}{2}$ of $1.

Aliquot parts may be used when the unit price is a combination of an aliquot part and the base or a multiple of the base.

Example: What is the cost of 32 lb. @ $1.10?

$$32 \times \$1.10 = \quad 32 \times \$1 = \$32.00$$
$$+ \tfrac{1}{10} \times \$32 = \quad 3.20$$
$$\overline{\quad\quad\quad}$$
$$\$35.20 \text{ cost}$$

Example: What is the cost of 16 yd. @ $2.50?

$$16 \times \$2.50 = \quad 16 \times \$2 = \$32$$
$$+ \tfrac{1}{2} \times \$16 = \quad 8$$
$$\overline{\quad\quad}$$
$$\$40 \text{ cost}$$

The following problems provide practice in using combinations of aliquot parts. Do the work mentally and complete the problems as rapidly as you can.

1. 12 @ $1.50 = _____
2. 40 @ 1.12\frac{1}{2}$ = _____
3. 20 @ $1.25 = _____
4. 16 @ $1.50 = _____
5. 32 @ 1.12\frac{1}{2}$ = _____

6. 26 @ $1.50 = _____
7. 48 @ 1.12\frac{1}{2}$ = _____
8. 15 @ $1.10 = _____
9. 16 @ $1.25 = _____
10. 25 @ $1.10 = _____

11. 18 @ $2.50 = _____
12. 72 @ 1.12\frac{1}{2}$ = _____
13. 44 @ $1.25 = _____
14. 42 @ $1.50 = _____
15. 22 @ $2.50 = _____

DRILL 90. (Combinations of aliquot parts)

When the figures are too difficult to handle mentally and written calculations are necessary, combinations of aliquot parts can often be used to advantage.

In the example at the right, notice that the work under Solution 1 ($135 + $\frac{1}{4}$ of $135) is much shorter than under Solution 2 (135 × $1.25).

Example: What is the cost of 135 yd. @ $1.25?

Solution 1	Solution 2
4) $135	1 35
33.75	$1.25
$168.75	6 75
	27 0
	135
	$168.75

Solve the following problems using combinations of aliquot parts.

1. 568 @ 1.12\frac{1}{2}$ = _____
2. 628 @ $1.25 = _____
3. 245 @ $1.10 = _____
4. 158 @ 1.12\frac{1}{2}$ = _____

5. 158 @ $1.50 = _____
6. 175 @ $1.25 = _____
7. 84 @ 1.12\frac{1}{2}$ = _____
8. 375 @ $1.10 = _____

9. 130 @ 1.12\frac{1}{2}$ = _____
10. 215 @ $1.25 = _____
11. 242 @ $1.50 = _____
12. 325 @ $1.25 = _____

SECTION 56. Figuring Trade Discounts

Manufacturers and wholesalers, when selling to retailers, may allow one or more discounts from list prices. These discounts are called trade discounts because they are given only to dealers in the trade. The discounts usually serve two purposes. They make it possible for dealers to sell at, or near, list prices and make a satisfactory profit when the list price is the manufacturer's suggested or advertised retail price. Secondly, they make it possible for the manufacturer or wholesaler to avoid frequent changes in catalog prices. The discounts are adjusted to meet any changes in market conditions. For example, the Progress Manufacturing Co. may have discounts of 25%, 15%, and 10% on a cabinet sink that lists at $255. If the cost of production increases, the company can reduce the discounts to 20%, 10%, and 10% instead of changing the list or catalog price.

Where two or more discounts are involved, the invoice price, or invoice cost, of an article may be found by deducting each discount separately. This method is shown at the left. The cabinet sink is listed at $255 less 25%, 15%, and 10%. Each discount is figured on the balance remaining after the previous discount has been deducted. A second method of finding the invoice price is to find the invoice price in percent by applying the discounts to the list price expressed as 100%. The list price in dollars is then multiplied by the invoice price in percent to find the dollar amount of the invoice price. This method is shown at the right.

Method 1

List Price	= $255.00
25% of $255	= 63.75
	191.25
15% of $191.25	= 28.688
	162.562
10% of $162.562	= 16.256
Invoice Price	= $146.306
	= $146.31

Method 2

List Price	= 100%
25% of 100%	= 25%
	75%
15% of 75%	= 11.25%
	63.75%
10% of 63.75%	= 6.375%
Invoice Price	= 57.375%
57.375% of $255	= $146.30625
	= $146.31

The amount of the trade discount in the above example may be found by any one of the following methods:

1. Add the individual discounts, $63.75, $28.688, and $16.256. The sum is $108.694, or $108.69, which is the total trade discount.

2. Subtract $146.31, the invoice price, from $255, the list price. The remainder, $108.69, is the amount of the trade discount.

3. Subtract the invoice price percent, 57.375% from the list price percent, 100%. The remainder, 42.625%, represents the single discount equivalent to the series. Multiply $255 by 42.625%, giving $108.69375, or $108.69, the amount of the trade discount.

EXERCISE. (Practical problems)

In the following problems, find the invoice price by one method, then prove your answer by the other method. Make the calculations in the space after each problem.

1. The Home Remodelers Company buys shower cabinets listed at $95 less discounts of 20%, 10%, and 5%. The invoice price is $_____.

2. An oil heater unit lists at $840 and is subject to discounts of 15%, 10%, and 10%. It costs the dealer $_____.

Section 56. (concluded)

3. The Downhill Ski Shop buys merchandise from the All Sports Supply Co. as listed in the invoice below. You are to complete the invoice by showing the amount of the trade discount and the invoice price of the goods.

ALL SPORTS SUPPLY CO. Benton, Vermont 05201		CUST. ORDER NO. 1231 DATE OF ORDER October 13, 19-- INVOICE NO. B325 DATE Oct. 20, 19-- DATE SHIPPED Oct. 20, 19-- SHIPPED BY Our Truck TERMS Net 30 days		
SOLD TO	Downhill Ski Shop 52 Main Street Milton, NH 03302			
QUANTITY	DESCRIPTION		UNIT PRICE	AMOUNT
6	Skis, 142B		55.00	330.00
8	Ski boots, 1243A		42.50	340.00
				670.00
		Less 20% and 20%		....
				....

DRILL 91. (Applying trade discounts)

The problems below will provide further practice in finding the invoice price.

1. $60 less 20%, 5% = _____

2. $1,275 less 20%, $16\frac{2}{3}$% = _____

3. $2,500 less 15%, 15% = _____

4. $400 less 30%, 20%, $12\frac{1}{2}$% = _____

5. $800 less 40%, $12\frac{1}{2}$%, 10% = _____

6. $96 less 20%, $16\frac{2}{3}$%, 10% = _____

SECTION 57. Figuring Cash Discounts

To encourage customers to pay their bills promptly, some businesses allow customers to deduct a cash discount if payment is made within a specified time. For example, Phelps & Porter may sell to the Norwood Store merchandise invoiced at $380.75, with the following terms:2/10, n/30. This means 2%/10 days, net/30 days. In other words, if payment is made within 10 days from the date of the invoice, a 2% cash discount may be deducted; otherwise, the entire amount of the invoice becomes due in 30 days. If payment is made within 10 days, the amount paid will be $380.75 − 2% of $380.75 = $380.75 − $7.62 = $373.13.

EXERCISE. (Practical problems)

1. Goods amounting to $642.85 are sold on April 9. The terms are 1/15, n/30. If the invoice is paid by check on April 24, the amount of the check is $_____.

2. Cash discount is always figured on the invoice price; that is, on the amount remaining after subtracting the trade discount and before adding the transportation charges.

If the Victor Garden Shop pays the invoice shown at the right by check on May 20, the amount of the check is $_____.

Mangrum Tree Farm
Fairfield, Vermont 05201

DATE May 12, 19--

SOLD TO Victor Garden Shop
202 Mason Ave.
Glendale, VT 05201

SHIPPED VIA Truck
TERMS 2/10, n/30

QUANTITY	DESCRIPTION	UNIT PRICE	AMOUNT
50	Blue Spruce Trees	15.50	775.00
	Less 20% and 10%		217.00
			558.00
	Delivery		25.00
			583.00

3. The Aurora Corporation allows retail dealers trade discounts of 20% and 10%. Credit terms are 3/10, n/30. It sells the Hite Appliance Company an air conditioner listed at $325. The invoice, dated June 3, is paid by the Hite Appliance Company on June 13. The payment amounts to $_____.

4. The Mayfair Store always tries to take advantage of cash discounts offered. If it pays a $750 invoice by tomorrow, it will be entitled to take a 2% cash discount. The store has a temporary cash shortage; but in order to save this 2%, it borrows $735 at the bank for 50 days at 7%.

(a) The discount saved on the invoice is $_____.

(b) The interest on the bank loan is $_____.

(c) The net saving by borrowing to pay the invoice is $_____.

SECTION 58. Figuring Buying Expense

The cost of merchandise includes the invoice price plus the merchant's expenses of purchasing the merchandise and getting it delivered to the place of business. These expenses consist mostly of the freight or other transportation charges on the shipment.

EXERCISE.   (Practical problems)

1. Green's Hardware buys from Benson Garden Supply the merchandise listed in the invoice at the right. The shipment weighs 610 pounds, and the truck freight is $6.25 a 100 pounds.

You are to complete the invoice by showing (a) the amount of the trade discount, (b) the invoice price, (c) the freight cost, and (d) the total of the invoice.

BENSON GARDEN SUPPLY

| SOLD TO | Green's Hardware
122 Garner Ave.
Tindale, MA   03217 | | | | 323 King Street
Boston, Mass. 02117 | |

SHIPPED VIA	DATE	INVOICE NO.	YOUR ORDER	F.O.B.	TERMS
Truck Prepaid	Feb.27,19--	C4104	743	Boston	2/10, n/30

QUANTITY	STOCK NO.	DECRIPTION	UNIT PRICE	AMOUNT	
10	415x	Wheelbarrows	17.50	175.00	
12	A182	Lawnmowers	45.00	540.00	
15	BW107	Lawn sweepers	15.50	232.50	947.50
		Less 40% and 10%			....
					....
		Freight Prepaid			....
					....

2. As buyer for the Barnard Store, you find that the terms on which you can purchase the following items are as shown below. You are to show (a) the invoice price of each article, and (b) the total cost.

	LIST PRICE OF ARTICLE	DISCOUNTS	INVOICE PRICE OF ARTICLE	ESTIMATED FREIGHT	TOTAL COST OF ARTICLE
a	$ 750	25%-10%		$18.55	
b	220	20%-5%		6.35	
c	1,240	10%-10%-5%		27.53	
d	720	25%-12½%-10%		15.65	

UNIT THIRTEEN   The Retailer: Selling

SECTION 59. Sales Records

Whenever a cash register is used, a record of each cash transaction is printed on an audit strip. Totals are printed on the strip and the cash balance in the cash drawer is proved at the end of each day. A record of the proof is reported on a daily balance slip.

EXERCISE.   (Practical problems)

1. The daily balance slip of the Men's Department of the Myer's Department Store is shown below. You are to complete the slip. "Total cash in drawer" consists of the total of all denominations of money listed on the slip. "Total cash received" equals "Total cash in drawer" plus "Cash paid out." "Cash short" equals the amount by which "Total cash received on audit strip" exceeds "Total cash received." "Cash over" equals the amount by which "Total cash received" exceeds "Total cash received on audit strip."

2. You are in charge of the shoe department of the Boyer Store and at the end of the day find in your cash register the following items: 15¢ in pennies, $1.20 in nickels, $2.40 in dimes, $6.75 in quarters, $2.50 in half dollars, 13 one-dollar bills, 12 five-dollar bills, 19 ten-dollar bills, and a check for $15. The detailed audit strip shows $6.25 paid out and $297.25 total cash received. You are to enter these items correctly on the slip below, complete the slip, and show the amount of cash short or over.

DAILY BALANCE SLIP		
DENOMINATION	DOLLARS	CENTS
Pennies		35
Nickels		95
Dimes	3	40
Quarters	6	75
Halves	3	50
Paper Money	157	00
Checks	34	85
Total Cash in Drawer		
Add Cash Paid Out	2	45
Total Cash Received		
Total Cash Received on Audit Strip	214	35
Cash Short		
Cash Over		

DAILY BALANCE SLIP		
DENOMINATION	DOLLARS	CENTS
Pennies		
Nickels		
Dimes		
Quarters		
Halves		
Paper Money		
Checks		
Total in Cash Drawer		
Add Cash Paid Out		
Total Cash Received		
Total Cash Received on Audit Strip		
Cash Short		
Cash Over		

3. The Westgate Gift Shop keeps a record of the daily sales totals in a book called a record of sales. The daily sales totals for the first week in December have been entered in the record of sales shown at the right.

RECORD OF SALES

DATE 19--	CASH SALES			CHARGE SALES			TOTAL NET SALES
	GROSS SALES	RET. & ALLOW.	NET SALES	GROSS SALES	RET. & ALLOW.	NET SALES	
Dec. 1	266 95	5 85		236 65	7 10		
2	378 65	6 45		213 55	6 45		
3	318 50	6 10		271 85	8 15		
4	446 75	12 50		350 70	10 50		
5	420 80	13 15		290 65	8 55		
6	361 45	10 20		269 35	7 95		
TOTALS					48 70		

plete the record by showing each day's (a) net cash sales, (b) net charge sales, and (c) total net sales, and by showing (d) the columnar totals for the week.

SECTION 60. Figuring Retail Discounts

To keep goods moving, it is sometimes necessary to offer them at reduced prices. The amount of the discount, or markdown, is often expressed as a percent of the original marked price. A topcoat, for example, marked to sell at $75 at the beginning of the season, may be marked down at the end of the season to $60. The amount of the discount is $15 ($75 − $60); and the rate of discount, or rate of markdown, is 20% ($15 ÷ $75).

EXERCISE.   (Practical problems)

1. A newspaper advertisement reads as follows:

COLONIAL LOUNGE CHAIR — WAS $200 — NOW $150

The amount of the price reduction is (a) $_____, which is (b) _____% of the original marked price.

2. At the Powers Store, ties that are regularly priced at $4 each are offered during a special sale at 2 ties for $7.20. If you purchase 2 ties at the special sale price, you obtain a discount of _____% from the regular price.

3. Richard Frost purchased at Sheridan's Clothing Shop a jacket priced at $49.55 and a suit priced at $95. With the purchase he was given, free of charge, a necktie worth $2.95. This was equivalent to a discount of _____%.

4. The bus fare from Nelson to Wakefield is $16.50. A round-trip ticket costs $29.70. If you wish to travel from Nelson to Wakefield and return, you would save _____% by buying a round-trip ticket instead of two one-way tickets.

5. The Fairfield Ski Center put an ad in the newspaper listing a pair of skis at 20% discount from the regular price. A coupon was included worth $5 in trade. Fred Wilson purchased skis regularly priced at $169 and presented the coupon in part payment. The amount of money Fred paid for the skis was $_____.

SECTION 61. Figuring Profits on Sales

The owner of a retail business often wants to know how much profit is made on the sale of an article and what percent the profit is of the selling price. Jules Levin, for example, owner of a dress shop, pays $12 each for dresses that he retails at $20. He estimates that operating expenses average $5 per dress. On the sale of each dress, his gross profit, which is often called markup, is $8 ($20 − $12), and his estimated net profit is $3 ($8 − $5). His markup, $8, is 40% of the selling price ($8 ÷ $20); and his net profit, $3, is 15% of the selling price ($3 ÷ $20).

EXERCISE.   (Practical problems)

1. The Rosen Luggage Store buys a certain line of tote bags at $10 each, less 30% and 10%, and sells them at $10.50 each. The store's markup is (a) $_____ each, which is (b) _____ % of the selling price.

2. The Rogers Department Store purchased a quantity of automatic blankets at $19.50 each, less 40%, and marked them to sell at $25. During a special sale the store offered the blankets at 20% off the marked price. On each blanket sold during the special sale the company realized a markup of (a) $_____, which was (b) _____% of the special sale price.

3. A retailer purchased 300 dresses at $9.95 each and marked them to sell at $16.95. He sold 240 at that price and then closed out the remaining dresses at $10.95 each. His average markup per dress was $_____.

4. Carol Snyder, a retail clothier, buys men's suits at $60.45 each and sells them at $99.95. Operating expenses average $30 per suit. (a) The markup on each suit is $_____. (b) The net profit is $_____. (c) The net profit is _____% of the selling price.

5. The Conway Furniture Company sells a certain style of chair for $142.50. The chair costs the company $96.90, and the company's operating expenses average 26% of the selling price. The company's net profit on each chair is (a) $_____, or (b) _____% of the selling price.

6. A dealer purchased an electric water heater listed at $125 less 20% and 10%, and sold it for $125. He estimated his operating expenses at 15% of the selling price and paid his salesman a commission of 6% of the selling price. The dealer's net profit on the heater was _____% of the selling price.

Name _____

SECTION 62. Pricing Goods — Sales Price Basis

The owner of a store must price the merchandise so that the markup will cover the operating expenses and the desired net profit. Operating expenses and net profit are usually expressed as percents of the selling price. In Lee's Clothing Store, for example, operating expenses are 33% of the selling price and the store desires a net profit of 7% of the selling price. The store's markup on an article should therefore be 33% + 7%, or 40% of the selling price. To stock a line of suits to retail at $90, the store's markup on each suit should be $36 (40% of $90); and the most the store can afford to pay for the suits is $54 ($90 − $36).

● On the other hand, if the store buys a line of suits at $60 each, the cost price, $60 represents 100% − 40%, or 60% of the selling price. The store's selling price should therefore be $100 ($60 ÷ 60%).

EXERCISE. (Practical problems)

1. Wilson Hall, owner of a men's wear store, wishes to stock a line of shirts that he can retail at $4.45. His expenses average 34% of the selling price, and he wants to make a net profit of 4% of the selling price.

a. His markup must be _____% of the selling price.

b His markup on each shirt must be $_____.

c The most he should pay for each shirt is $_____.

2. Bernice King, proprietor of a jewelry store, buys a certain line of necklaces at $9.75 each. She wants to sell them at a price that will yield a net profit of 8% on the selling price. Operating expenses average 40% of the selling price.

a Her markup must be _____% of the selling price.

b The cost price represents _____% of the selling price.

c The price at which she should sell each bracelet is $_____.

● 3. The Anderson Appliance Store buys an electric oven for $55.50. The store must sell the oven for $_____ in order to realize a markup equal to 40% of the selling price.

● 4. If a dealer pays $6.60 for an article and desires to realize a markup of 45% on the selling price, the lowest price at which he should sell the article is $_____.

● 5. The table at the right shows the cost price for seven articles and the required percent of markup based on the selling price of each. You are to show for each article the selling price needed, to the nearest cent, to yield the required markup.

COST	MARKUP % OF SELLING PRICE	SELLING PRICE
$ 7.50	40%	
.83	30%	
3.50	$33\frac{1}{3}$%	
5.50	45%	
.85	$37\frac{1}{2}$%	
41.25	34%	
42.90	45%	

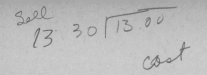

Sell
13. 30)13.00
cost

Name_____

SECTION 63. Pricing Goods — Cost Price Basis

The rate of markup on selling price may be converted to an equivalent rate based on cost. To do so, you express the markup and the cost as percents of the selling price, and then divide the markup percent by the cost percent. For example, if the desired markup on an article is 20% of the selling price, 80% of the selling price represents the cost. Dividing 20% by 80% gives 25% (.20 ÷ 80 = .25 = 25%), the equivalent rate of markup based on cost. Hence, if the cost of the article is $40, the markup should be 25% of $40, or $10. Adding the markup, $10, to the cost, $40, gives $50, the price at which the article should be sold.

EXERCISE. (Practical problems)

1. A dealer buys slide projectors at $65 each. She wants to sell them at a price that will yield a gross profit equal to 55% of the cost. (a) Her markup on each projector should be $_____. (b) The selling price should be $_____.

2. The Colfax Builders Supplies Company pays $11.25 each for stepladders. If the company desires 56% markup on the cost, it should sell the ladders at $_____ each.

3. By purchasing a model airplane for $29 and selling it for $44.95, the Bedell Hobby Shop realized a gross profit of (a) $_____, which was (b) _____% of the cost price.

4. A markup of _____% on the cost is equivalent to a markup of 30% on the selling price.

5. (a) If a retailer wishes to sell an article so as to realize a markup equal to 40% of his selling price, the markup should be _____% of the cost. (b) On an article costing the dealer $4.50, the dealer's markup should be $_____. (c) His selling price should be $_____.

6. To simplify the work of converting rate of markup based on selling price to the equivalent rate based on cost, markup tables have been prepared. A portion of such a table is shown at the right. Suppose a jeweler buys a watch for $20 and desires a markup equal to 42% of the selling price. In the table, opposite 42% in the first column, there appears 72.4% in the second column. This means that a markup of 72.4% of the cost must be added to the cost to produce the desired selling price. $20 + 72.4% of $20 = $20.00 + $14.48 = $34.48, selling price.

The lower table at the right shows the cost price of four articles and the desired rate of markup on the selling price. You are to show (a) the required amount of markup and (b) the selling price. Use the upper table in finding the amount of the markup.

MARKUP % OF S.P.	MARKUP % OF COST
36	$56\frac{1}{4}$
38	61.3
40	$66\frac{2}{3}$
42	72.4
44	78.6
46	85.2

COST PRICE	MARKUP % OF S.P.	MARKUP	SELLING PRICE
$ .60	38%		
4.50	46%		
10.50	40%		
3.00	44%		

UNIT FOURTEEN   The Wholesaler

SECTION 64. Sales Invoice

In an earlier section you saw that sales slips are widely used in retail stores. Wholesale stores usually use a more formal record, like the one below, called an invoice. Invoices may be filled out by hand or on a typewriter, but often they are completed on a billing machine or some form of automated equipment.

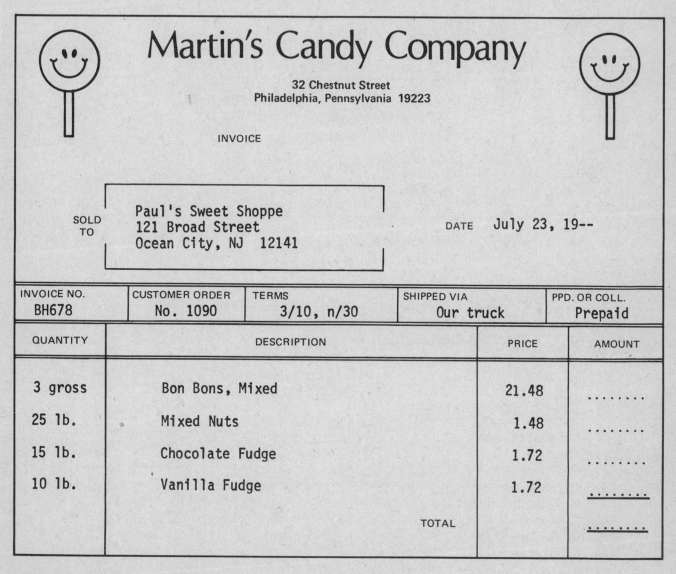

Martin's Candy Company

32 Chestnut Street
Philadelphia, Pennsylvania 19223

INVOICE

SOLD TO

Paul's Sweet Shoppe
121 Broad Street
Ocean City, NJ 12141

DATE   July 23, 19--

INVOICE NO. BH678	CUSTOMER ORDER No. 1090	TERMS 3/10, n/30	SHIPPED VIA Our truck	PPD. OR COLL. Prepaid

QUANTITY	DESCRIPTION	PRICE	AMOUNT
3 gross	Bon Bons, Mixed	21.48	. . . .
25 lb.	Mixed Nuts	1.48	. . . .
15 lb.	Chocolate Fudge	1.72	. . . .
10 lb.	Vanilla Fudge	1.72	. . . .
	TOTAL		. . . .

EXERCISE.   (Practical problems)

1. The sales invoice above has been completed except for the extended total amount for each item and the total for the invoice. You are (a) to make each extension and (b) to show the total of the invoice.

2. The invoice in Problem 1 was paid by check on August 2. The amount of the check was $_____.

3. Complete the following invoice by showing (a) the extension of each item, (b) the total list price, (c) the trade discount, and (d) the invoice price.

PARKER OFFICE SUPPLIES CO.
INVOICE
Peoria, Illinois 61601

INVOICE NO.	C1045
DATE	May 5, 19--
SHIP VIA	Mack's Express
TERMS	2/10, n/30

SOLD TO Day's Dept. Store
259 N. Main
Godfrey, IL 62234

QUANTITY	STOCK NO.	DESCRIPTION	UNIT PRICE	EXTENSION	TOTAL
5 doz.	B64	Ring Binders 11 x 8½	32.50	. . . .	
3 gr.	N27	Composition Notebooks	33.40	. . . .	
2 gr.	N14	Stenographer's Notebooks	28.60	. . . .	. . . .
		Less 40%			. . . .
					. . . .

4. Complete the following invoice by showing (a) the extensions, (b) the total list price, (c) the trade discount, (d) the invoice price, and (e) the total of the invoice.

excello paint manufacturing co.
ATLANTA, GEORGIA 30319

Craftsman Paint Shop
610 South Street
Gainsville, GA 30501

INVOICE NO. K1466   SHIP VIA EZ Motor Freight
DATE May 11, 19-- TERMS 2/10, n/30

QUANTITY	DESCRIPTION	UNIT PRICE	EXTENSION	TOTAL
24	Gal. House Paint, White #3-235	7.60	. . . .	
48	Qt. Wall Paint, Ivory #6-276	2.85	. . . .	
18	Pt. Spar Varnish #8-121	1.60	. . . .	. . . .
	Less 25% and 10%			. . . .
				. . . .
	Freight Prepaid			7.32
				. . . .

Name_____

Section 64. (concluded)

5. The Craftsman Paint Shop paid the invoice in Problem 4 by check on May 21 to take advantage of the cash discount. The discount was taken on the merchandise but not on the prepaid freight charges. The amount of the check drawn in payment of the invoice was $_____.

6. A wholesaler keeps an account record with each customer to show how much the customer owes. Shown below at the left is the Parker Office Supplies Co's. record of transactions with Day's Department Store for May. The entry of May 5 is the record of the invoice in Problem 3.

NAME		Day's Department Store			
ADDRESS		259 North Main, Godfrey, IL 62234			
DATE		EXPLANATION	CHARGES	CREDITS	BALANCE
19—					
May	1	Balance			68 58
	5	2/10, n/30	191 94		260 52
	14	Return		5 10	255 42
	14	Check		68 58	186 84
	16	Check		186 84	— —
	17	2/10, n/30	168 32		
	20	2/10, n/30	115 74		
	24	Return		22 40	
	27	Check		143 00	
	29	2/10, n/30	79 13		
	31	Check		118 66	

The amount of each sale to the customer is recorded in the "Charges" column. The same amount is added to the preceding balance, and the sum is entered in the "Balance" column.

The amount of each payment or return of merchandise received from the customer is entered in the "Credits" column. The same amount is subtracted from the preceding balance, and the difference is entered in the "Balance" column.

The account at the left is complete except for the balances after the last six transactions. You are to complete the account by figuring and entering those balances.

DRILL 92. (Aliquot parts of 100)

You have solved problems in previous sections involving multiplication by an aliquot part of $1. The same short method may be used to multiply by an aliquot part of 100. That is, you may multiply by the fraction and the base.

For example, 75 is $\frac{3}{4}$ of 100. To find the cost of 75 yd. at $1.60, first multiply $1.60 by $\frac{3}{4}$. This gives $1.20. Then multiply $1.20 by 100, giving $120. The cost is $120.

Example: What is the cost of 75 yd. @ $1.60?
$$75 = \tfrac{3}{4} \text{ of } 100$$
$$\tfrac{3}{4} \times \$1.60 = \$1.20$$
$$100 \times \$1.20 = \$120 \text{ cost}$$

The following problems provide practice in using aliquot parts of 100. Do the work mentally and complete the problems as rapidly as you can.

1. 25 yd. @ $3.60 = _____
2. 75 doz. @ .64 = _____
3. $12\frac{1}{2}$ gross @ 3.20 = _____
4. $37\frac{1}{2}$ lb. @ .40 = _____
5. $62\frac{1}{2}$ bu. @ .88 = _____
6. $87\frac{1}{2}$ doz. @ 1.60 = _____
7. $33\frac{1}{3}$ yd. @ 1.50 = _____
8. $66\frac{2}{3}$ yd. @ 2.10 = _____

9. 50 gal. @ $2.10 = _____
10. $16\frac{2}{3}$ yd. @ 1.80 = _____
11. 20 yd. @ 3.50 = _____
12. 40 doz. @ 2.50 = _____
13. $33\frac{1}{3}$ yd. @ 4.50 = _____
14. $37\frac{1}{2}$ bu. @ .80 = _____
15. 60 ft. @ .25 = _____
16. 80 bu. @ 1.50 = _____

DRILL 93. (Combinations of aliquot parts of 100)

Numbers such as 125, 150, and 175 are combinations of 100 and an aliquot part of 100. Thus, 125 equals $100 + \frac{1}{4}$ of 100; 150 equals $100 + \frac{1}{2}$ of 100; 175 equals $100 + \frac{3}{4}$ of 100. 250 represents a combination of 200 and $\frac{1}{2}$ of 100.

The principle of multiplication by an aliquot part may be used when the multiplier is a combination of an aliquot part and the base or a multiple of the base.

Example: What is the cost of 175 yd. @ $1.60?

$$175 \text{ yd. @ } \$1.60 = 100 \times \$1.60 = \$160$$
$$+ \frac{3}{4} \times \$160 = \underline{120}$$
$$\$280 \text{ cost}$$

Example: What is the cost of 250 yd. @ $.16?

$$250 \text{ yd. @ } \$.16 = 200 \times \$.16 = \$32$$
$$+ \frac{1}{2} \times \$16 = \underline{8}$$
$$\$40 \text{ cost}$$

Using combinations of aliquot parts of 100, solve the following problems mentally.

1. 125 doz. @ $3.60 = _____
2. 150 ft. @ 1.40 = _____
3. 175 gal. @ 2.80 = _____
4. 250 ft. @ .22 = _____
5. 125 yd. @ .40 = _____
6. 150 bu. @ 1.20 = _____
7. 120 gal. @ $2.50 = _____
8. 140 doz. @ 4.00 = _____
9. 160 yd. @ 5.00 = _____
10. 175 ft. @ 1.20 = _____
11. 180 gal. @ 3.00 = _____
12. 150 doz. @ 1.80 = _____

DRILL 94. (Aliquot parts of 100 and combinations of aliquot parts of 100)

When the figures are too difficult to handle mentally and written calculations are necessary, aliquot parts of 100 or combinations of aliquot parts can be used to advantage. In each case, multiply first by 100 by moving the decimal point two places to the right, and then multiply that result by the fraction.

Example: What is the cost of $37\frac{1}{2}$ yd. @ $1.42?

$$\begin{array}{r} \$142 \\ 3 \\ \hline 8)\overline{\$426} \\ \hline \$53.25 \text{ Ans.} \end{array}$$

Example: What is the cost of 125 yd. @ $1.42?

$$\begin{array}{r} 4)\overline{\$142} \\ 35.50 \\ \hline \$177.50 \text{ Ans.} \end{array}$$

Solve the following problems using aliquot parts or combinations of aliquot parts of 100.

1. $37\frac{1}{2}$ pt. @ $ .95 = _____
2. $62\frac{1}{2}$ yd. @ 1.25 = _____
3. 75 bu. @ 2.38 = _____
4. 25 qt. @ 1.45 = _____
5. $12\frac{1}{2}$ doz. @ 9.40 = _____
6. $33\frac{1}{3}$ yd. @ 8.65 = _____
7. 25 gal. @ 4.35 = _____
8. $16\frac{2}{3}$ yd. @ $11.55 = _____
9. 125 lb. @ 1.37 = _____
10. 150 gal. @ 3.53 = _____
11. 25 doz. @ 9.75 = _____
12. 75 bu. @ 1.58 = _____
13. 120 lb. @ 1.75 = _____
14. 125 doz. @ .89 = _____

SECTION 65. Promissory Notes and Bank Discount

A promissory note is a written promise to pay a sum of money at a definite date called the date of maturity. The seller may require a customer either to pay cash or sign a promissory note for the amount of the purchase. If payment of a customer's account is overdue, the seller may ask the customer to sign a note for the amount due. These notes usually bear interest at an agreed rate.

If a seller has a customer's note and needs the money before the note comes due, the seller may discount the note at the bank; that is, the note may be sold to the bank and cash received for it. On the date the note is discounted, the bank will deduct interest in advance, called bank discount, at an agreed rate and give the seller the proceeds. The proceeds of such a note consist of the maturity value of the note less discount on the maturity value from the date of discount to the maturity date.

Example: The Patterson Company received from a customer a 90-day note for $400 dated March 1 and bearing 5% interest. It discounts this note at the bank on March 31, the discount rate being 6%. What are the proceeds?

Date of maturity, March 1 + 90 days = May 30

Face of note..........................	$400.00
Interest at 5% for 90 days.............	5.00
Value at maturity.....................	$405.00
Term of discount, March 31 to May 30 = 60 days	
Bank discount at 6% on $405 for 60 days	4.05
Proceeds of note......................	$400.95

When the customer's note is non-interest-bearing, the proceeds are found in the same way. However, no calculations are needed for obtaining the value at maturity. The maturity value of a non-interest-bearing note is the same amount as the face of the note.

If a seller in need of cash does not have any customer's notes to discount, the seller may discount a personal non-interest-bearing note. The proceeds are found in the same way as the proceeds of a customer's non-interest-bearing note.

EXERCISE. (Practical problems)

1. Complete the following solution by showing, in the appropriate blank spaces, (a) the date of maturity, (b) the value at maturity, (c) the term of discount, (d) the bank discount, and (e) the proceeds.

Date of note	November 13
Time	80 days
Date of maturity	_____
Face of note	$1,410
Rate of interest	6%
Value at maturity	_____
Date of discount	December 18
Term of discount	_____
Rate of discount	6%
Bank discount	_____
Proceeds	_____

2. Complete the following solution by showing, in the appropriate blank spaces, (a) the date of maturity, (b) the value at maturity, (c) the term of discount, (d) the bank discount, and (e) the proceeds.

Date of note	May 15
Time	3 months
Date of maturity	_____
Face of note	$1,150
Rate of interest	Without interest
Value at maturity	_____
Date of discount	June 6
Term of discount	_____
Rate of discount	7%
Bank discount	_____
Proceeds	_____

3. (a) From the following data, write a promissory note, using the blank below. Face of note, $530; date, May 14; time, 3 months; interest, 6%; made payable to James C. Brian; payable at The Citizens Trust, Memphis; maker, George B. Anderson.

$_____ _____19_____

_____ AFTER DATE _____ PROMISE TO PAY TO

THE ORDER OF_____

_____DOLLARS

PAYABLE AT_____

VALUE RECEIVED WITH INTEREST AT_____%

NO. 165   DUE_____   _____

(b) James Brian discounts the above note at his bank on June 15, the discount rate being 6%. The bank credits his account for the proceeds which amount to $_____.

Section 65. (concluded)

4. (a) From the following data, write a promissory note, using the blank below. Face of note, $1,210; date, July 10; time, 90 days; made payable to Anthony Franco; payable at First National Bank of Fargo, without interest; number 128; maker, Richard Harris.

```
┌─────────────────────────────────────────────────────────────────────────┐
│ $_____          AFTON, MICHIGAN_____19_____     │
│                                                                           │
│ _____ AFTER DATE_____ PROMISE TO PAY TO │
│                                                                           │
│ THE ORDER OF_____ │
│                                                                           │
│ _____DOLLARS   │
│                                                                           │
│ PAYABLE AT_____ │
│                                                                           │
│ VALUE RECEIVED WITH INTEREST AT_____%    _____  │
│                                                                           │
│ NO._____ DUE_____  _____ │
└─────────────────────────────────────────────────────────────────────────┘
```

(b) Anthony Franco discounts the above note at his bank on July 25, the discount rate being 7%. The bank credits his account for the proceeds which amount to $_____.

DRILL 95: (Discounting notes)

The problems below will give you further practice in handling calculations involved in discounting interest-bearing and non-interest-bearing notes. You are to find for each note: (a) date of maturity, (b) value at maturity, (c) term of discount, (d) bank discount, and (e) proceeds. Make all your calculations on a separate sheet of paper.

NO.	FACE OF NOTE	INT. RATE	DATE OF NOTE	TIME OF NOTE	DATE OF MATURITY	VALUE AT MATURITY	DIS-COUNT DATE	TERM OF DISCOUNT	DIS-COUNT RATE	DISCOUNT	PROCEEDS
1.	$785	6%	Mar. 3	6 mo.			May 6		6%		
2.	868	6%	June 12	80 da.			June 26		6%		
3.	268		April 22	90 da.			June 21		6%		
4.	635		Sept. 1	75 da.			Sept. 26		5%		
5.	475		Aug. 12	90 da.			Aug. 12		7%		
6.	390		Sept. 21	3 mo.			Sept. 21		5%		
7.	950	5%	Jan. 3	30 da.			Jan. 10		6%		
8.	740	7%	July 6	2 mo.			July 23		7%		

SECTION 66. Bankruptcy of a Customer

If a business cannot pay its debts when they are due, a court may be asked by the business itself or its creditors to declare the business bankrupt. A trustee is then appointed to convert the property into cash, which is used first to pay the bankruptcy proceedings and certain claims that have priority. The remaining cash is then divided among the creditors in proportion to their claims. The percent paid to each creditor is found by dividing the total cash available by the total claims.

Example: At the request of its creditors, the Argus Stationery Store, having assets of $5,200 and liabilities of $10,000, is declared bankrupt. After selling all the assets and paying the bankruptcy costs, the trustee has $3,000 cash for distribution to the creditors. How much will the Weston Paper Company receive from the trustee in full settlement of its claim of $400?

$$\frac{\$3,000}{\$10,000} = .30 = 30\%, \text{ percent of each claim that can be paid}$$

$.3 \times \$400 = \$120$ payment to Weston Paper Co.

EXERCISE. (Practical problems)

1. Larry Brown, a druggist who is unable to pay his debts, is forced into bankruptcy. A trustee is appointed to handle the affairs for the benefit of the creditors. After selling all assets, the trustee has cash on hand sufficient to pay creditors 32.16% of their claims. If Mr. Brown owes Amco Paper Company $820, the company should receive $_____.

2. R. B. Weidman & Co. has assets valued at $26,500 and liabilities amounting to $32,500. The company goes into bankruptcy and, under forced sale, the assets are turned into $14,300 cash. (a) This cash amounts to _____% of liabilities. (b) The cash being distributed proportionately, Ralston Bros., with a claim of $822.50, will receive $_____.

3. In winding up the affairs of Olsen's Brick Yard, a bankrupt concern with liabilities of $17,350, the trustee has $5,685 cash for payment to the creditors. Calculated correct to three decimal places, the percent to be used as the basis for settlement with the creditors is _____%.

4. The Levy Sign Company, one of the creditors in Problem 3, will receive $_____ in settlement of its claim of $120.

SECTION 67. The Commission Merchant

The seller may ship goods to a commission merchant for sale, allowing the merchant a certain percent of sales as a *commission*. The seller is known as the *principal* and the merchandise sent for sale is a *consignment*.

After the goods have been sold, the commission merchant sends to the principal a statement known as an *account sales*. This statement lists the items sold, the amount received from the sale, the charges for making the sale, the commission deducted, and the net proceeds owed to the principal. *Net proceeds* equal the total amount of the sale less the commission and other charges.

Instead of acting as a seller, a commission merchant may act as a buyer of goods for a principal. After making the purchase as ordered and shipping the goods to the principal, the merchant sends the principal a statement known as an *account purchase*. This statement lists the items purchased, the amount paid for them, the charges for buying and shipping, the commission added, and the total amount due the commission merchant. The amount due, or *gross cost*, equals the prime cost of the goods plus the commission and other charges.

EXERCISE. (Practical problems)

1. The Durand Orchards, Inc., shipped a consignment of 750 boxes of pears to the Pacific Brokerage Company to be sold on commission. The pears were sold by the Pacific Brokerage Company as reported on the account sales below. You are to complete the account sales by showing (a) the commission, which is 7% of the total receipts, (b) the total charges, and (c) the net proceeds.

PACIFIC BROKERAGE COMPANY
541 Front Street, San Francisco, California 94104

NO. __1341__

DATE __Sept. 10__ 19 __--__

SALES FOR THE ACCOUNT OF   Durand Orchards, Inc.

Sunnyvale, CA 94086

Sept.	7	400 Boxes Pears		6	50	2,600	00
	9	350 Boxes Pears		6	25	2,187	50
						4,787	50
		EXPRESS					
		FREIGHT					
		DRAYAGE		134	70		
		STORAGE		98	40		
		COMMISSION ____					
		TOTAL CHARGES		....	...	....	...
		NET PROCEEDS				....	...

2. The schedule at the right shows the gross sales, the percent commission, and the other charges involved in four sales. You are to show (a) the amount of each commission, and (b) the net proceeds.

| NO. | GROSS SALES | COMMISSION | | OTHER CHARGES | NET PROCEEDS |
		PERCENT	AMOUNT		
1.	$ 473.28	9%		$23.68	
2.	1,742.65	10%		56.27	
3.	1,321.65	7%		69.29	
4.	856.16	8%		82.42	

ACCOUNT PURCHASE

ATLANTA, GA July 20, 19--

PURCHASE OF MERCHANDISE

FOR ACCOUNT OF   Dixie Food Markets
Chattanooga, TN 37401

BY Clifton Frazier

July 19 300 boxes peaches	@3.25	975.00	
50 crates cantaloupes	@4.85	242.50	1,217.50
Charges:			
Freight		49.72	
Commission, 5% of 1,217.50		··········	··········
Total charged to your account			··········

3. Clifton Frazier, agent, located in Atlanta, Georgia, purchases and sends to the Dixie Food Markets, Chattanooga, Tenn., 300 boxes of peaches and 50 crates of cantaloupes. With the shipment he sends the statement or account purchase at the left. The account purchase shows the total cost of the purchase to the Dixie Food Markets, including the freight on the shipment and the agent's commission, which is 5% of the total price of the items purchased.

You are to enter on the account purchase (a) the amount of the commission, (b) the total of freight and commission (enter in right-hand column), and (c) the total charged to the account of Dixie Food Markets.

Section 67. (concluded)

4. On May 23, Paul Seim, agent located in Milwaukee, Wisconsin, purchases and sends to Fisher & Sons, Madison, WI 53704, 750 lbs. cheese @ $.53, and 80 crates celery @ $3.60.

Freight charges on the shipment amount to $27.51. Seim's commission is 6% of the total price of the goods bought. With this information you are to complete the account purchase at the right which Mr. Seim sends to Fisher & Sons. The account purchase should be dated May 23.

Use the form shown in Problem 3 as a guide.

```
ACCOUNT PURCHASE

PURCHASE OF MERCHANDISE

        FOR ACCOUNT OF

BY
_____

    Charges:




    Total charged to your account
```

NO.	PRIME COST	COMMISSION		OTHER CHARGES	GROSS COSTS
		PERCENT	AMOUNT		
1	$ 453.35	7%		$ 15.72	
2	867.24	8%		36.86	
3	3,453.81	6%		132.14	
4	1,242.56	5%		58.74	

5. The schedule at the left shows the prime cost, the percent commission, and the other charges involved in four purchases. You are to show (a) the amount of each commission, and (b) the gross cost.

UNIT FIFTEEN   The Manufacturer

SECTION 68.   Figuring Cost of Manufacturing

In a manufacturing plant, raw materials or partly manufactured goods are made into finished products. The cost of the finished product consists of the cost of the raw materials, direct labor, and factory expense or overhead.

Direct labor means the wages of the skilled mechanics or other workers who work directly on the finished product as it moves through the factory.

Factory overhead, or factory expense, includes those production expenses that cannot be charged directly to a particular product; for example, taxes, rent, depreciation, insurance, power, heat, maintenance, and salaries paid to superintendents and foremen. The sum of the costs of the materials, direct labor, and factory expense gives the total factory cost.

For each order moving through the factory, a record is kept of the cost of the materials used and the direct labor, and an estimate is made of the factory expense, so that the total cost of filing the order may be known.

Department expense records are also kept by apportioning the factory expense to each factory department. The basis of the apportionment depends upon the type of expense to be distributed. The cost of the factory rent is usually distributed on the basis of the floor space each department occupies.

For example, the Siebert Manufacturing Co. pays $6,400 rent a year on its factory. It has 9,600 sq. ft. of floor space divided into the following departments: Dept. A, 3,600 sq. ft.; Dept. B, 3,000 sq. ft.; Dept. C, 1,800 sq. ft.; Dept. D, 1,200 sq. ft. The rent is apportioned as follows:

Dept. A $\frac{3,600}{9,600}$ or $\frac{3}{8} \times \$6,400 = \$2,400$ Dept. C $\frac{1,800}{9,600}$ or $\frac{3}{16} \times \$6,400 = \$1,200$

Dept. B $\frac{3,000}{9,600}$ or $\frac{5}{16} \times \$6,400 = \$2,000$ Dept. D $\frac{1,200}{9,600}$ or $\frac{1}{8} \times \$6,400 = \$800$

EXERCISE.   (Practical problems)

1. Itemized at the right are the costs of making 50 shirts in a factory. You are to find (a) direct labor cost, (b) factory expense, and (c) total cost of manufacturing the 50 shirts.

Raw materials..........................	$256.72
Direct labor	
32 hours @ $3.24 =	
28 hours @ 2.90 =	
$18\frac{1}{2}$ hours @ 3.06 =	
9 hours @ 3.35 =	
Direct labor cost =	
Factory expense, 25% of direct labor =	
Total cost of manufacturing 50 shirts =	

2. The costs to manufacture 250 dozen novelty flower holders were: raw materials, $490; direct labor, $660; factory expense at 10% of the combined cost of the direct labor and materials. (a) The total factory cost was $_____. (b) The factory cost per dozen was $_____.

Name _____

Section 68. (continued)

3. The Brooks Tool Co. pays $18,000 a year rent for its factory. This building has an area of 15,000 sq. ft. divided into four departments as follows: Dept. A, 6,000 sq. ft.; Dept. B, 4,500 sq. ft.; Dept. C, 2,500 sq. ft.; Dept. D, 2,000 sq. ft. You are to show in the correct spaces below (a) the fractional part to be apportioned to each department and (b) the actual amount apportioned to each department.

	FRACTION IN LOWEST TERMS	TOTAL RENT	DEPARTMENTAL RENT
Dept. A $\frac{6,000}{15,000}$ or	_____	× $18,000 =	_____
Dept. B $\frac{4,500}{15,000}$ or	_____	× $18,000 =	_____
Dept. C $\frac{2,500}{15,000}$ or	_____	× $18,000 =	_____
Dept. D $\frac{2,000}{15,000}$ or	_____	× $18,000 =	_____

4. When the factory building is owned instead of rented, the depreciation, taxes, and insurance on the factory are distributed on the same basis as rent would be; that is, according to floor space. Depreciation on the factory of the Auto Parts Co., built at a cost of $225,000, is estimated to be $9,000 annually. The factory contains three departments with the following floor space: Dept. A, 18,000 sq. ft.; Dept. B, 15,000 sq. ft.; Dept. C, 7,000 sq. ft. You are to show in the proper spaces below (a) the fractional relationship of each department's floor space to total floor space, (b) the fraction in lowest terms, and (c) the depreciation apportioned to each department.

	FRACTIONAL RELATIONSHIP TO TOTAL FLOOR SPACE	FRACTION IN LOWEST TERMS	TOTAL DEPRECIATION	DEPARTMENTAL DEPRECIATION
Dept. A	$\frac{18,000}{\dots\dots}$ or	_____	× $_____	= $_____
Dept. B	$\frac{15,000}{\dots\dots}$ or	_____	× $_____	= $_____
Dept. C	$\frac{7,000}{\dots\dots}$ or	_____	× $_____	= $_____

5. A factory has three departments with machinery valued as follows: Dept. A, $27,000; Dept. B, $18,000; Dept. C, $15,000. Taxes on this machinery are $2,500, and are apportioned on the basis of the value of the machinery in each department. You are to show in the correct spaces below (a) the fractional relationship of each department's machinery valuation to the total, (b) the fraction in lowest terms, and (c) the tax apportioned to each department.

	FRACTIONAL RELATIONSHIP TO TOTAL	FRACTION IN LOWEST TERMS	TOTAL TAX	DEPARTMENTAL TAX
Dept. A	$\frac{27,000}{\dots\dots}$ or	_____	× $2,500	= $_____
Dept. B	$\frac{18,000}{\dots\dots}$ or	_____	× $2,500	= $_____
Dept. C	$\frac{15,000}{\dots\dots}$ or	_____	× $2,500	= $_____

Many kinds of manufacturing equipment depreciate more during the first years of use than during the later years of use. Thus, some manufacturers like to use methods of depreciation which allow higher amounts of depreciation during the early years of the life of their equipment. One such method is called the *sum-of-the-years-digits method*.

Suppose that you expect a hydraulic lift, which originally cost $10,000, to be used five years and then traded in for $4,000. The total depreciation would be $6,000. Using the sum-of-the-years-digits method, you would add: 1 year + 2 years + 3 years + 4 years + 5 years = 15 years. Then you would depreciate the lift $\frac{5}{15}$ of $6,000, or $2,000, the first year; $\frac{4}{15}$ of $6,000, or $1,600, the second year; $\frac{3}{15}$ of $6,000, or $1,200, the third year; and so on. For example:

$10,000 − $4,000 = $6,000 total depreciation
1 + 2 + 3 + 4 + 5 = 15 years
$\frac{5}{15}$ × $6,000 = $2,000 depreciation, end of first year
$10,000 − $2,000 = $8,000 book value, end of first year
$\frac{4}{15}$ × $6,000 = $1,600 depreciation, end of second year
$8,000 − $1,600 = $6,400 book value, end of second year

The original cost of an item less the total depreciation to date is called the *book value*.

EXERCISE. (Practical problems)

1. The Nadler Tool Corporation purchases a large electric motor for $15,000. They estimate that the motor will be used for four years and then traded in for $5,000. Using the sum-of-the-years-digits method, find the amount of depreciation for the first year $_____, second year $_____, third year $_____, fourth year $_____.

2. Your company buys an automatic press for $60,000. The company plans to use the press for six years and then trade it in for $18,000. Using the sum-of-the-years-digits method, the total amount the press is estimated to depreciate for the first three years is $_____.

3. The Blandford Company buys three delivery trucks for $5,000 each. The company estimates that they will use the trucks three years and then trade them in for $2,300 each. Using the sum-of-the-years-digits method, the book value of the three trucks at the end of the second year will be $_____.

SECTION 69. Pricing Manufactured Articles

A manufacturer's gross profit on an article is found by subtracting the cost (factory cost) from the selling price. The net profit is found by subtracting the selling and administrative expenses from the gross profit.

Selling Price − Cost = Gross Profit

Gross Profit − Selling and Administrative Expenses = Net Profit

The manufacturer determines the selling price of an article the same way a retailer does.

For example, the cost of manufacturing a certain radio is $21, and the manufacturer wants to make a gross profit equal to $33\frac{1}{3}\%$ of the cost. The calculation of the selling price would be:

$$\$21 + 33\tfrac{1}{3}\% \text{ of } \$21 = \$21 + \$7 = \$28, \text{ selling price}$$

● If the manufacturer desires a gross profit equal to 25% of the selling price, the calculation would be:

$$\$21 \div (100\% - 25\%) = \$21 \div 75\% = \$28, \text{ selling price}$$

● The manufacturer's list price or catalog price is determined by dividing the selling price in dollars by the selling price expressed as a percent of the list price. For example, if the manufacturer desires to get $28 for a radio after allowing the dealer a discount of 30% from the list price, $28, is 70% of the list price (100% − 30% = 70%). The calculation of the list price would be:

$$\$28 \div 70\% = \$28 \div .7 = \$40, \text{ list price}$$

EXERCISE.   (Practical problems)

1. A manufacturer sells workbenches at $34.60 each. The manufacturing costs per bench are: material, $9.22; labor, $11.43; overhead, $6.77. (a) The factory cost per bench is $_____. (b) The manufacturer's gross profit per bench is $_____.

2. Posters that a manufacturer sells at $6 a dozen cost $2.80 a dozen to make. The manufacturer estimates the selling and administrative expenses at 23% of the selling price. The net profit per dozen is $_____.

3. In filling an order for 940 hats at $3.75 each, the manufacturer had the following manufacturing costs: material, $832.26; labor, $942.68; overhead, $312.90. (a) The manufacturer's gross profit on the order was $_____. (b) The average factory cost per hat was $_____.

4. A manufacturer sells a desk lamp at $15, less $33\frac{1}{3}\%$ and 10%. The manufacturing costs are: materials, $2.25; labor, $2.70; overhead, $.90. The selling and administrative expenses amount to 28% of the selling price. The manufacturer's rate of net profit on the selling price is _____%.

5. At the factory of the Brockton Company the factory cost of a certain picture frame is $4.50. To make a gross profit of 28% on the cost, the company should sell the picture frame at $_____.

● **6.** The factory cost of a stepladder is $6.46. If the manufacturer desires 32% gross profit on the selling price, the selling price of the stepladder should be $_____.

● **7.** The Republic Electric Manufacturing Company manufactures a motor on which it wants to realize a gross profit of 24% of the selling price after allowing the dealer 20% discount on the catalog price. The factory cost of the motor is $15.20. (a) The company should sell the motor for $_____. (b) The motor should be listed in the company's catalog at $_____.

● **8.** The factory cost, desired percent of profit on selling price, and the trade discounts to be allowed on four articles produced by the Kendall Manufacturing Corporation are given below. For each article you are to show (a) the appropriate selling price and (b) the catalog price.

STOCK NUMBER	FACTORY COST	DESIRED GROSS PROFIT ON SELLING PRICE	SELLING PRICE	TRADE DISCOUNT	CATALOG PRICE
1.	$13.50	25%		25%	
2.	14.56	35%		30%	
3.	17.85	30%		25% and 20%	
4.	30.52	20%		20% and 12½%	

● **9.** It costs $16.56 to manufacture and sell a particular rifle. The manufacturer desires to make a net profit of 8% on the selling price after allowing trade discounts of 20% and 10%. The rifle should be listed in the manufacturer's catalog at $_____.

● **10.** A manufacturer sells radios to retail dealers at $10 less 35%. To reduce the invoice price to $5.85, he must allow an additional discount of _____%.

UNIT SIXTEEN   Special Business and Farm Problems

SECTION 70.   Office Costs

Although businesses differ greatly, they all have some type of office operations which cost money. There are different types of costs in the office. Items such as desks and calculators (office equipment) have a long life and depreciate in value each year. The depreciation of such items is part of the office costs.

Items such as pencils and paper are quickly used up and are called office supplies. The value of the office supplies used is a cost of the office. Often the greatest office cost is labor, sometimes comprising 70 percent or more of the total office budget.

EXERCISE.   (Practical problems)

1. Leonard Beacon, manager of a branch office, wanted to compare his yearly office costs, excluding labor, per employee with the company average of $1,560. There were 25 employees in the office including Mr. Beacon. Office space was rented for $2,000 a month. There was $20,000 of office equipment which Mr. Beacon estimated would last an average of 5 years. The yearly budget for office supplies was $7,500. The average yearly office cost per employee was (more or less) _____ than the company average. It was $ _____ (more or less).

2. Sally Werner, a clerk in a local business firm, earns $3.50 per hour. In addition, fringe benefits, such as insurance and retirement benefits, amount to an extra 25% of her cash wage. Miss Werner is paid for 2,080 hours of work during one year. Her cash wage for the year amounts to $_____. Her total wage, including fringe benefits, is $_____.

3. A computer office manager needs five keypunch stations. The cost of each station includes:
Wages: 1,760 hours per year @ $3.40 per hour
Space: 90 square feet @ $21.50 per square foot per year
Keypunch rental: $92 per month
Supplies: $750 per year

The total yearly cost of the five keypunch stations is $_____.

4. In figuring his yearly office budget, Denver Lawrence allotted 75% of the total budget to employee labor expense; 15% to rent, heat, and light; and 10% to office supplies, telephone, and postage. If the yearly budget was $20,000, Mr. Lawrence allotted $_____ for labor; $_____ for rent, heat, and light; and $_____ for office supplies.

5. The Wilson Research Company pays 5¢ per page for its office copying machine. In addition, paper costs $5 a ream (500 sheets). A local printer offers to print 100 copies of a 50-page report for a price of $225. Should Wilson go to the printer or use its own machine? _____.

SECTION 71. Distributing Partnership Income

Many small businesses are organized as partnerships. A partnership agreement should specify the investment, duties, and responsibilities of each partner. It should also describe the way in which the net income (net profit) or net loss is to be distributed among the partners.

EXERCISE. (Practical problems)

1. Saban and Cohn are partners in a wholesale jewelry business. Their partnership agreement provides that net income shall be shared in the ratio of 8 to 7 in favor of Saban. This means that the net income is to be divided into fifteen equal parts, with eight parts going to Saban and seven to Cohn. In sharing a profit of $18,000, Saban will receive $_____, and Cohn will receive $_____.

2. Reed and Butler are partners sharing profits and losses in proportion to their investments. Reed's investment is $18,000, and Butler's is $14,000. A profit of $22,000 is to be divided between the partners. You are to show in the proper spaces below (a) the fractional relationship of each partner's investment to the total investment, (b) the fraction in lowest terms, (c) the total profit to be divided, and (d) each partner's share of the profit.

	FRACTIONAL RELATIONSHIP TO TOTAL		FRACTION IN LOWEST TERMS	TOTAL PROFIT	PARTNER'S SHARE OF PROFIT
Reed	$\frac{18,000}{\cdots}$	or	____ ×	____ =	____
Butler	$\frac{14,000}{\cdots}$	or	____ ×	____ =	____

3. Haney and Mills are partners in a retail business with investments of $36,000 and $48,000, respectively. Their agreement provides that the net income is to be divided by allowing each partner 10% interest annually on his investment and dividing the remainder of the net income equally. At the end of one year, the net income to be divided between the partners is $39,000. In the spaces in the form at the right, you are to show (a) each partner's interest on investment and the total of the interest, (b) each

PARTNER	INTEREST ON INVESTMENT	SHARE OF REMAINDER	TOTAL SHARE OF NET INCOME
Haney			
Mills			
TOTALS			

partner's share of the remainder and the total remainder, and (c) each partner's total share of the net income and the total net income.

4. In the partnership of Turco and Reese, a net profit of $22,700 for one year is to be divided between the partners in the following manner: (A) Turco is to be allowed an annual salary of $9,600, and Reese, $7,800; (B) the remainder of the net profit is to be shared equally. (a) On this basis, Turco's total share of the net profit is $_____. (b) Reese's total share is $_____.

SECTION 72. Distributing Corporation Income

A large business is usually organized as a corporation. Capital for establishing the business is obtained from the sale of shares of capital stock. The net income of a corporation is distributed among the shareholders in the form of dividends. Usually, only a part of the net income is distributed to the shareholders. The remainder is kept in a retained earnings account for future emergencies.

A cooperative, such as a farmers' cooperative, is a corporation that is owned by its patrons. The net income is divided among the shareholders in two parts. One part is in the form of a dividend on the capital stock. The other part is in the form of a patronage or participation dividend that is based on the amount of business the shareholder has done with the cooperative.

EXERCISE. (Practical problems)

1. The outstanding capital stock of the Banfill Corporation consists of 250,000 shares, each with a par value of $10. For the first quarter of the current year, the corporation's net income is $81,462.17. The directors vote to pay a quarterly dividend of $1\frac{1}{2}\%$ of the capital stock to the shareholders and to keep the remainder of the income in the retained earnings account. (a) The total par value of the 250,000 shares of stock is $_____. (b) The total dividend paid to the shareholders amounts to $_____. (c) The amount of income kept in the retained earnings account is $_____.

2. A corporation with 250,000 shares of capital stock outstanding earns in one quarter a net income of $87,465.13. The directors vote to pay the regular quarterly dividend of 25 cents a share and to keep the remainder of the profit in the retained earnings account. (a) The total dividend paid to the shareholders amounts to $_____. (b) The amount kept in the retained earnings account is $_____.

3. The outstanding capital stock of the Bowmar-Regis Company consists of 25,000 shares of 6% preferred stock (par value $50) and 50,000 shares of common stock (no-par-value). For the first half of the year, the corporation's net income is $87,511.71. The directors declare the regular 3% semiannual dividend on the preferred stock, a dividend of 40¢ a share on the common, and vote to keep the remainder of the income in the retained earnings account. (a) The total dividend on the preferred stock is $_____. (b) The total dividend on the common stock is $_____. (c) The amount kept in the retained earnings account is $_____.

4. Peter Howell owns 50 shares of the preferred stock and 80 shares of the common stock referred to in Problem 3. The total dividend he should receive is $_____.

5. At the end of one year's operations, the directors of the Concord Retail Cooperative declare a 6% dividend on the capital stock and a 5% patronage dividend to the store's customers. Henry Simpson, a farmer, owns 45 shares of the capital stock, par value $10 per share, and during the year has purchased $818.20 worth of goods from the cooperative. He should receive a total dividend amounting to $_____.

SECTION 73. Problems of the Farmer

The efficient farmer keeps a complete, accurate record of farm income and expenses. In this way the net profit or loss for the farm can be determined as a whole for each kind of product raised.

EXERCISE. (Practical problems)

1. During one year, Evan Long, a farmer had the following farm income: produce sales, $15,605; milk sales, $7,860; miscellaneous farm income, $4,290. His farm expenses for the year were: hired labor, $4,322; fertilizer, $2,103; seeds and plants, $2,063; feed, $1,575; fuel and oil, $925; taxes and insurance, $750; repairs and depreciation, $1,782; interest expense, $485; other expenses, $820. (a) The gross farm income for the year was $_____. (b) The net farm income was $_____.

2. On an 80-acre orchard, Lucy Denton harvested 1,628 bushels of lemons and sold the entire crop at $8.25 a bushel. Production, harvesting, and marketing costs were: land use, $884; spraying, $1,160; labor, $4,265; equipment rental, $565; interest, $151; storing and selling, $658. Her net profit on the entire crop was $_____.

3. In Problem 2, (a) the net profit per bushel was $_____, and (b) the net profit per acre was $_____.

4. A farmer is considering the profitability of using five acres of his land for the production of onions. He estimates that the land will yield an average of 320 bags (50 lb. per bag) per acre, that production expenses up to the time of harvest will average $874 per acre, and that the cost of harvesting and marketing the crop will average $2.10 a bag. He also estimates that the maximum market price of the onions will be about $4.75 a bag. (a) In order that he may meet expenses, or break even, the market price would have to be $_____ a bag. (b) On the basis of the foregoing estimates, would the onion enterprise be a profitable undertaking? _____.

5. Milt Barnes, a poultry farmer, has five crates of eggs to sell to retailers. Each crate contains 30 dozen eggs. The local price of the eggs is $13.20 a crate, whereas the price in a nearby city is 53¢ a dozen. If he ships the eggs to the city, transportation and other expenses will cost him $1.15 a crate. (a) Would he gain or lose by shipping the five crates to the city rather than selling them locally? _____. (b) How much would he gain or lose? $_____

UNIT SEVENTEEN   Metric and United States Measurements

SECTION 74.   The United States System

A denominate number is one that specifies a certain number of units of measure, such as 3 feet, 9 gallons, 7 pounds, etc. In working with denominate numbers, you will frequently find it necessary to change units of one denomination to units of a lower or higher denomination. To do this you must be familiar with the various standard tables of weights and measures. It is strongly advised that you obtain and memorize the commonly used tables in the same manner that you have memorized the multiplication table.

DRILL 96.   (Changing denominate numbers to lower denominations)

A denominate number is changed to units of lower denomination by multiplication. Thus, since 1 ft. = 12 in., the number of inches in 7 ft. = $7 \times 12 = 84$ in. The number of inches in 7 ft. 5 in. = $(7 \times 12) + 5 = 89$ in.

Change each of the following to the denomination indicated and write your answer in the space provided.

1. 8 ft. 10 in. = _____ in.   5. 9 bu. 3 pk. = _____ pk.   9. 4 lb.   7 oz. = _____ oz.
2. 11 yd. 2 ft. = _____ ft.   6. 7 bu. 2 pk. = _____ qt.   10. 4 min. 20 sec. = _____ sec.
3. 7 qt. 1 pt. = _____ pt.   7. 5 qt. 1 pt. = _____ pt.   11. 2 hr. 45 min. = _____ min.
4. 6 pk. 5 qt. = _____ qt.   8. 4 gal. 3 qt. = _____ qt.   12. 10 da. 8 hr. = _____ hr.

DRILL 97.   (Changing denominate numbers to higher denominations)

A denominate number is changed to units of higher denomination by division. Thus, since 12 in. = 1 ft., the number of feet in 84 in. = $84 \div 12 = 7$ ft. The number of feet and inches in 89 in. = $89 \div 12 = 7$ ft. 5 in.

Change each of the following to the denominations indicated and write your answer in the spaces provided.

1. 75 in. = ____ ft. ____ in.   5. 35 pk. = ____ bu. ____ pk.   9. 100 oz. = ____ lb. _____ oz.
2. 40 ft. = ____ yd. ____ ft.   6. 152 qt. = ____ bu. ____ pk.   10. 425 sec. = ____ min. _____ sec.
3. 27 pt. = ____ qt. ____ pt.   7. 19 pt. = ____ qt. ____ pt.   11. 375 min. = ____ hr. _____ min.
4. 69 qt. = ____ pk. ____ qt.   8. 50 qt. = ____ gal. ____ qt.   12. 130 hr. = ____ da. _____ hr.

DRILL 98.   (Addition of denominate numbers)

It is sometimes necessary to add two or more denominate numbers, such as 5 ft. 9 in.; 4 ft. 8 in.; and 3 ft. 10 in. The numbers of the same denominations are written in the same column, as shown in the solution at the right, and then added. Since the sum of the inches column, 27, is equal to 2 ft. 3 in. (27 in. ÷ 12), the final result is 14 ft. 3 in.

5 ft.	9 in.
4	8
3	10
12 ft.	27 in.
14 ft.	3 in.

Find the sum in each of the following problems.

1. 8 ft. 7 in.   2. 6 lb. 12 oz.   3. 2 yd. 1 ft. 11 in.   4. 3 bu. 3 pk. 7 qt.
   3   11   4   9   5   2   9   9   1   2
   5   3   7   14   3   2   10   4   2   4

DRILL 99. (Subtraction of denominate numbers)

```
      8      17
      9 ft.   5 in.
      2      10
      6 ft.   7 in.
```

Denominate numbers are subtracted in the manner shown at the left, which shows the subtraction of 2 ft. 10 in. from 9 ft. 5 in. Since 10 in. cannot be subtracted from 5 in., one foot (12 in.) is borrowed from 9 ft. and added to 5 in., making the new minuend 8 ft. 17 in., from which 2 ft. 10 in. may be subtracted, leaving 6 ft. 7 in. as the remainder.

Perform subtraction in each of the following and write the remainder.

1. 8 ft. 2 in.
   3   9

2. 11 lb. 3 oz.
   2   9

3. 7 yd. 1 ft. 4 in.
   4   2   9

4. 12 bu. 2 pk. 3 qt.
   7   3   6

DRILL 100. (Multiplication of denominate numbers)

The procedure for multiplying a denominate number is indicated by the illustration at the right, which shows the multiplication of 13 ft. 7 in. by 4. As indicated, each part of the denominate number is multiplied separately by the multiplier. Since the product in the inches column, 28, is equal to 2 ft. 4 in. (28÷12), the final result is 54 ft. 4 in.

```
13 ft.   7 in.
          4
52 ft.  28 in.
54 ft.   4 in.
```

Perform multiplication in each of the following problems.

1. 3 ft. 5 in.
          5

2. 3 yd. 2 ft.
          7

3. 6 pk. 5 qt.
          4

4. 2 gal. 3 qt.
          9

5. 6 lb. 7 oz.
          8

6. 3 yd. 2 ft. 11 in.
              4

7. 2 bu. 3 pk. 7 qt.
              3

8. 4 gal. 3 qt. 1 pt.
                5

DRILL 101. (Division of denominate numbers)

```
          41
4 ) 11 ft.  5 in.
    2 ft. 10¼ in.
```

The method of dividing a denominate number is shown at the left, which shows the division of 11 ft. 5 in. by 4. Beginning at the left, each part of the denominate number is divided separately by the divisor. Thus, 11 ft. divided by 4 gives 2 ft. for the quotient in the first column, with a remainder of 3 ft. The remainder, 3 ft., is changed to 36 in., and then added to 5 in., giving 41 in. Dividing 41 in. by 4 gives 10¼ in. for the quotient in the inches column.

Divide each of the following problems.

1. 3) 28 ft. 9 in.

2. 8) 42 ft. 5 in.

3. 4) 35 qt. 1 pt.

4. 12) 15 lb. 6 oz.

5. 2) 7 yd. 2 ft. 3 in.

6. 4) 15 yd. 1 ft. 9 in.

7. 5) 19 gal. 1 qt. 1 pt.

SECTION 75. The Metric System: Length and Distance

The basic unit of length or distance in the metric system is the meter (m). The meter is equivalent to about 39.37 inches in the United States system, or slightly more than one yard. In the metric system each unit is 10 times less than the next higher unit and 10 times more than the next lower unit. For example, the meter equals 10 decimeters (dm). It also equals one-tenth of one dekameter (dam) and .001 kilometers (km). In the same way, one decimeter equals 10 centimeters (cm), and one centimeter equals 10 millimeters (mm). One meter, then equals 10 × 10 × 10 or 1 000 millimeters. A space is used to separate large numbers into groups. The comma, where used, is recognized as a decimal point.

DRILL 102. (Equivalent metric measurements)

In the following problems, write the value of the missing number.

a 1 meter = _____ centimeters   **e** 1 decimeter = ____ meters   **i** 10 millimeters = _____ meters

b 20 dekameters = ___ hectometers   **f** .3 decimeters = ___ centimeters   **j** 2 kilometers = _____ meters

c 5 m = _____ cm   **g** 400 mm = ___ m   **k** 3 500 m = _____ km

d .05 dm = ___ mm   **h** .008 km = ___ m   **l** 16 000 mm = ____ m

DRILL 103. (Adding, subtracting, multiplying, and dividing metric numbers)

To add, subtract, multiply, or divide metric values, first express the values in equivalent units. Then, perform the arithmetic as you would with other decimal values. For example, to subtract .08 meters from 150 millimeters, convert the .08 meters to the equivalent in millimeters (80), then subtract:

$$\begin{array}{r} 150 \text{ mm} \\ - 80 \text{ mm} \\ \hline 70 \text{ mm} \end{array}$$

1. Add each of the following problems.

a 2.5 km + .8 km = _____ km   **c** 2.7 m + 350 cm = _____ cm   **e** 52 km + 29 km + 620 m = _____ km

b 4.75 m + 8.50 m = _____ m   **d** 1 500 mm + 3.2 m = _____ m **f** 2.5 m + 750 cm + 1 250 mm = _____ m

2. Subtract each of the following problems.

a 8.92 m − 6.48 m = _____ m   **c** 4.25 m − 315 cm = _____ cm   **e** .03 km − 22.7 m = _____ m

b 12.47 km − 9.62 km = _____ km   **d** 1 650 mm − 1.25 m = _____ mm **f** 772 cm − 5 280 mm = _____ mm

3. Multiply each of the following problems.

a 4.25 m × 4 = ___ m   **b** 22.7 cm × 5 = _____ cm   **c** 500 m × 20 = ___ km   **d** 75 cm × 50 = _____ m

4. Divide each of the following problems.

a 50 m ÷ 4 = _____ m   **b** 1 600 km ÷ 4 = _____ km   **c** 8 000 mm ÷ 100 = ___ mm   **d** 2 km ÷ 5 = _____ m

EXERCISE. (Practical problems)

1. Rita Long bought several pieces of fabric to use in her sewing. She bought 2.5 meters of wool, 3.25 meters of cotton, 4.35 meters of denim, and 1.75 meters of tweed. How many meters did she buy all together? _____ .

2. Fred Owens and his family took a winter cruise. After they returned, Mr. Owens wanted to find out the total distance they had traveled on their vacation. He estimated that they had driven 175 kilometers, flown 1 250 kilometers and sailed on a ship for 2 125 kilometers. How many kilometers did they travel in total? _____ .

3. A new coil of electric wire was 300 meters in length. Pieces of wire of the following lengths were cut off and sold at 45¢ per meter: 33 meters, 16.5 meters, 50 meters, and 68 meters.
   a How many meters of wire were sold? _____ m .
   b What was the total selling price of the wire that was sold? $ _____ .
   c How much wire was left in the coil? _____ m .

4. Carl Garrett planned to put a fence around the outside of his property. In looking at the plan of his lot, he found that each of the two sides of the lot measured 37.5 meters in length. One end was 22.5 meters long, and the other end was 25.2 meters long. The sidewalk and driveway entrances, a length of 5.2 meters, were not to be fenced. If the fence Mr. Garrett used cost $2.70 per meter, how much did the fence cost? $ _____ .

5. Sara Knight knew that the distance of a trip from her home to Chicago was 780 kilometers. Before starting the trip, Sara wrote down that the car had traveled 25 732 kilometers according to the odometer on the instrument panel. At the end of the first day of her trip, Sara found that the odometer read 26 151 kilometers. How far from Chicago was she at that time? _____ km .

6. Hale Cline wanted to see how far he walked when he mowed his lawn. His front yard was 35 meters wide, and he crossed it 25 times when mowing it. The back yard was only 25 meters wide, but he had to cross it 42 times to mow it. Each of the two sides was 15 meters long and required 10 trips with the mower. How many kilometers did Mr. Cline walk to mow the lawn? _____ km .

Section 75. (concluded)

7. A pile of duplicator paper is 1.8 meters high. If a ream (500 sheets) of the paper measures 4.5 centimeters in height, (a) how many reams of paper are there in the pile? _____. (b) How many sheets of paper are there in the pile? _____.

8. Ken Porter, owner of an art gallery, bought three new paintings. One painting measured 75 cm × 80 cm, one measured 1 m on each side, and the third was 120 cm × 125 cm. If Mr. Porter were to buy framing wood for the three pictures, how many meters would he need? _____ m. At $2.50 per meter, how much would it cost Mr. Porter to frame the three pictures? $_____.

9. Leonard Denton, a salesman, planned an automobile sales trip of 2 200 kilometers. Making two sales calls a day, he could drive 200 kilometers each day. Mr. Denton estimated it would cost him $35 per day for motels and food. Mr. Denton's car got 25 km to a gallon of gas. If gas cost 55¢ per gallon, what would be the total cost of the sales trip? $_____.

10. Four-inch by six-inch cards are used for many personal and business records. If one inch is approximately equal to 2.5 centimeters, what is the approximate size of those cards when expressed in the metric system? _____

11. In track and field meets, some events are measured using the metric system and some using the United States system. Mount Henry High School wanted to measure all events according to the metric system.

a How many meters would there be in a 100-yard dash? (1 meter = 1.09 yards) _____ m.
b If Clayton Harris high-jumped 6 feet 2 inches, how many centimeters high did he jump? (1 centimeter = .39 inches). _____ cm.

12. Mount Henry High School (see problem above) competed against Chilton Central School in a track meet. Chilton preferred to keep records by the United States system. In the pole vault, Sam Myers of Mount Henry vaulted 4.25 meters high. Phil Larsen of Chilton vaulted 14 feet 5 inches. Who won the event? (1 meter = 39.37 inches). _____.

SECTION 76. The Metric System: Capacity and Weight

The liter (l) is the basic metric measurement of capacity. A liter is slightly more than one quart. The most commonly used metric measures of capacity are the milliliter (ml) and the liter (1 liter = 1 000 milliliters). Other subdivisions and multiples of the liter are identified by the same prefixes as those used with the meter (deci, deka, etc.). A part of a liter is usually expressed as a common or decimal fraction of a liter. For example, 750 milliliters would be expressed as .75 liters or as $\frac{3}{4}$ liter.

DRILL 104. (Arithmetic with metric measures of capacity)

Do the following. Use the space at the right for calculations.

1. 625 ml + 120 ml + 55 ml + 810 ml + 440 ml = _____ ml = _____ l

2. 6.30 l + 750 ml + 2.75 l + 1 550 ml = _____ l

3. 722 ml − 436 ml = _____ ml

4. 7.85 l − 860 ml = _____ l

5. 65 l × 5 = _____ l

6. 850 ml × 7 = _____ ml = _____ l

7. 1 230 ml ÷ 30 = _____ ml

8. 7.5 l ÷ 25 = _____ l = _____ ml

EXERCISE 1. (Practical problems)

1. On a trip to visit their son, Mr. and Mrs. Nelson stopped for gas five times, buying the following quantities: 62.5 liters; 73.35 liters; 58.4 liters; 68.95 liters; and 66.8 liters. At 14¢ per liter, how much did the Nelsons spend for gas? $_____ If they traveled a total of 2 310 kilometers, how many kilometers per liter did they average? _____ km

2. Harvey Fenwick delivers fuel oil to his customers in a truck which will hold 5.95 kiloliters. If each of his customers has a tank holding 850 liters, how many customers can Mr. Fenwick serve without refilling his tank? _____

3. In comparing the prices of different sizes of the same product, Mrs. Wills saw that a one liter container cost $1.49 and a 250 ml jar cost 40¢. Which should Mrs. Wills buy to save money? _____

Section 76. (continued)

4. In order to save money when building his new home, Matt Gregory decided to paint some of the rooms himself. He figured that he would need 6.2 liters of paint for the living room, 4.7 liters for the dining room, 5.8 liters for the kitchen and 15.7 liters for the bedroom. The local hardware store normally charged $2.80 per liter for paint. Because of the large quantity Mr. Gregory bought, the store gave him a 15% discount. How much did Mr. Gregory save? $_____.

5. On an automobile trip, Arnie Crawford traveled 1 220 kilometers and used 182 liters of gasoline. To the nearest mile, how many miles did Mr. Crawford travel per gallon of gas? (1 km = .62 miles; 1 liter = .26 gallons) _____ miles.

6. In her home, Mary Stewart used 3,560 gallons of fuel oil during the year. In her office, Mary Stewart used 1,874 gallons. At 3.2¢ per liter, how much did Mary spend all year for fuel oil (1 liter = .26 gallons)? $_____.

The most commonly used metric measurement of weight is the kilogram (kg). A kilogram is about 2.2 United States pounds. As with length or distance and capacity, the same prefixes (milli, centi, etc.) are used. The kilogram, therefore, is 1 000 grams. The gram (g) is another common metric unit and equals about $\frac{1}{28}$ of a U. S. ounce.

DRILL 105 . (Arithmetic with metric units of weight)

Do the following. Use the space at the right for calculations.

1. 4 kilograms + 16 kilograms + 2.5 kilograms = _____ kilograms

2. 25 grams + .5 grams + 2.25 grams = _____ grams

3. 560 g + 1.2 kg + 1 220 g + 2.82 kg = _____ kg

4. 27.3 kg + 2 430 g + 3.4 kg + 28 400 mg = _____ g

5. 1 530 g − 780 g = _____ g

6. 2.72 kg − 1 340 g = _____ kg

7. 3.8 kg × 4 = _____ kg

8. 3 420 g × 8 = _____ kg

9. 540 g ÷ 90 = _____ mg

10. 7.2 kg ÷ 320 = _____ g

EXERCISE 2. (Practical problems)

1. Janet Farnsworth was asked to buy some food for her company picnic. She bought the following items at a supermarket: potatoes, 18.2 kilograms; sliced ham, 12.7 kilograms; onions, 5.3 kilograms; black pepper, 55 grams; celery salt, 78.2 grams. What was the total weight of her purchase, expressed to the nearest kilogram? _____ kg.

2. Five kilograms of shrimp were bought for $2.80 per kilogram. However, when the shrimp were deheaded and reweighed, they only weighed 3.5 kg. What was the real cost per kg? $_____.

3. Larry Walker ordered 8 rolls of wallpaper to redecorate his home. Two rolls weighed 1.4 kg each and cost $8.50 per roll; two rolls weighed 1.6 kg each and cost $9.70 per roll; and four rolls weighed 1.3 kg each and cost $6.75 per roll. If shipping cost 12¢ per kilogram, or fraction thereof, what was the total cost of his purchase? $_____.

4. Greg Howell paid a state automobile registration fee based on the weight of his car. For one year he paid $28.80 for a car that weighed 1 440 kg. At the same rate, how much will he pay for the registration of a new car weighing 1 890 kg? $_____.

5. In shopping for meat, Paula Reed finds that Mack's Market is selling steak at $1.79 per pound. The Greatway Discount Store is selling the same quality meat at $4.07 per kilogram. How much does Greatway Discount charge per pound? (1 kg = 2.2 lbs.) $_____. In which store is the meat less expensive? _____.

6. Allen Milton competed in the shot put for his high school track team. The shot he used weighed 12 pounds. What was the equivalent weight of the shot in kilograms? (1 kg = 2.2 pounds) _____ kg.

UNIT EIGHTEEN   Computer Mathematics and Probability

SECTION 77.   Decimal System of Numeration

Under the decimal system of numeration, which we use in our everyday computations, each position a digit may occupy in a numeral has a place value. The top row in the place-value chart at the right shows the place value of each position. Note that each position has ten times the place value of the position on its right. For example, the place value of the first position at the right is one; of the second position, ten times one, or ten; of the third, ten times ten, or one hundred; of the fourth, ten times one hundred, or one thousand.

1,000	100	10	1
2	4	6	3

In the numeral 2,463, for example, which has also been entered in the chart, the 2 stands for $2 \times 1,000$, or 2,000; the 4, for 4×100, or 400; the 6, for 6×10, or 60; the 3, for 3×1, or 3. Hence, we may write either $2,463 = (2 \times 1,000) + (4 \times 100) + (6 \times 10) + (3 \times 1)$ or $2,463 = 2,000 + 400 + 60 + 3$.

The expressions "$(2 \times 1,000) + (4 \times 100) + (6 \times 10) + (3 \times 1)$" and "$2,000 + 400 + 60 + 3$" are each called an *expanded form* of the numeral 2,463. 2,463 is called the *standard* or *basic form*.

DRILL 106.   (Analyzing numerals)

Express each of the following standard numerals in expanded form by writing the appropriate numerals in the spaces at the right.

Example 1: $379 = (\underline{\quad 3 \quad} \times 100) + (\underline{\quad 7 \quad} \times 10) + (\underline{\quad 9 \quad} \times 1)$

Example 2: $268 = (2 \times \underline{\quad 100 \quad}) + (6 \times \underline{\quad 10 \quad}) + (8 \times \underline{\quad 1 \quad})$

1. $3,795 = (3 \times \underline{\quad}) + (7 \times \underline{\quad}) + (9 \times \underline{\quad}) + (5 \times \underline{\quad})$

2. $840 = (8 \times \underline{\quad}) + (4 \times \underline{\quad}) + (0 \times \underline{\quad})$

3. $15,682 = (1 \times \underline{\quad}) + (5 \times \underline{\quad}) + (6 \times \underline{\quad}) + (8 \times \underline{\quad}) + (2 \times \underline{\quad})$

4. $9,103 = (9 \times \underline{\quad}) + (1 \times \underline{\quad}) + (0 \times \underline{\quad}) + (3 \times \underline{\quad})$

5. $2,648 = (\underline{\quad} \times 1,000) + (\underline{\quad} \times 100) + (\underline{\quad} \times 10) + (\underline{\quad} \times 1)$

6. $902 = (\underline{\quad} \times 100) + (\underline{\quad} \times 10) + (\underline{\quad} \times 1)$

7. $18,570 = (\underline{\quad} \times 10,000) + (\underline{\quad} \times 1,000) + (\underline{\quad} \times 100) + (\underline{\quad} \times 10) + (\underline{\quad} \times 1)$

Express each of the following standard numerals in expanded form by writing the appropriate numerals in the spaces at the right.

Example: $47 = \underline{\quad 40 \quad} + \underline{\quad 7 \quad}$

8. $235 = \underline{\quad} + \underline{\quad} + \underline{\quad}$ 9. $4,982 = \underline{\quad} + \underline{\quad} + \underline{\quad} + \underline{\quad}$

10. $27,674 = \underline{\quad} + \underline{\quad} + \underline{\quad} + \underline{\quad} + \underline{\quad}$

In the space at the right of each of the following, write the standard numeral that is equal to the given expanded numeral.

11. $(7 \times 1,000) + (9 \times 100) + (3 \times 10) + (8 \times 1) = \underline{\quad}$

12. $(1 \times 1,000) + (1 \times 100) + (0 \times 10) + (9 \times 1) = \underline{\quad}$

13. $(3 \times 10,000) + (4 \times 1,000) + (3 \times 100) + (1 \times 10) + (0 \times 1) = \underline{\quad}$

14. $8,000 + 900 + 40 + 6 = \underline{\quad}$ 15. $10,000 + 3,000 + 400 + 80 + 7 = \underline{\quad}$

SECTION 78. Binary System of Numeration

The decimal system of numeration, which we use in our everyday computations, uses the ten basic symbols, 0 through 9, and is referred to as a *base-ten system*. The binary system, which is used in many electronic computers, uses just two symbols, 0 and 1, and is called a *base-two system*. As indicated by the top row in the place-value chart at the right, the place value of each position is two times the place value of the position on its right.

16	8	4	2	1
1	1	0	1	1

In the base-2 numeral, 11011, which has been entered in the place-value chart, the 1 in the first position at the left stands for 1×16, or 16; the 1 in the second position, for 1×8, or 8; the 0 in the third position, for 0×4, or 0; the 1 in the fourth position, for 1×2, or 2; and the 1 in the last position, for 1×1, or 1. The numeral 11011, base 2, is therefore equal to $16 + 8 + 0 + 2 + 1$, or 27, base 10.

DRILL 107. (Changing a base-2 numeral to a base-10 numeral)

As shown above, a base-2 numeral can be changed to a base-10 numeral by entering the binary digits in a place-value chart and then adding the place values of the digits.

Using the place-value chart below, you are to find the base-10 numeral for each base-2 numeral, listed at the left, and write it in the "Base-10" column at the right.

Problem 1, with the base-2 numeral 1101, has been completed as a sample. The 1 in the first place at the right end of 1101 was entered in the "1" column. The 0 in the second place in 1101 was entered in the "2" column. The 1 in the third place in 1101 was entered in the "4" column. The 1 in the fourth place in 1101 was entered in the "8" column. The values of these four binary digits from left to right are 8, 4, 0, and 1, respectively. These values were added; and their sum, 13, was entered in the "Base-10" column.

	Base 2	512	256	128	64	32	16	8	4	2	1		Base 10
1.	1101							1	1	0	1	=	13
2.	100110											=	
3.	10101001											=	
4.	1100100											=	
5.	100010011											=	
6.	100101100											=	
7.	1000100110											=	

DRILL 108. (Changing a base-2 numeral to a base-10 numeral)

Without using a formal place-value chart, a base-2 numeral can be changed to a base-10 numeral by writing the place values above the digits in the base-2 numeral and then adding the place values of the digits.

Example: 101101, base 2 = $\overset{32}{1}\ \overset{16}{0}\ \overset{8}{1}\ \overset{4}{1}\ \overset{2}{0}\ \overset{1}{1}$ = $32 + 0 + 8 + 4 + 0 + 1 = 45$, base 10

The place value of each digit is identified by starting with the first digit on the right and writing 1, 2, 4, 8, 16, 32, 64, etc., in that order, above the successive digits, from right to left, as shown in the example.

For each base-2 numeral, find the base-10 numeral equal to it and write it in the blank space provided.

Base 2	Base 10		Base 2	Base 10		Base 2	Base 10
1. 1 1 0 0 1 1 =	_____	4. 1 0 0 1 0 1 =	_____	7. 1 1 0 1 0 1 1 =	_____
2. 1 0 1 0 1 0 0 =	_____	5. 1 1 1 0 1 1 =	_____	8. 1 1 1 1 0 0 =	_____
3. 1 0 0 0 1 1 1 =	_____	6. 1 0 1 1 1 0 1 =	_____	9. 1 0 1 1 0 0 1 =	_____

Section 78 (concluded)

DRILL **109.** (Changing a base-10 numeral to a base-2 numeral)

The procedure for using a place-value chart to change a base-10 numeral, such as 50, to a base-2 numeral is explained below.

In 50 there is 1 thirty-two and 18 left over. Write 1 in the "32" column in the place value chart. In the 18 left over, there is 1 sixteen and 2 left over. Write 1 in the "16" column. In the 2 left over, there is 1 two and nothing left over. Write 1 in the "2" column. Insert 0's in the spaces where there are no 1's. Reading the second row in the place-value chart gives 110010 as the base-2 numeral equal to the base-10 numeral 50.

32	16	8	4	2	1
1	1	0	0	1	0

Check:

$$32 + 16 + 0 + 0 + 2 + 0 = 50$$

Using the place-value chart below, find the base-2 numeral for each base-10 numeral listed at the left and write it in the "Base-2" column at the right.

Base 10	512	256	128	64	32	16	8	4	2	1		Base 2
1. 26											=	_____
2. 58											=	_____
3. 73											=	_____
4. 122											=	_____
5. 175											=	_____
6. 217											=	_____
7. 488											=	_____
8. 695											=	_____
9. 277											=	_____

DRILL **110.** (Changing a base-10 numeral to a base-2 numeral)

A base-10 numeral can also be changed to a base-2 numeral by dividing the base-10 numeral and the successive quotients by 2, and recording the remainders. This method of changing the base-10 numeral 50 to a base-2 numeral is explained below.

Dividing 50 by 2 gives a quotient of 25 and a remainder of 0.
Dividing 25 by 2 gives a quotient of 12 and a remainder of 1.
Dividing 12 by 2 gives a quotient of 6 and a remainder of 0.
Dividing 6 by 2 gives a quotient of 3 and a remainder of 0.
Dividing 3 by 2 gives a quotient of 1 and a remainder of 1.
Dividing 1 by 2 gives a quotient of 0 and a remainder of 1.

2) 50
2) 25, remainder 0
2) 12, remainder 1
2) 6, remainder 0
2) 3, remainder 0
2) 1, remainder 1
2) 0, remainder 1

The remainders, read from the bottom up, represent the base-2 numeral. Reading them in this manner and writing them from left to right gives 110010 as the base-2 numeral equal to the base-10 numeral 50.

Using the division method, find the base-2 numeral equal to each base-10 numeral listed below.

Base 10	Base 2		Base 10	Base 2		Base 10	Base 2
1. 21	= _____		4. 49	= _____		7. 97	= _____
2. 42	= _____		5. 85	= _____		8. 45	= _____
3. 52	= _____		6. 56	= _____		9. 122	= _____

SECTION 79. Binary Arithmetic

Addition, subtraction, multiplication, and division with base-2 numerals are performed in the same manner as with base-10 numerals.

DRILL 111. (Addition with base-2 numerals)

In performing addition with base-2 numerals, we make use of the addition facts shown at the right.

0	0	1	1	11
+0	+1	+0	+1	+1
0	1	1	10	100

The way we use these addition facts is explained below in obtaining the sum of $111 + 111 + 11$.

1. Beginning with the ones column and adding from the bottom up, $1 + 1 = 10$; $10 + 1 = 11$. Write 1; carry (1).

2. In the twos column, $(1) + 1 = 10$; $10 + 1 = 11$; $11 + 1 = 100$. Write 0; carry (10).

3. In the fours column, $(10) + 1 = 11$; $11 + 1 = 100$. Write 100.

Find the sum with the base-2 numerals in each problem given below.

Check Base 10

```
1 1 1 =   7
1 1 1 =   7
  1 1 =   3
      10 1
1 0 0 0 1 =  17
 16 + 1 =  17
```

1.	2.	3.	4.	5.	6.
1 0 1 0	1 0 0	1 0 1 0	1 0 1 0	1 1 0	1 1 1 0
1 0 1	1 1 0	1 1	1 0 1 1	1 1	1 1 1

7.	8.	9.	10.	11.	12.
1 0 1 1	1 1 1 0	1 1 1 1	1 1 1 1	1 0 1 1	1 1 0
1 0 1	1 1 1	1 1 1	1 1 1 1	1 1 0 0	1 1 1
				1 1 1	1 1 1

DRILL 112. (Multiplication with base-2 numerals)

In performing multiplication with base-2 numerals, we make use of the multiplication facts shown at the right. The way we use these facts and perform the multiplication is explained below in finding the product of $101 √ó 1011$. We first obtain the partial products, in the same manner as with base-10 numerals, and then add them.

0	0	1	1
√ó0	√ó1	√ó0	√ó1
0	0	0	1

1. $1 √ó 1011 = 1011$, the first partial product.
2. $0 √ó 1011 = 0$. Write 0 in the twos column of the second partial product.
3. $1 √ó 1011 = 1011$. Write 1011 to the left of the 0 in the second partial product.
4. Add the partial products and write the sum, 110111.

Find the product with the base-2 numerals in each problem given below. Make the necessary calculations on a separate piece of paper.

Check Base 10

```
1 0 1 1 =  11
  1 0 1 =   5
1 0 1 1
1 0 1 1 0
      1
1 1 0 1 1 1 =  55
32 + 16 +
 4 + 2 + 1 =  55
```

1.	2.	3.	4.	5.	6.	7.	8.	9.
1001	101	1101	1011	1011	1111	1011	10101	1011
111	101	1001	1001	11	1001	10	111	111

Section 79 (concluded)

DRILL 113. (Subtraction with base-2 numerals)

In performing subtraction with base-2 numerals, we make use of the subtraction facts shown at the right. The way we perform the subtraction is explained below in subtracting 10101 from 1001000.

0	1	1	10
−0	−0	−1	−1
0	1	0	1

1. The 1 in the ones column of the subtrahend cannot be subtracted from the 0 in the minuend.

2. To meet this situation, move to the left in the minuend until a 1 is reached. This 1 is in the eights column. Change this 1 to 0, and change each intervening 0 to 1. Change the 0 in the ones column to 10, and subtract until a point is reached where a 1 must again be subtracted from 0. This point is in the sixteens column.

3. Move to the left in the minuend until the next 1 is reached, and proceed again in the manner described above.

Find the difference with the base-2 numerals in each problem given below.

```
1 0 0 1 0 0 0
  1 0 1 0 1
_____

        0 1 1 10
1 0 0 1 0 0 0
    1 0 1 0 1
_____
      0 0 1 1

0 1 10 0 1 1 10
1 0 0 1 0 0 0
    1 0 1 0 1
_____
1 1 0 0 1 1
```

Check: Base 2   Base 10
        1001000 =   72
          10101 =   21
         110011 =   51

32 + 16 + 2 + 1 = 51

1. 1 1 1 1 0
     1 0 1 0

2. 1 1 0 1 1
     1 0 1 0

3. 1 1 0 0 0
       1 1 1

4. 1 1 0 0 0
      1 0 1

5. 1 1 0 0 0
     1 0 1 1

6. 1 1 0 0 1
     1 0 1 0

7. 1 1 1 0 1
     1 0 1 0

8. 1 1 0 1 1
     1 1 0 0

9. 1 0 0 0
     1 1 0

10. 1 0 1 1 0
      1 1 0 1

11. 1 0 1 0 0
      1 1 1 1

12. 1 0 1 1 0
      1 1 1 1

DRILL 114. (Division with base-2 numerals)

Division with base-2 numerals is performed in the same way as with base-10 numerals as illustrated in the two examples given below.

Example 1 shows the division of 1111 by 101.

Example 2 shows the division of 10010 by 11. Notice in Example 2 that the divisor, 11, cannot be subtracted from 10, the first two digits in the dividend. It is therefore placed under and subtracted from the first three digits, 100.

```
Example 1.        11
              101)1111
                  101
                  ___
                  101
                  101
                  ___
```

```
Example 2.        110
               11)10010
                  11
                  __
                  11
                  11
                  __
                  00
```

Check: Base 2 Base 10
Dividend 1111 = 15
Divisor   101 =   5
Quotient   11 =   3

Check: Base 2 Base 10
Dividend 10010 = 18
Divisor   11 =   3
Quotient   110 =   6

Find the quotient with the base-2 numerals in each problem given below. Make the necessary calculations on a separate piece of paper.

1. 11)11110 2. 11)1111 3. 101)11110 4. 101)101101 5. 111)111111

6. 101)11001 7. 10)10010 8. 110)101010 9. 111)1000110 10. 1101)1000001

SECTION 80. Probability

Suppose a box contains six marbles that are identical in size. Four are red and numbered 1, 2, 3, and 4, respectively, as shown at the right. Two are blue and numbered 5 and 6, respectively. Without looking, you are to draw one marble from the box. Since you cannot tell one marble from another, each one is as likely to be drawn as any other.

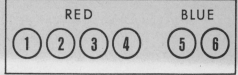

Among the six marbles, there is only one marked "4." There is one chance out of six that you will draw the "4" marble. So we say that the probability of your drawing the "4" marble is one out of six, which we usually express in fraction form, $\frac{1}{6}$. Since four of the marbles are red, there are four chances out of six for drawing a red marble. The probability of drawing a red one is therefore $\frac{4}{6}$, or $\frac{2}{3}$. The probability of *not* drawing a red one is $\frac{2}{6}$, or $\frac{1}{3}$. Since all are either red or blue, the probability of drawing either a red or blue one is $\frac{6}{6}$, or 1. Since none are white, the probability of drawing a white one is $\frac{0}{6}$, or 0.

EXERCISE.   (Practical problems)

1. Assume that you are to draw one marble from the box of marbles described above. In the blank space provided, write the numeral that expresses the probability of each of these events:

a. Drawing a blue marble. _____   **d.** Drawing a marble marked 5. _____

b. Drawing a green marble. _____   **e.** Drawing a marble not marked 3. _____

c. Not drawing a blue marble. _____   **f.** Drawing a marble numbered either 3 or 5. ____

g. Drawing a marble marked with a number less than 7. _____

h. Drawing a marble marked with a number greater than 6. _____

i. Drawing a marble marked with an even number. _____

j. Drawing a marble marked with a number not greater than 4. _____

2. From the records of deaths among their policyholders, life insurance companies compile mortality tables showing the number still living in each age group. A portion of a mortality table is shown below at the right.

From the table we can determine the probability that a person will live to a certain age. For example, the table shows that 92,000 of the original 100,000 reached the age of 40. This means that at birth the probability of living to be 40 is 92,000 ÷ 100,000, which we may express in decimal form, .92. Of the 92,000 living at age 40, 26,000 were still living at age 80. Hence, the probability that a person now 40 will reach age 80 is 26,000 ÷ 92,000, or .28, to the nearest hundredth.

You are to complete the following table by showing in the last column the probability, to the nearest hundredth, of reaching the projected age indicated in the "Projected Age" column for each individual.

Mortality Table	
Age	Number Living
0	100,000
10	98,000
18	97,000
30	95,000
40	92,000
50	88,000
60	77,000
70	56,000
80	26,000

	Name	Present Age	Projected Age	Probability of Reaching Projected Age
a	E. Baxter	Born today	70	
b	G. Doan	50	80	
c	S. Hood	10	70	
d	C. Larkin	18	80	
e	M. Simon	30	60	